Detroit Tigers

— LISTS AND MORE —

For Reference

Not to be taken from this room

Great Lakes Books
*A complete listing of the books in this series
can be found at the back of this volume.*

Philip P. Mason, Editor
Department of History, Wayne State University

Dr. Charles K. Hyde, Associate Editor
Department of History, Wayne State University

Detroit Tigers

— LISTS AND MORE —

RUNS, HITS, AND ERAS

MARK PATTISON
AND
DAVID RAGLIN

With an Introduction by Dale Petroskey,
President, National Baseball Hall of Fame

WAYNE STATE UNIVERSITY PRESS
DETROIT

∞ The paper used in this publication meets the minimum
requirements of the American national Standard for Information
Sciences—Permanence of Paper for Printed Library Materials,
ANSI Z39.48-1984

Library of Congress Cataloging-in-Publication Data
Pattison, Mark, 1956–
    Detroit Tigers lists and more : runs, hits, and eras / Mark
    Pattison and David Raglin ; with an introduction by Dale
    Petroskey.
        p. cm. — (Great Lakes books)
Includes bibliographical references and index.
    ISBN 0-8143-3040-1 (pbk. : alk. paper)
    1. Detroit Tigers (Baseball team) — Miscellanea. 2. Detroit
    Tigers (Baseball team) — Statistics. I. Raglin, David. II. Title.
    III. Series.
GV875.D6 P38 2002
796.357'64'0977434—dc21
                                                2001008423

Cover and interior book design by
Sanford J. Barris, Business Graphic Services, Inc.
Bloomfield Hills, MI

CONTENTS

PREFACE

This is a fine kettle of fish. Here I am, a journalist who's spent his entire adult life making his living as a writer and editor, and I'm having a hard time trying to put words together for this preface.

How do you say how much you like the Detroit Tigers in a few hundred words, or even a few thousand? If we could have done so, David Raglin and I wouldn't have assembled a book that runs into the hundreds of pages from all sorts of reference journals, David's background in statistics, and our fertile imaginations.

I can remember when my parents took my sister, my brother and me to our first game at Tiger Stadium. It was 1962. We sat in the reserved seat section; I remember how I tried to grab a foul ball but was too afraid to really make a play for it even though we sat in the front row of the section. I also remember that the Tigers won.

And I also remember my second outing with my family to the ballpark the following year. It was a Sunday doubleheader against the Red Sox, and the Tigers won both ends of the doubleheader. It must have left some kind of impression on me. My "what I did on my summer vacation" report when I entered second grade at St. David Grade School in Detroit was our trip to the ballpark. Not content to just give the game summaries, I also drew pictures of each of the Tigers on the team in the margins of my ruled paper. I still have that report—which has a lot more spelling and grammar errors than I remembered at the time—tucked away in one of those "(Your Name Here)'s School Days" folders.

And so it goes. At St. David, we were allowed to watch the 1968 World Series between the Tigers and the St. Louis Cardinals on the televisions we had in each of our classrooms. I had to watch the first couple of games from home, though. In my giddy exuberance over the Tigers' obvious superiority while at my safety-boy post, I had an unfortunate bout of poor timing while jumping a fire hydrant, and went on my own personal disabled list. But I was back at school for games five through seven, and got home—from chastened safety-boy duty after school—in time to see Jim Northrup's triple over Curt Flood's head in center field, which proved to be the decisive hit of the final game.

Flash forward twenty-one years later to 1989. When I got a job in Washington, I asked my then-wife (who was still in Detroit) to look up a newspaper item about the Mayo Smith Society. I remembered that it had been founded in Washington in the early 1980s, and I reasoned that there must be some Tigers fans in the nation's capital. One thing led to another, and I met the Mayo Smith Society sabermetrician, David Raglin, who became my friend and now co-author.

In the years since, a lot of things have changed for me. I've been divorced and have since remarried, and have lived in more dwellings in a dozen years in Washington than I ever did in thirty-three years in Detroit. Every prime-time TV show I regularly watched as a Detroiter has since gone off the air. But the Tigers, win or lose—and they've lost a lot this past decade—remain an emotional anchor to our youth, a reason to squint at the agate type of a box score in the sports section, a reason to see if you can pull in a strong-enough station on the car radio to listen to a Tigers game after a late night at the office. It's that constancy that keeps together the fraternity of Tigers fans. It's when that constancy is disrupted, such as in the closing of Tiger Stadium, that can give fans ever greater pause to think that all's not right with the world.

While more seems to have gone wrong than right with the Tigers in recent years, the balance sheet over a century is still well on the plus side of the ledger. Tigers fans have been graced to witness the exploits of such greats as Ty Cobb, Harry Heilmann, Hank Greenberg, Charlie Gehringer, Hal Newhouser, George Kell and Al Kaline—Hall of Famers all—plus stars who may yet make the Hall and some superb supporting casts. We've even taken the club's broadcasters under our collective, protective wing.

Though this book is made up largely of lists, David and I chose in every possible instance to put the players first, with the numbers and dates close behind. Other books may organize their information differently, and that's their valid choice. But because of the Detroit orientation of our book, we wanted to feature the players who did the deeds.

It's unlikely that either of us will be around to chronicle the entire second century of the Tigers, but we like how we've chronicled the first century. We hope you agree, but if you don't—if you believe we've dropped a name, blown a stat, left a blank unfilled, missed important lists and dates altogether, or even have memories different than our own—we encourage you to write us at Wayne State University Press. One of baseball's benefits is that it's a good conversation starter.

Mark Pattison

Something that Jim Bouton said comes to mind. I don't remember the exact wording but it was something like: All of these years you grip a baseball before you realize it was the other way around all along.

I'm not sure why someone has such a passion for something, whether it be coins from the time of the American Revolution, Jane Austen, a Bach cantata, or baseball and the Detroit Tigers. I don't have anything against any of those other things, but I'm glad my passion is for baseball, and the greatest team ever (in my very biased opinion), the Detroit Tigers.

I have had the privilege to communicate my passion for the Tigers the last sixteen years by writing "Tigers Stripes," the newsletter of the Mayo Smith Society. The Mayo Smith Society is a Tiger fan club founded in 1983 in Washington, D.C., by expatriate Michiganians who missed their favorite team. The name came from two facts: At that time, Mayo was the last man to lead the Tigers to a World Series championship, and despite that, he was not overly famous, so only loyal Tiger fans would know who Mayo was. I joined the group in its second year at its weekly breakfast on Capitol Hill, and immediately knew I was in the right place. I helped found "Tiger Stripes," which was designed to be a Tigers version of the work Bill James, the famous sabermetrician, was doing.

Soon after the 2000 season started, I was at a local Society of American Baseball Research meeting, and a friend of mine was describing his book of Baltimore Orioles lists. He said his publisher was interested in doing other teams, and a light bulb went off in my head. I called Mark Pattison, my longtime friend with whom I had shared many a Tigers win (and loss) at my house, watching on the satellite dish. I figured that Mark would be interested in such a book, and anyway, I know he'd do a much better job at the funny lists than I, given his creative sense of humor.

The vision I had for this book was that it would have four purposes. First was the humorous lists. This is baseball, not brain surgery, and it's easy to take it too seriously. It's a GAME! Where else would you find a Tigers odd couple like Donie Bush and Greg Gohr (say their last names and remember the 2000 presidential race)?

Second was the information you cannot find elsewhere, like the starting eight Mayo Smith used for all seven games of the 1968 World Series or the 1986 Tigers infield that was the first infield (including the catcher) where everyone hit twenty or more home runs in a season.

Third was information that may be available elsewhere, but usually with a twist. We give the information on Tigers' retired numbers that is presented well in the Tigers' own media guide, but we add who (other than the honoree) wore it last.

Fourth is lists based on our opinions. Lists in that category include the best Tiger to wear each uniform number and the best team of Tigers-Red Sox players (players who played for each team).

Enjoy the book. As I said, it honors a team that plays a game. Don't walk over to the section of the bookstore where they have books on wars and scandals and murders. Pick up this book, laugh a little, howl a little, learn a little, and have fun.

David Raglin

Acknowledgments

The authors are grateful for the assistance of, among others, Gordon Olson, Marc Okkonen and William Anderson for reviewing draft versions of this book and making suggestions to improve it.

We are thankful for the aid of many at Wayne State University Press, principally Jane Hoehner, for shepherding this book to completion.

We are deeply appreciative of the efforts of Jim Gates and Patricia Kelly of the National Baseball Hall of Fame and Museum's library in helping the authors sift through Detroit Tigers-related material in the library's holdings.

Similarly, we thank David Lee Poremba of the Burton Historical Collection at the main branch of the Detroit Public Library for giving ready access to, and assistance with, the Ernie Harwell Collection.

We acknowledge a debt of gratitude to George Waldman for his photographic expertise.

The authors thank the Mayo Smith Society for giving them an initial outlet to develop their interest in Detroit Tigers history and statistics, and to its members—not the least of which include Gordon "Mickey" Schubert and Todd Miller—for their insights.

We also thank Ray Formosa of Brooks Lumber and George Eichorn of the *Detroit Monitor* for their contributions.

Mark Pattison cannot say enough nice words about his wife, Judith McCullough, who never had to feign interest in her husband's latest research findings, and so dedicates his portion of the book to her.

Dave Raglin, who owns dedication rights for his portion of the book, dedicates it to his father, Art and to the memory of his mother, Anne, for everything they did for him, including nurturing a love for baseball, to his brother, Phil, and to his fiancée, Barb Mantegani.

The authors also wish to acknowledge the contributions in their lives of the friends and others who helped shape them. While a few were foul balls, the rest have been eminently fair.

INTRODUCTION

When I was named president of the National Baseball Hall of Fame and Museum in Cooperstown, N.Y., in 1999, I was told it's OK to have a favorite team. So I tell people, "I love twenty-nine teams equally—and one a lot more than the rest."

I grew up in the Detroit area, and since I was five in 1960, I have been in love with the Tigers. I followed Al Kaline, Bill Freehan, Willie Horton, Mickey Stanley, Jim Northrup, Denny McLain, and Mickey Lolich like they were family. What a team! My favorite was Rocky Colavito, the flat-footed slugger with the rifle arm. I was such a fan that I took the name "Rocco" as my Confirmation name in the Catholic Church. Saint Rocco's feast day is August 16; you can look it up!

I also loved playing The Game, and played as much as possible. In fact, I was fortunate to play on two national championship teams based in Detroit in 1971 and 1972. My teammates on those Kowalski Sausage teams included future major league pitcher Lary Sorensen and shortstop Todd Cruz, and we were managed by a wonderful man named Thom Engel.

In between playing, I took the bus to Tiger Stadium for every home game with my buddies to volunteer as a boy usher. We worked for tips only—no hourly wage—just to be in the ballpark and see my heroes as often as I could. My supervisor was Emory Fasano, another fine man.

Fast forward. My wife, Ann, and I moved to Washington, D.C., in 1981. Living in a city far from Detroit, without a major league team, before the days of instant cable news and the Internet, it was mighty tough to keep track of the Tigers. In spring 1983, with my brother Dennis and our good friend, Bill Mackay, we founded the Mayo Smith Society on Capitol Hill. We hosted Friday morning breakfasts for Democrats and Republicans to talk baseball, and more specifically Tigers baseball. The Society quickly became popular—mirroring the Tigers' success at that time. The reason we named the group the Mayo Smith Society was to immortalize the forgettable manager of the 1968 Tigers, then the last championship baseball team in

Detroit. The name was a litmus test, of sorts. We describe our-
selves as "loyal and knowledgeable Tigers fans." No Johnny-
ne-latelys need apply.

ourse, the next year, 1984, the Tigers won their first
world championship in sixteen years. And that's where David
Raglin stepped in. David, originally from Rochester, Michigan,
and a statistician for the U.S. Census Bureau, is a talented and
passionate baseball analyst. Month after month, he was able to
tell the story behind the Tigers' successes and shortcomings in
the Society's monthly publication, "Tigers Stripes." And he's
been doing it ever since.

The Mayo Smith Society is in very good hands today with
administrator Todd Miller, originally from Ann Arbor, David,
and Mark Pattison, who has spent half his life as a professional
journalist. He's a fine writer, and always fair in his approach.

David and Mark have been able to distill more than 100 years
of Detroit baseball history into some four hundred categories.
Their obvious loyalty to the Old English "D" is evident by the
great care they've taken to present a wealth of information not
only about the American League Tigers, but also the National
League Wolverines of the nineteenth century, and the Stars—
the respected Negro leagues club that played in Detroit. In
2000, we inducted its best player, Turkey Stearnes, into the
Baseball Hall of Fame.

Runs, Hits, and Eras is a must for any self-respecting Tigers fan.
I can't wait to put it on my bookshelf in Cooperstown!

Dale Petroskey, President
National Baseball Hall of Fame and Museum

LET'S GO TO THE HIGHLIGHTS!

Reader beware: We couldn't include every single highlight in this chapter. Had we, there wouldn't be any other chapters! For other notable performances not found here, you will want to consult such chapters as "Pennants and Postseason Play," "Pitching and Defense," "Homer, Sweet Homer" and "More Hitting and Offense" among others. Still, in the first century of Detroit Tigers baseball, there have been plenty of noteworthy, heroic, and downright quirky things, both on and off the field of play. This chapter offers a glimpse into that history.

We start with the most basic information on the Tigers— their won-lost record each season. Note the column with ties; no, we're not talking about the Detroit Red Wings, the other Mike Ilitch-owned team. There are ties in baseball—any game of five or more innings that ends with a tie score is a tie and is replayed when possible from the beginning. All statistics count, but most books do not show you these games. This one does.

We also show the Tigers' runs scored (RS/G) and allowed (RA/G) per-game average for each season. Why did the 1997 Tigers post one of the biggest one-season gains in team history? The table shows they scored about the same number or runs per game as the year before but allowed about two runs per game less. On the other hand, the 1961 Tigers posted a 26–game improvement from the season before largely on the strength of the extra run per game they tallied.

THE HISTORY OF THE DETROIT TIGERS

Year	W	L	T	Pct.	GB/GA	Finish	RS/G	RA/G
1901	74	61	1	.548	8-1/2	3rd (of 8) AL	5.45	5.10
1902	52	83	2	.385	30-1/2	7th (of 8) AL	4.13	4.80
1903	65	71	1	.478	25	5th (of 8) AL	4.14	3.93
1904	62	90	10	.408	32	7th (of 8) AL	3.12	3.87
1905	79	74	1	.516	15-1/2	3rd (of 8) AL	3.32	3.91
1906	71	78	2	.477	21	6th (of 8) AL	3.43	3.97
1907	92	58	3	.613	+1-1/2	1st (of 8) AL	4.54	3.48
1908	90	63	1	.588	+-1/2	1st (of 8) AL	4.20	3.55
1909	98	54	6	.645	+3-1/2	1st (of 8) AL	4.22	3.12
1910	86	68	1	.558	18	3rd (of 8) AL	4.38	3.75
1911	89	65	0	.578	13-1/2	2nd (of 8) AL	5.40	5.04
1912	69	84	1	.451	36-1/2	6th (of 8) AL	4.68	5.05
1913	66	87	0	.431	30	6th (of 8) AL	4.08	4.68
1914	80	73	4	.523	19-1/2	4th (of 8) AL	3.92	3.94
1915	100	54	2	.649	2-1/2	2nd (of 8) AL	4.99	3.83
1916	87	67	1	.565	4	3rd (of 8) AL	4.32	3.84
1917	78	75	1	.510	21-1/2	4th (of 8) AL	4.15	3.75
1918	55	71	2	.437	20	7th (of 8) AL	3.72	4.35
1919	80	60	0	.571	8	4th (of 8) AL	4.41	4.13
1920	61	93	1	.396	37	7th (of 8) AL	4.21	5.37
1921	71	82	1	.464	27	6th (of 8) AL	5.73	5.53
1922	79	75	1	.513	15	3rd (of 8) AL	5.34	5.10
1923	83	71	1	.539	16	2nd (of 8) AL	5.36	4.78
1924	86	68	2	.558	6	3rd (of 8) AL	5.44	5.10
1925	81	73	2	.526	16-1/2	4th (of 8) AL	5.79	5.31
1926	79	75	3	.513	12	6th (of 8) AL	5.05	5.29
1927	82	71	3	.536	27-1/2	4th (of 8) AL	5.42	5.16
1928	68	86	0	.442	33	6th (of 8) AL	4.83	5.22
1929	70	84	1	.455	36	6th (of 8) AL	5.97	5.99
1930	75	79	0	.487	27	5th (of 8) AL	5.08	5.41
1931	61	93	0	.396	47	7th (of 8) AL	4.23	5.43
1932	76	75	2	.503	29-1/2	5th (of 8) AL	5.22	5.14
1933	75	79	1	.487	25	5th (of 8) AL	4.66	4.73
1934	101	53	0	.656	+7	1st (of 8) AL	6.22	4.60
1935	93	58	1	.616	+3	1st (of 8) AL	6.05	4.38
1936	83	71	0	.539	19-1/2	2nd (of 8) AL	5.98	5.66
1937	89	65	1	.578	13	2nd (of 8) AL	6.03	5.43

Year	W	L	T	Pct.	GB/GA	Finish	RS/G	RA/G
1938	84	70	1	.545	16	4th (of 8) AL	5.56	5.13
1939	81	73	1	.526	26 - 1/2	5th (of 8) AL	5.48	4.92
1940	90	64	1	.584	+1	1st (of 8) AL	5.73	4.63
1941	75	79	1	.487	26	4th (of 8) AL	4.43	4.79
1942	73	81	2	.474	30	5th (of 8) AL	3.78	3.76
1943	78	76	1	.506	20	5th (of 8) AL	4.08	3.61
1944	88	66	2	.571	1	2nd (of 8) AL	4.22	3.72
1945	88	65	2	.575	+1 - 1/2	1st (of 8) AL	4.08	3.65
1946	92	62	1	.597	12	2nd (of 8) AL	4.54	3.66
1947	85	69	4	.552	12	2nd (of 8) AL	4.52	4.06
1948	78	76	0	.506	18 - 1/2	5th (of 8) AL	4.55	4.71
1949	87	67	1	.565	10	4th (of 8) AL	4.85	4.23
1950	95	59	3	.617	3	2nd (of 8) AL	5.33	4.54
1951	73	81	0	.474	25	5th (of 8) AL	4.45	4.81
1952	50	104	2	.325	45	8th (of 8) AL	3.57	4.73
1953	60	94	4	.390	40 - 1/2	6th (of 8) AL	4.40	5.84
1954	68	86	1	.442	43	5th (of 8) AL	3.77	4.28
1955	79	75	0	.513	17	5th (of 8) AL	5.03	4.27
1956	82	72	1	.532	15	5th (of 8) AL	5.09	4.51
1957	78	76	0	.506	20	4th (of 8) AL	3.99	3.99
1958	77	77	0	.500	15	5th (of 8) AL	4.28	3.94
1959	76	78	0	.494	18	4th (of 8) AL	4.63	4.75
1960	71	83	0	.461	26	6th (of 8) AL	4.11	4.18
1961	101	61	1	.623	8	2nd (of 10) AL	5.16	4.12
1962	85	76	0	.528	10 - 1/2	4th (of 10) AL	4.71	4.30
1963	79	83	0	.488	25 - 1/2	5th (of 10) AL	4.32	4.34
1964	85	77	1	.525	14	4th (of 10) AL	4.29	4.16
1965	89	73	0	.549	13	4th (of 10) AL	4.20	3.72
1966	88	74	0	.543	10	3rd (of 10) AL	4.44	4.31
1967	91	71	1	.562	1	3rd (of 10) AL	4.19	3.60
1968	103	59	2	.636	+12	1st (of 10) AL	4.09	3.00
1969	90	72	0	.556	19	2nd (of 6) AL East	4.33	3.71
1970	79	83	0	.488	29	4th (of 6) AL East	4.11	4.51
1971	91	71	0	.562	12	2nd (of 6) AL East	4.33	3.98
1972	86	70	0	.551	+-1/2	1st (of 6) AL East	3.58	3.29
1973	85	77	0	.525	12	3rd (of 6) AL East	3.96	4.16
1974	72	90	0	.444	19	6th (of 6) AL East	3.83	4.74
1975	57	102	0	.358	37 - 1/2	6th (of 6) AL East	3.58	4.94
1976	74	87	0	.460	24	5th (of 6) AL East	3.78	4.40
1977	74	88	0	.457	26	4th (of 7) AL East	4.41	4.64
1978	86	76	0	.531	13 - 1/2	5th (of 7) AL East	4.41	4.03
1979	85	76	0	.528	18	5th (of 7) AL East	4.78	4.58

Year	W	L	T	Pct.	GB/GA	Finish	RS/G	RA/G
1980	84	78	1	.519	19	5th (of 7) AL East	5.09	4.64
1981	60	49	0	.550	2	4th (of 7) AL East*	3.92	3.71
1982	83	79	0	.512	12	4th (of 7) AL East	4.50	4.23
1983	92	70	0	.568	6	2nd (of 7) AL East	4.87	4.19
1984	104	58	0	.642	+15	1st (of 7) AL East	5.12	3.97
1985	84	77	0	.522	15	3rd (of 7) AL East	4.53	4.27
1986	87	75	0	.537	8-1/2	3rd (of 7) AL East	4.93	4.41
1987	98	64	0	.605	+2	1st (of 7) AL East	5.53	4.54
1988	88	74	0	.543	1	2nd (of 7) AL East	4.34	4.06
1989	59	103	0	.364	30	7th (of 7) AL East	3.81	5.04
1990	79	83	0	.488	9	3rd (of 7) AL East	4.63	4.65
1991	84	78	0	.519	7	2nd (of 7) AL East	5.04	4.90
1992	75	87	0	.463	21	6th (of 7) AL East	4.88	4.90
1993	85	77	0	.525	10	4th (of 7) AL East	5.55	5.17
1994	53	62	0	.461	18	5th (of 5) AL East	5.67	5.83
1995	60	84	0	.417	26	4th (of 5) AL East	4.54	5.86
1996	53	109	0	.327	39	5th (of 5) AL East	4.83	6.81
1997	79	83	0	.488	19	3rd (of 5) AL East	4.84	4.88
1998	65	97	0	.401	24	5th (of 5) AL Cent.	4.46	5.33
1999	69	92	0	.429	28	3rd (of 5) AL Cent.	4.64	5.48
2000	79	83	0	.488	16	3rd (of 5) AL Cent.	5.08	5.10
2001	66	96	0	.407	25	4th (of 5) AL Cent.	4.47	5.41
Tot.	7980	7644	93	.511			4.63	4.54

*The 1981 season was declared a "split season" due to the players' midseason strike. The Tigers finished 31-26, good for fourth place, in the first half—all games before the strike—and tied for second place in the second half with a 29-23 record.

THE 1900S

April 25, 1901: With 10,023 crammed into 6,000-capacity Bennett Park, the Tigers staged a ninth-inning rally the likes of which the team, the American League, or the majors has not seen since. Down 13-4 in the bottom of the ninth, the Tigers rallied, crowning it with Pop Dillon's fourth double of the game, which drove in Doc Casey and Kid Gleason for the winning runs in a thrilling 14-13 win over Milwaukee. The fans danced on the field for an hour afterward to celebrate the victory.

April 28, 1901: The Tigers and the Milwaukee Brewers (soon to become the St. Louis Browns) played the first Sunday game in the American League, with Detroit prevailing 12-11.

July 27, 1901: The Tigers recorded the American League's first 1-0 game, a win vs. Baltimore (later to become the New York Yankees).

September 15, 1901: The Tigers recorded their most lopsided shutout victory, a 21-0 shellacking against Cleveland, in the second game of a doubleheader. Imagine if they had played it all the way through; because it was the nightcap, it was ended after the Indians had batted in the eighth inning so they could catch a train.

August 11, 1902: The Tigers were on the losing end of not only the AL's first extra-inning shutout, but its first extra-inning 1-0 shutout, losing to the Philadelphia Athletics 1-0 in 13 innings.

January 12, 1903: Detroit pitcher Win Mercer, who had been recently named manager of the Tigers, committed suicide by inhaling gas in a San Francisco hotel.

April 26, 1904: Ty Cobb made his professional debut, hitting a double and a home run for Augusta in the Sally League in an 8-7 loss to Columbus (Ga.).

August 9, 1905: Three weeks before Cobb's debut with the Tigers, his mother, mistaking her husband for a burglar, shot and killed him. She would be tried and found not guilty on a charge of involuntary manslaughter.

August 30, 1905: In Cobb's big-league debut, he doubled off the New York Highlanders' ace, Jack Chesbro, in a 5-3 win over New York.

June 4, 1906: Third baseman Bill Coughlin became the first Tiger to steal second base, third base and home plate in the same inning in the seventh inning of a game against the Senators.

August 2, 1907: Ty Cobb got the first hit—a bunt single—off future Hall of Famer Walter Johnson, making his big-league bow, in a 3-2 win over Washington. It was Sam Crawford's inside-the-park home run that beat the "Big Train."

September 30, 1907: In an AL pennant fight, the Tigers recovered from a 7-1 deficit to tie the game at 8-8 on a two-run homer by Cobb in the ninth inning. Both teams scored in the 11th, making it 9-9. In the 14th inning, the Athletics' Harry Davis hit a long fly into the standing-room-only crowd in the outfield. It was usually scored as a ground-rule double, but the base umpire contended a policeman in the crowd had interfered with center fielder Sam Crawford. Davis was ruled out. The next hitter slapped a single that would have certainly scored Davis. After 17 innings, it grew too dark to play. The 9-9 tie stood; the scheduled second game of the doubleheader was never played. The Bengals swept the Senators in Washington to win the pennant by a game and a half.

July 16, 1909: The Tigers and Senators played the longest scoreless game in AL history—18 innings. Ed Summers went the distance for the home-team Detroiters, giving up just seven hits. But "long" is a relative term; the game took just 3:15 to play.

THE 1910S

July 31, 1910: A month after Comiskey Park in Chicago opened, Ty Cobb hit the first home run by a visiting player in the fifth inning of 6-5 Tigers win over the White Sox. Chisox infielder Lee Tannehill had hit a three-run homer in the bottom of the fourth to tie the game; the ball went through the pickets in a gate in the left-field corner, despite the fact that a ball barely fit through the pickets. Cobb's ball went through the same pickets. It turned out to be the game-winner. Likewise, it was another Detroiter who hit the first visitor's homer in the current Comiskey Park: Cecil Fielder, with one out in the third inning of the Tigers' 16-0 shellacking of the Pale Hose.

October 9, 1910: Ty Cobb beat Nap Lajoie in a close race for the batting title, .385 to .384. Cobb sat out the last two games to preserve his lead, but Lajoie's backers, including a sympathetic St. Louis Browns scorer, gave him an 8-for-8 day (plus a sacrifice) during a doubleheader thanks to questionable fielding, and third

Ty Cobb, spikes high—about six inches off the ground—at home plate
in an undated photo. Perhaps Cobb's hell-bent-for-leather sliding
style inspired Kung Fu. (Photo courtesy Ernie Harwell
Collection/Burton Historical Collection, Detroit Public Library)

baseman Red Corriden purposely stationed too deep to make
plays on bunted balls. The Chalmers automobile company,
embarrassed, gave cars to both players.

July 4, 1911: Cobb's 40-game hitting streak was snapped by
Ed Walsh in a 7-3 White Sox win. Cobb had hit .456 since the
streak started May 15.

September 10, 1911: In the last game played at Bennett Park,
Detroit edged the Indians 2-1.

April 20, 1912: In the debut of Navin Field, the Tigers beat
Cleveland 6-5 in 11 innings before an overflow crowd of 24,384.

More attention was paid in the newspapers, though, to the recent sinking of the Titanic.

July 12, 1913: Ty Cobb played the first of his two games at second base, making three errors in a 16-9 loss to the Athletics. Cobb played second to get Hugh High's bat into the lineup, and High did go 1-for-3 with three walks, but Cobb made an error on the first play of the game, helping the Athletics to a 3-0 lead they would not relinquish. Cobb played second one more time, July 8, 1918, and made two errors that day. He was in at second that day for the same reason: to get another bat into the lineup. It should be noted that Cobb's fielding problems did not affect his bat—he went 6-for-8 in the two games.

August 11, 1914: Because of the raiding threat posed by the Federal League, the Tigers signed Ty Cobb to a three-year deal at $20,000 a year. The contract lasted longer than the Federal League, which survived just two years.

June 18, 1915: Cobb stole home twice in a game against Washington. One was the front end of a double steal. The other was the front end of a triple steal. Cobb's derring-do on the bases came in the midst of a stretch that month during which he stole 29 bases in 25 games.

October 3, 1915: The Tigers became the first 100-win team to not claim the pennant, as their 100-54 record was 2-1/2 games behind the Red Sox's 101-50 mark. Also that day, Ty Cobb stole his 96th base, a record that would stand for 47 years.

May 9, 1916: The Tigers set a one-game record for walks with 18 in a game against the Philadelphia Athletics.

August 19, 1917: Ty Cobb, coaching third base, shoved Detroit runner "Tioga George" Burns toward home after he stopped at third base on a long hit in a 1-1 game against the Senators. The Nats' Clark Griffith protested, and AL president Ban Johnson agreed with Griffith, since new rules prevented a coach from touching a runner. In the replayed game, Washington won 2-0.

August 24, 1919: Babe Ruth of the Boston Red Sox hit his second massive home run of the season out of Navin Field.

The ball landed in a lumber yard across Trumbull Avenue—mangled beyond recognition—after sailing out of the stadium in right-center field. In the bottom half of that inning, the third, the Tigers' Ty Cobb performed his own wizardry, leading a triple steal with Bobby Veach on second and Harry Heilmann on first. The Tigers won the game 8-4.

THE 1920s

August 8, 1920: Tigers pitcher Howard Ehmke hurled the fastest game in AL history, a 1:13, 1-0 whitewashing of the Yankees.

December 18, 1920: Ty Cobb was named manager of the Tigers on his 34th birthday. Cobb replaced longtime skipper Hughie Jennings, who resigned after the 1920 season. Cobb had to be talked into taking the job; in part, he took it because of rumors that Clarence "Pants" Rowland, the former White Sox manager whom Cobb did not feel qualified, would get it if Cobb turned it down.

July 17, 1922: Cobb got his fourth five-hit game of the season (the others occurred May 7, July 7 and July 12) to set an American League record.

August 11, 1923: AL President Ban Johnson banned Babe Ruth from using his "Sam Crawford" bat, which was made of four pieces of wood glued together; henceforth, only one-piece bats would be legal. The Tigers' Harry Heilmann, then tied with Ruth, pulled away from him to win the batting championship.

May 5, 1925: Ty Cobb, in his 21st year as a Tiger, hit three home runs en route to a 6-for-6 day—and a new record of 16 total bases in one game—in a 14-8 smothering of the Browns. Cobb, who had a huge dislike for Babe Ruth, reportedly pulled off the feat to prove that it wasn't all that difficult to hit home runs. Cobb then hit two more homers the next game, becoming the first player to hit five home runs in two consecutive games.

October 4, 1925: Harry Heilmann got six hits in a twin-bill sweep of St. Louis to push him ahead of Cleveland's Tris Speaker, .393 to .389, for his third AL batting title in five years.

January 27, 1927: Ty Cobb and Tris Speaker ware cleared of charges that they conspired to fix a game played on September 25, 1919. Former Tigers pitcher Dutch Leonard had claimed that Smokey Joe Wood, then an Indians pitcher, was also involved in the plan. Some believed Cobb's defense was a vigorous offense: threats to reveal embarrassing information about team accounting and turnstile counting practices. Cobb had already departed as Tigers manager the previous November, and played the last two years of his career with the Philadelphia Athletics.

THE 1930S

July 13, 1934: Navin Field was the site of Babe Ruth's 700th home run, a game-winner off Tommy Bridges, for a 4-2 Yankees victory.

July 14, 1934: Lou Gehrig kept his consecutive-game streak alive, after having been helped off Navin Field with a lumbago seizure the day before, by being listed as the shortstop and the leadoff batter against the Tigers. The lefthanded hitter and thrower hit a single and left the game, never taking the field. The Tigers beat New York, 12-11.

August 25, 1934: Sophomore sensation Schoolboy Rowe tied the AL record of Lefty Grove, Walter Johnson and Smokey Joe Wood by winning his 16th straight game, a 4-2 victory over Washington.

September 21, 1935: The Tigers won both ends of a double-header over the Browns to clinch the pennant; they'd finish three games ahead of the Yankees.

August 14, 1937: Outfielder Pete Fox scored eight of Detroit's record-setting 36 runs in a doubleheader sweep of the St. Louis Browns.

August 31, 1937: Tigers rookie catcher Rudy York blasted his 17th and 18th home runs of the month of August, the highest one-month homer mark until the Cubs' Sammy Sosa broke it June 24, 1998 (in an interleague game in Detroit), in a 12-3 thumping of Washington. York drove in seven runs in the game.

September 19, 1937: Hank Greenberg hit the first-ever home run into the center field stands in Yankee Stadium in an 8-1 win over New York.

October 2, 1938: On the last day of the season, Greenberg, with 58 home runs, had a chance to tie or break Babe Ruth's record of 60 in a season. But the doubleheader against Cleveland was moved from cozy League Park to cavernous Municipal Stadium to accommodate the crowds. Greenberg hit a double off Bob Feller in the opener that would have been a homer in any other park, but Feller struck out 18 that game. Greenberg was stalled at 58 when the second game was called after seven innings due to darkness.

May 2, 1939: In Detroit, Lou Gehrig benched himself to end his 2,130-game streak that began June 2, 1925. The Briggs Stadium crowd gave him a two-minute standing ovation when he walked out to give the lineup card to the umpire. The Yankees, with Babe Dahlgren at first base, clobbered the Tigers 22-2. Wally Pipp, whom Gehrig had replaced at first base, was in the stands that day.

THE 1940s

January 14, 1940: Baseball commissioner Kenesaw Mountain Landis gave free agency to 91 Detroit players and farmhands, saying the Tigers covered up player movement within the organization. He ordered compensation paid to 14 players, who shared a $47,250 pot. Of the farmhands, 23 made it to the majors, most notably Johnny Sain. Big-league Tigers given their freedom included Benny McCoy, Roy Cullenbine and Lloyd Dietz. The Tigers had traded McCoy and George Coffman to Philadelphia for

Wally Moses but Landis nullified the deal. A's owner Connie Mack not only kept Moses but signed McCoy as well.

September 27, 1940: Floyd Giebell's last major-league victory—he had only three—was a shutout over Bob Feller and the Cleveland Indians to win the AL pennant.

May 6, 1941: Hank Greenberg, playing his last game before joining the Army, hit two home runs as Detroit beat New York 7-4. Because of a later law banning the drafting of men over age 30, Greenberg was discharged from the service on December 5, 1941, two days before the Japanese attack on Pearl Harbor. Greenberg re-upped and didn't appear in a Detroit uniform again until 1945.

June 23, 1943: Because of race rioting in Detroit, the first use of armed troops at a baseball game occurred this day. The Tigers and Indians split a doubleheader—a 3-1 Tigers win in the opener but a 9-6 11-inning loss in the nightcap—with 350 troops present to guard 5,210 fans.

September 30, 1944: On two days' rest, Hal Newhouser shut down the Senators 7-3 in a key pennant-race game and tied George Mullin's team single-season win mark at 29. Teammate Dizzy Trout added 27 wins that year; Hal and Diz finished 1-2 in AL MVP voting.

October 1, 1944: Dizzy Trout and the Tigers lost to Washington, 4-1, unable to score until the ninth inning, while the largest crowd in St. Louis Browns history—37,815— watched the Browns beat the Yanks, 5-2 to capture the only AL flag they'd ever win. St. Louis finished 89-65, which was to that point the worst won-lost record of any pennant winner. Detroit finished a game back at 88-66.

July 1, 1945: Hank Greenberg, in his first game back from the military, hit a home run off Philadelphia's Charlie Gassaway before a crowd of 47,000 at Briggs Stadium in a 9-5 Tigers win.

July 21, 1945: In an era when pitch counts didn't matter, Tigers starter Les Mueller pitched 19.2 innings of a 24-inning, 1-1 tie against Philadelphia—still the longest tie in AL history. Dizzy Trout pitched the rest of the game until it was called on account of darkness.

September 30, 1945: In the first game of a doubleheader between Detroit and St. Louis, Greenberg hit a grand slam in the ninth inning to clinch the pennant for Detroit.

June 15, 1948: The Tigers, the last AL team to install lights, drew 54,480 for the first night game at Briggs Stadium, beating the Athletics 4-1. Tigers owner Walter Briggs had once lamented, "It's artificial without the sun." The Cubs had plans to put in their own lights at Wrigley Field in 1942, but shelved them in a show of sacrifice for the war effort. The no-lights policy subsequently became the stuff of legend until the Cubs' first night game in 1988.

September 8, 1949: The Tigers played their first-ever day-night doubleheader against Cleveland and took both games against the Indians.

October 2, 1949: On a day when the Tigers set an all-time single-season attendance record (since broken) of 1,821,204, George Kell nosed out Ted Williams for the AL batting crown, .34291 to .34276, the second-closest race in major-league history. It cost Williams the Triple Crown. Against starter Bob Lemon of Cleveland, Kell hit a double and a single, but recorded an out against reliever Bob Feller. "The manager (Red Rolfe) was going to take me out of the game," said Kell more than a half-century later. Thanks to a sportswriter's tipoff on the numbers, Rolfe was prepared to have Joe Ginsberg pinch-hit for Kell. Kell was waiting in the on-deck circle when word filtered from the press box that Williams had gone 0-for-2 (plus two walks) in Boston's game against the Yankees. "I had the title. But I didn't want to come out. I didn't bat again, though. (Eddie Lake had hit into a double play to end the inning, the game and the season.) In the batting circle, I threw my bats in the air and let out a yell. I knew I had the title."

THE 1950s

June 23, 1950: The Tigers and Yankees combined for a major-league record 11 home runs (since broken) before a crowd of 51,400, with the Tigers winning 10-9 in the bottom of the ninth on Hoot Evers' inside-the-park homer.

July 9, 1951: Harry Heilmann, the Tigers' star outfielder of the 1920s and a fixture in their broadcast booth during the 1930s and '40s, died at his home in Southfield, Mich., a Detroit suburb, of the cancer which had prevented him from doing play-by-play for any games that season. It was the day before the All-Star game in Detroit, and Heilmann had been picked by baseball commissioner Happy Chandler to broadcast it. Before Heilmann's death, former teammate and manager Ty Cobb told Heilmann he had been elected to the Hall of Fame, even though the vote had not been taken yet.

January 17, 1952: Longtime owner Walter O. Briggs died. He was lauded in the press as a "sportsman" who was "just another fan," ecstatic when the Tigers won, despondent when they lost. In his penultimate season, 1950, the Tigers came close to giving Briggs the one additional pennant that was his dream. Many of the articles about him following his death noted how he put up the $100,000 to acquire Mickey Cochrane, who led the Tigers to the top of the standings in 1934 and '35.

April 26, 1952: Art Houtteman blanked the Cleveland Indians on a one-hit gem, 13-0. Harry "Suitcase" Simpson broke up the no-hitter in the ninth inning with a solid single to left field. A walk and an error by George Kell, both in the second inning, were the only other hitters Houtteman allowed on base.

June 3, 1952: Detroit pulled off a blockbuster midseason trade with Boston. The multiplayer deal didn't make that much of a difference to either club. The Tigers sent third baseman Kell, shortstop Johnny Lipon, outfielder Hoot Evers and pitcher Dizzy Trout to the Red Sox for first baseman Walt Dropo, third baseman Fred Hatfield, shortstop Johnny Pesky, outfielder Don Lenhardt and pitcher Bill Wight.

July 14–15, 1952: Tigers first baseman Walt Dropo got 12 consecutive hits—tying the major-league record—starting with five consecutive singles in a game against New York in an 8-2 win, and completing the feat the next day in a doubleheader against the Senators, going 4-for-4 (all singles again) in the first-game, 8-2 loss. He added a triple, a single and a double in the nightcap before fouling to the catcher on a first-pitch offering from Washington's Lou Sleater. Dropo got some revenge on Sleater, driving him from the game in the ninth inning with a single to knock in two runs and close the Washington lead to 9-8, the eventual final score. Dropo finished that second game a home run short of the cycle, but with a 4-for-5 performance and five RBI.

August 25, 1952: Virgil Trucks' second no-hitter of the season, a 1-0 win over the Yankees, was nearly a one-hitter. Here's why: A grounder by Phil Rizzuto was scooped up by Tigers shortstop Johnny Pesky, who had trouble getting it out of his glove. Official scorer John Drebinger at Yankee Stadium charged Pesky with an error. But writer Dan Daniel of the New York World Telegram convinced Drebinger that since the ball was already in Pesky's glove, it couldn't be considered an error. Three innings later, Drebinger called Pesky in the dugout; Pesky said he should be given an error rather than Rizzuto be credited with a hit. With that, the call was changed for the second and last time.

September 25, 1952: Before Briggs Stadium's smallest-ever crowd—569—Hal Newhouser picked up his 200th (and last) win as a Tiger with a 3-2 win over the Browns. It was a small ray of light in a season that saw the Tigers finish last for the first time. They were the last original AL team to finish in the cellar in the league's history.

June 18, 1953: Detroit pitchers allowed the dubious distinction of letting Boston rookie outfielder Gene Stephens to get three hits—in one inning—as the Red Sox scored 17 times in the seventh inning of a 23-3 rout of the Tigers.

April 17, 1955: Al Kaline became the only Tiger to hit two home runs in one inning, a solo shot off Kansas City Athletics starter Bob Spicer and a two-run blast off reliever Bob Trice. The Tigers won 16-0.

September 25, 1955: Kaline became the youngest-ever batting champion in major-league history, beating out Ty Cobb, with his .340 average. Under 1955 rules, walks did not count toward eligibility for the batting title, so the BoSox's Ted Williams—with 71 walks—did not have enough plate appearances to qualify for the title for the second year in a row. The rules were changed to keep this from happening again. Kaline's birthday is Dec. 19; Dec. 17 is the birthday of Cobb, who also won a batting title at age 20. Even so, Cobb's 1907 season ended in October.

June 6, 1958: Ozzie Virgil, Detroit's first nonwhite player— and the first major leaguer from the Dominican Republic— debuted at third base for the Tigers on the road and went 1-for-5 with a ground-rule double in an 11-2 Detroit victory at Washington. Eleven days later, he made his home debut, also against the Senators, and went 5-for-5.

THE 1960S

April 19, 1960: The Tigers and Indians tied the AL mark for longest Opening Day game at 15 innings, with Detroit coming out on top 4-2 at Municipal Stadium in Cleveland.

May 12, 1961: Rocky Colavito was ejected in the eighth inning after he went into the stands behind third base at Yankee Stadium to go after a drunken heckler who was aiming his barbs at Colavito's wife and father. In the ninth inning, pitcher Frank Lary hit a home run to beat the Yanks, running Lary's lifetime record against New York to 25-8. The day after his ejection, The Rock hit two homers of his own plus two singles in an 8-3 Detroit drubbing of the Bronx Bombers.

June 20, 1961: Manager Bob Scheffing installed Al Kaline at third base due to infield injuries. Kaline responded by fielding both of his chances cleanly, while hitting a single and a double, scoring a run and driving in two more, in a 5-4 win over the Senators.

July 17, 1961: Ty Cobb died, after a yearlong battle with cancer, at Emory University Hospital in Atlanta.

September 1–3, 1961: The Tigers, 1-1/2 games behind the Yankees, went to New York anticipating a sweep. Instead, Detroit was the team that got swept. It was part of an eight-game losing streak that left them nine games behind the Yankees and effectively out of the pennant chase.

May 26, 1962: Al Kaline made a diving, game-saving catch to preserve the Tigers' 2-1 win over New York, but he broke his right collarbone in the process, sidelining him for four weeks.

July 2, 1962: In a remarkable comeback from cancer, Sad Sam Jones, also known as "Toothpick," struck out 10 White Sox to get his first win as a Tiger, 2-1. He had been sidelined while getting treatment for cancer in his neck.

April 8, 1963: The Tigers claimed Denny McLain from the White Sox for the $25,000 waiver price.

May 19, 1963: Bill Bruton hit four consecutive doubles to pace the attack in a 5-1 Tigers win over Washington, giving Bill Faul his first major league victory.

April 24, 1964: Manager Charlie Dressen picked up the team's $385 dinner tab at Schick's Café after Mickey Lolich threw his first major league shutout, 5-0, over the Twins in Minnesota. The tab could have been higher, but Tigers Dave Wickersham and Don Demeter, both members of the Fellowship of Christian Athletes, begged off to attend a Youth for Christ rally in Minneapolis.

June 15, 1965: Denny McLain, in a relief appearance, struck out the first seven batters he faced to set a major league record as the Tigers came back to beat Boston, 6-5. In all, McLain struck out 15 in 6.2 innings of relief.

September 24, 1965: The Tigers, the first American League team to play 10,000 games, trumpeted their achievement by honoring 1900s outfielder Davy Jones, sportswriter E. A. Batchelor and grounds crew member Gilbert Claeys. But the Bengals lost to Cleveland 3-2 in 10 innings.

17

March 12, 1966: The Tigers dedicated Joker Marchant Stadium in Lakeland, Fla., their new spring training home, with a 4-2 win over Minnesota in front of a crowd of 4,919.

August 29, 1966: Denny McLain threw an unbelievable 229 pitches in a nine-inning complete-game victory over Baltimore, 6-3. He walked nine, struck out 11 and gave up eight hits.

June 17, 1967: The Tigers and the Kansas City A's played 28 innings of baseball in the longest doubleheader in American League history. It took nine hours and five minutes to get both games in.

October 1, 1967: On the last day of the regular season, in a doubleheader against California, Detroit needed a sweep to tie for first place with Boston, which had beaten Minnesota earlier that day, and force a playoff. The Tigers won the first game 6-4. In the second game, behind 8-5 in the bottom of the ninth inning with two men on and one out, Dick McAuliffe hit into his only double play over a two-year span to end the game and the season. The Bosox finished 92-70 to win the flag. Detroit and Minnesota finished one game back at 91-71, while Chicago finished three games out at 89-73 to cap one of the tightest pennant races in history.

May 18, 1968: In a day of notable home runs, Al Kaline hit his 307th career home run, putting him in first place past Hank Greenberg among all Tigers, as the Tigers lost 8-4 to Washington. The Senators' Frank Howard hit a homer in his sixth consecutive game to set an AL record; he had 10 home runs in the streak.

June 24, 1968: Jim Northrup hit grand slams in consecutive at-bats vs. Cleveland. It was his son's birthday.

August 6, 1968: John Hiller struck out the first six hitters to start a game vs. Cleveland.

September 14, 1968: Denny McLain won his 30th game, the last pitcher—and the only one since Dizzy Dean in 1934—to do so, in a 5-4 win over the Oakland A's on a rally in the bottom of the ninth.

September 17, 1968: With the magic number to clinch the AL pennant at one—either one Tiger win against the Yankees or one Baltimore Orioles loss at Boston—Detroit led 1-0 going into the ninth inning on a run driven in by starter Joe Sparma. The Yanks scored a run in their half of the ninth to tie the game. But the Tigers clinched the pennant on a clutch Don Wert single driving in Al Kaline to beat New York, 2-1. The Red Sox had already beaten Baltimore 2-0, but that fact was kept off the scoreboard—and from the fans. The stadium erupted after the Tigers won, with Ernie Harwell instructing over the radio, "Let's listen to the bedlam here at Tiger Stadium."

May 15, 1969: Willie Horton, after hearing a growing crescendo of boos in the early part of the Tigers' World Championship defense season, went AWOL from the team after coming in from left field after the first half of the seventh inning of a game in Detroit. He missed the entire series in Minnesota against the Twins, but rejoined the club in Chicago for a series against the White Sox. Horton cited unspecified "personal problems" as the reason for his walkout. Detroit general manager Jim Campbell fined Horton $1,360 for his disappearing act.

July 18, 1969: Horton tied an American League record for a left fielder with 11 putouts in a nine-inning game and hit a two-run homer to give Denny McLain and the Tigers the win, 4-0.

THE 1970S

June 21, 1970: Cesar Gutierrez, the Tigers' shortstop, went 7-for-7 in a 12-inning, 9-8 win over Cleveland. It was Mickey Stanley's home run that won it, though.

July 1, 1970: Denny McLain returned from a season-to-date suspension for bookmaking in front of a Tiger Stadium crowd of 53,863. He was pulled from the game against New York in the sixth inning, but the Tigers rallied in the 11th inning to win 6-5.

July 2, 1970: Tigers hurler Joe Niekro had a no-hitter in the ninth inning broken up by the Yanks' Horace Clarke, the third time Clarke had done so in the past month.

January 11, 1971: Detroit pitcher John Hiller suffered a heart attack and had to sit out the season to recuperate.

June 26, 1972: Bill Slayback pitched seven no-hit innings vs. New York in his first game in the big leagues.

August 5, 1972: Shortstop Ed Brinkman committed an error for the first time in 72 games and 331 total chances in a 4-3 win over Cleveland.

September 30, 1973: The Tigers' Marvin Lane became the last player to hit a home run in Yankee Stadium before the 1974–75 refurbishing which brought in the fences.

September 24, 1974: Al Kaline, back in his home town of Baltimore, got his 3,000th career hit, a double off the Orioles' Dave McNally, as the Tigers won 5-4.

August 16, 1975: Ray Bare broke a team 19-game losing streak with a two-hit, 8-0 shutout vs. California.

May 1, 1976: Willie Horton's consecutive-game RBI streak reached its peak of 10 (with 17 RBI since the streak started April 18).

September 9, 1977: "Sweet Lou" Whitaker and Alan Trammell made their Tigers debut together. Whitaker went 3-for-5 and Trammell 2-for-3 in their first game. They would be teammates for 19 years, holding down the keystone positions.

April 21, 1979: A Tigers-Blue Jays game was nearly canceled after unionized electricians, concession workers and service employees refused to cross the umpires' picket line. The umps eventually relented and let the game be played "in the best interest of the fans." But it may not have been in the Tigers' best interest, as they lost 5-4.

May 31, 1979: Pat Underwood, in his major-league debut for the Tigers, pitched 8.1 innings of shutout ball against his brother, Tom, winning a 1-0 decision against the Toronto Blue Jays.

June 12, 1979: The Tigers hired Sparky Anderson as manager. The fired Les Moss, who had a 27-26 record in his first season as a manager, was offered another position with the club, but he declined.

THE 1980S

October 3, 1981: The Tigers contended for the second-half American League East title set up by the players' strike, and were in the race to the second-to-last day of the season. The Tigers were a half-game behind the Brewers as they headed into Milwaukee for the final three games of the season, but the Tigers lost the first two games 8-2 and 2-1, giving the Brewers the second-half title.

September 20, 1983: The Tigers scored 11 runs in the first inning en route to a 14-1 pasting of the Baltimore Orioles in a rain-shorted five-inning contest. Detroit got 11 straight runners in the opening frame by virtue of 10 hits and a walk.

December 16, 1983: On the heels of a solid second-place season, the Tigers showed they meant business by signing their first major free agent ever, 1B-3B Darrell Evans. (The Tigers had signed one other regular, second baseman Tito Fuentes in 1977, as a free agent, but he was only a stopgap until Lou Whitaker was ready.) The move paid off handsomely; Evans hit a three-run homer in his first game as the Tigers went on to win the World Series. Evans had five good seasons with the Tigers.

April 7, 1984: Jack Morris, pitching on national television, hurled a no-hitter to beat the White Sox, 4-0. The Tigers went to 5-0 on the season, this being the midpoint of a 9-0 streak.

June 4, 1984: The Tigers' Dave Bergman may have had the franchise's best-ever at-bat against Toronto's Roy Lee Howell. If not, it qualifies as the most-seen at-bat, happening as it did in a nationwide "Monday Night Baseball" telecast on ABC. It came after the Tigers began the season 35-5, with the Blue Jays furiously trying to keep pace. Even by winning twice as many games as they lost, they were still 3-1/2 games behind Detroit. The score was tied in the bottom of the 10th inning. Two men were on, two men were out. Howell got two quick strikes on Bergman, who fouled off seven straight two-strike offerings. On Howell's next pitch, Bergman blasted the ball into the upper deck in right field for a three-run homer to give the Tigers the victory.

September 18, 1984: Randy O'Neal won his first major league game as the Tigers clinched the AL East with a 3-0 shutout against the Milwaukee Brewers. Detroit was just the fourth team to be in first place every day of the season. The 1887 Detroit Wolverines were the first team to accomplish that feat.

April 16, 1985: The Tigers beat Milwaukee to start the season 6-0. Coming after the club's fabulous 1984 season and the 9-0 start that year, the fans are thinking in terms of "back-to-back" and "dynasty." However, by May 3, the Tigers slipped to 11-9 and third place, never to rise higher that year.

November 17, 1987: Alan Trammell was robbed of the AL Most Valuable Player award by Toronto's George Bell, who contributed nothing during the Jays' collapse in the final week of the season. Trammell hit .343 with 28 home runs and 105 RBI compared to Bell's .308 batting average, 47 homers and 134 RBI.

April 20, 1988: Hundreds of members and supporters of the Tiger Stadium Fan Club took part in a "stadium hug" in a show of love and support for the edifice which had been serving Tigers fans since 1912. The fan club kept up public, political and legal pressure against building a replacement for Tiger Stadium for the better part of a decade.

August 31, 1988: The first-place Tigers acquired Fred Lynn from Baltimore for a final playoff push. Major-league rules stated that a player had to report to his new club by midnight August 31 in order to be eligible for a postseason roster. With Lynn and the Orioles being in Southern California for a series against the Angels, Detroit chartered a plane for Lynn to fly to Chicago, where the Tigers were playing the White Sox. But the strategy didn't work. Lynn arrived after midnight, and the Tigers fell short of first place, losing out to Boston.

May 18, 1989: Manager Sparky Anderson took a leave of absence from the club after its dismal 13-24 start. In his place, Dick Tracewski led Detroit to a 9-9 record. Anderson returned June 6. While the Tigers cited exhaustion as the reason for Anderson's leave, Anderson said in 1996, the reason was not exhaustion but "a personal thing. Jim Campbell, who was my dear friend, the (Tigers') president, said, `We will call it exhaustion.' Jim went to his grave knowing what it was, and I know what it was. But it was not exhaustion."

THE 1990S

April 18, 1991: The Tigers opened the new Comiskey Park in Chicago, and proceeded to tear the house down, clobbering the White Sox 16-0.

April 13, 1993: In the biggest home-opener rout in Tigers history, Detroit demolished Oakland, 20-4. Four days later, the Tigers won another laugher by a bigger margin, this time against Seattle, 20-3.

June 19, 1994: The Tigers tied a major-league record by homering in their 25th straight game with a Mickey Tettleton blast against the Blue Jays.

July 27, 1994: Sparky Anderson passed Joe McCarthy to move into fourth place on the all-time managerial win list with 2,126 in a 3-1 win over the Seattle Mariners.

August 30, 1995: Lou Whitaker and Alan Trammell played in an AL-record 1,915th game together, but the Tigers lost to the White Sox, 10-7.

October 1, 1995: The Tigers were shut out in Baltimore for the third straight game to end the season, not scoring a run and allowing 22 in Sparky Anderson's last series as a manager.

May 3–4, 1996: The Tigers became the first AL team in 79 years to fall victim to consecutive one-hitters—and at home, yet—thrown by the Texas Rangers' Ken Hill and Roger Pavlik.

May 14–27, 1996: The Tigers endured a 12-game losing streak. During the streak they gave up the most hits that season (21 vs. Chicago in a 16-4 loss), the fewest hits that season (3 vs. Cleveland in a 5-0 loss), and fanned the most hitters (14 vs. Kansas City in a 13-inning, 5-4 loss).

September 18, 1996: Red Sox ace Roger Clemens struck out 20 Tigers. It was the second time Clemens had struck out 20 in a game, doing so a decade apart. For the Tigers, their loss to Clemens was the 11th loss in a row, en route to their second 12-loss streak of the season.

September 23, 1997: The Tigers beat Boston 6-0 to push their record to 79-78. It was the only time apart from the first week of the season the Tigers would have a winning record between July 16, 1995 (a 12-6 [first game] loss at home to California), and September 1, 2000 (a 7-5 win at home over Texas). Detroit lost the final five games of the season to finish 79-83.

April 17–19, 1998: Because of falling concrete in Yankee Stadium, a weekend series was hastily moved to Detroit. The move didn't faze the Yanks as they took the first two of the three-game series en route to an AL-record 112 wins.

July 20, 1998: In a homer-happy year, the Tigers were homer-unhappy as their pitchers gave up an AL record four two-out home runs to the Boston Red Sox in a 9-4 loss. Three of the dingers came in the fourth inning.

August 1, 1998: Tony Clark set an American League record by homering from both sides of the plate for the third time in a season as the Tigers shut out the Tampa Bay Devil Rays 8-0.

September 27, 1998: Bobby Higginson broke up a no-hitter by the Blue Jays' Roy Halladay on the season's final day with a home run. The Tigers lost 2-1 in a game that took only 1:45 to play.

September 27, 1999: In the last Tigers game at Tiger Stadium, rookie Rob Fick hit a grand-slam home run off the roof in the bottom of the eighth inning to put the icing on the cake in Detroit's 8-2 win over Kansas City.

THE 2000S (SO FAR)

June 29, 2000: Detroit gave up three sacrifice flies in an inning, tying a major league mark, in a game against the Yankees. A none-out fly ball was dropped by left fielder Bobby Higginson, but the official scorer ruled the play a sacrifice fly because the runner at third could not have anticipated the misplay. Two more fly balls Higginson's way brought in two more New York runs.

September 15, 2000: The Tigers and the Red Sox tied an American League record by using 42 players—in just nine innings—in a 7-6 Red Sox win. Boston had 34 players available and used 24 of them; Detroit had 33 players in uniform and used 18. It's a mark the Tigers would tie that October 1 in a game against Minnesota. Detroit used 23 players and the Twins 19.

October 1, 2000: The Tigers' Shane Halter played all nine positions in the field—not to mention getting his second career four-hit game and scoring the winning run—in a 12-11 season-ending contest against Minnesota.

May 4, 2001: Pinch-runners aren't so rare. But sending a pitcher to pinch-run is relatively rare. With no out in the ninth inning and with the Tigers down 7-5 to Anaheim, Steve Sparks pinch-ran for Robert Fick, who started the inning with a single. But here's where it gets truly rare: Phil Garner had Ryan Jackson pinch-run for pinch-runner Sparks; research shows this has happened only nine times since 1992. Rarer yet was that the last substitution took place during an at-bat (a 3-2 count to Jose Macias with one out), not between at-bats. Macias struck out after Jackson came in, as did Bobby Higginson to end the game.

HOMER, SWEET HOMER

Ah, there's nothing like a home run being lofted into the seats to make a fan stand up and cheer, then sit back down with smiling satisfaction. Given that Tiger Stadium acquired a reputation as a hitter's park, coupled with the fact that players cognizant of that tried harder to belt one into the stands—especially with a 10-foot overhang in the right-field upper deck—there are many individual and group statistics for which the Tigers can be proud. It doesn't hurt that batters swing for the fences to fatten their future paychecks.

THE TIGERS' RECORD-SETTING
HOME RUN INFIELD OF 1986

Player, Position	HR
Darrell Evans, 1B	29
Lou Whitaker, 2B	20
Alan Trammell, SS	21
Darnell Coles, 3B	20*
Lance Parrish, C	22**

*Home run #20 was hit the last game of the season in 1986.
**While the 1940 Red Sox infielders each hit 20 home runs, their catcher did not.

HOMERS IN RECORD-SETTING 12-HOMER GAME VS. WHITE SOX, MAY 28, 1995

1st inning:	Tigers, Chad Curtis off James Baldwin, 0 on
	Tigers, Cecil Fielder off Baldwin, 2 on
2nd inning:	Tigers, Curtis off Baldwin, 0 on
	Tigers, Fielder off Baldwin, 2 on
4th inning:	White Sox, Ray Durham off David Wells, 0 on
	White Sox, Ron Karkovice off Wells, 0 on
	White Sox, Craig Grebeck off Wells, 0 on
	Tigers, Kirk Gibson off Kirk McCaskill, 0 on
6th inning:	White Sox, Frank Thomas off John Doherty, 0 on
	Tigers, Gibson off Rob Dibble, 0 on
7th inning:	White Sox, Karkovice off Doherty, 0 on
8th inning:	Tigers, Lou Whitaker off Scott Radinsky, 0 on

The game set a record with 10 solo homers, and tied a mark of four players with multi-homer games.

THE TIGERS' CLUB-RECORD EIGHT HOME RUNS AT TORONTO, JUNE 20, 2000

1st inning:	Juan Gonzalez off Chris Carpenter, 2 on
	Juan Encarnacion off Carpenter, 0 on
2nd inning:	Bobby Higginson off Carpenter, 1 on
3rd inning:	Deivi Cruz off Matt DeWitt, 1 on
4th inning:	Tony Clark off DeWitt, 1 on
8th inning:	Clark off Darwin Cubillan, 1 on
9th inning:	Robert Fick off John Frascatore, 2 on
	Rich Becker off Frascatore, 0 on

TIGERS WHO HOMERED IN THEIR FIRST AT-BAT

Hack Miller*, April 23, 1944, at Cleveland off Al Smith
George Vico, April 20, 1948, at Chicago off Joe Haynes (first pitch)
Gates Brown**, June 19, 1963, at Boston off Bob Heffner
Bill Roman*, September 30, 1964, at New York off Jim Bouton
Gene Lamont, September 2, 1970, at Boston off Cal Koonce
Reggie Sanders, September 1, 1974, vs. Oakland off Catfish Hunter

*This was the only big-league homer he'd ever hit.
**Brown was the first black in the American League to homer in his first at-bat.

TOP HOMER HITTERS AT TIGER/BRIGGS STADIUM/NAVIN FIELD 1912–1999

Tigers	HR
Al Kaline	226
Norm Cash	210
Hank Greenberg*	187
Lou Whitaker	146
Rudy York	139
Cecil Fielder	127
Willie Horton	124
Dick McAuliffe	107
Bill Freehan	100

*Greenberg holds the single-season record of 39 in 1938, a major-league record for home runs by any hitter in any park.

Visitors	HR
Babe Ruth	60
Ted Williams	55
Jimmie Foxx**	52
Mickey Mantle	42
Yogi Berra	37
Carl Yastrzemski	36
Harmon Killebrew	35
Joe DiMaggio	30

**Foxx holds single-season record of 9.

Totals	HR
Al Kaline	226
Norm Cash	212
Hank Greenberg	187
Lou Whitaker	146
Rudy York	140
Cecil Fielder	130
Willie Horton	127
Dick McAuliffe	107
Lance Parrish	102
Bill Freehan	100

TOP PITCHERS SURRENDERING HOMERS

To Al Kaline

Pitcher	HRs Allowed
Jim Kaat	10
Tom Brewer	9
Pedro Ramos	8
Billy Pierce	7

To Hank Greenberg (as a Tiger)

Pitcher	HRs Allowed
Lefty Grove	9
Mel Harder	7
Nels Potter	7
Lefty Gomez	6
Bump Hadley	6
Red Ruffing	6

To Norm Cash (as a Tiger)

Pitcher	HRs Allowed
Bill Monbouquette	9
Catfish Hunter	8
Jim Grant	7
Gary Bell	6
Lee Stange	6
Ralph Terry	6

To Willie Horton (as a Tiger)

Pitcher	HRs Allowed
Dave McNally	10
Clyde Wright	9
Catfish Hunter	6
Luis Tiant	6

HOMER, SWEET HOMER

Two generations of Tigers greats meet as Ty Cobb (left) greets Harvey Kuenn (center) and Al Kaline. (Photo courtesy Ernie Harwell Collection/Burton Historical Collection, Detroit Public Library)

TOP BATTERS HITTING HOMERS

Off Hal Newhouser (as a Tiger)

Player	HR
Joe DiMaggio	9
Joe Gordon	9
Bobby Doerr	5
Luke Easter	4
Johnny Lindell	4
Vern Stephens	4

HOMER, SWEET HOMER

Off Mickey Lolich (as a Tiger)

Player	HR
Roy White	7
Carl Yastrzemski	7
Frank Howard	6
Harmon Killebrew	6
Joe Pepitone	6
Rico Petrocelli	6

Off Jack Morris (as a Tiger)

Player	HR
Kent Hrbek	7
Ernie Whitt	6
George Bell	5
Dwight Evans	5
Eddie Murray	5
Robin Yount	5

HOME RUNS CLEARING THE TIGER STADIUM RIGHT FIELD ROOF

Ted Williams, Boston, May 3, 1939, off Bob Harris
Mickey Mantle, New York, June 18, 1956, off Paul Foytack
Mickey Mantle, New York, September 17, 1958, off Jim Bunning
Mickey Mantle, New York, September 10, 1960, off Paul Foytack
Norm Cash, June 11, 1961, off Joe McClain, Washington
Norm Cash, May 11, 1962, off Don Schwall, Boston
Norm Cash, July 27, 1962, off Eli Grba, Los Angeles
Norm Cash, July 29, 1962, off Bob Botz, Los Angeles
Don Mincher, Minnesota, August 23, 1964, off Fred Gladding
Boog Powell, Baltimore, July 6, 1969, off Denny McLain
Jim Northrup, August 28, 1969, off George Lauzerique, Oakland
Jason Thompson, August 18, 1977, off Catfish Hunter, New York
Jason Thompson, September 17, 1977, off Dick Tidrow, New York
Kirk Gibson, June 14, 1983, off Mike Brown, Boston
Cecil Cooper, Milwaukee, October 2, 1983, off Dave Rozema
Reggie Jackson, California, May 12, 1984, off Juan Berenguer
Ruppert Jones, June 24, 1984, off Tom Tellmann, Milwaukee

HOMER, SWEET HOMER

Lou Whitaker, May 13, 1985, off Burt Hooton, Texas
Kirk Gibson, September 10, 1986, off Chris Bosio, Milwaukee
George Brett, Kansas City, April 17, 1988, off Jeff Robinson
Mickey Tettleton, June 21, 1991, off Kirk McCaskill, California
Mickey Tettleton, June 26, 1991, off Jaime Navarro, Milwaukee
Kirk Gibson, May 1, 1994, off Jack McDowell, Chicago
Chad Kreuter, May 21, 1994, off Jaime Navarro, Milwaukee
Melvin Nieves, May 17, 1996, off Alex Fernandez, Chicago
Carlos Delgado, Toronto, July 6, 1996, off Omar Olivares
Tony Clark, September 15, 1996, off Rocky Coppinger, Baltimore
Bobby Bonilla, Florida, June 17, 1997, off Todd Jones
Tony Clark, July 2, 1997, off Juan Acevedo, New York Mets
Karim Garcia, May 28, 1999, off Jaime Navarro, Chicago
Brant Brown, Pittsburgh, June 9, 1999, off Willie Blair
Jeromy Burnitz, Milwaukee, July 9, 1999, off Nelson Cruz

HOME RUNS CLEARING THE TIGER STADIUM LEFT FIELD ROOF

Harmon Killebrew, Minnesota, August 3, 1962, off Jim Bunning
Frank Howard, Washington, May 18, 1968, off Mickey Lolich
Cecil Fielder, August 25, 1990, off Dave Stewart, Oakland
Mark McGwire, Oakland, April 21, 1997, off Brian Moehler

PITCHERS ALLOWING THE MOST ROOF-CLEARING HOMERS AT TIGER STADIUM

Pitcher	HRs Allowed
Jaime Navarro	3*
Jim Bunning	2
Paul Foytack	2

*What makes Navarro's dubious feat even more distinctive is that he's given up all of the roof-clearing gopher balls as a member of the opposing team (twice with the Brewers, once with the White Sox), thus having had far fewer opportunities to pitch in Tiger Stadium than Tigers pitchers themselves.

HOME RUNS CLEARING THE
CENTER FIELD WALL AT COMERICA PARK

Richie Sexson, Cleveland, May 24, 2000, off Jeff Weaver
J. D. Drew, St. Louis, June 10, 2000, off Brian Moehler
Jim Thome, Cleveland, June 18, 2000, off Willie Blair
Tony Eusebio, Houston, July 15, 2000, off Willie Blair
Ben Grieve, Oakland, August 18, 2000, off Hideo Nomo
Billy McMillon, September 16, 2000 (game 1), off Rolando Arrojo,
        Boston
Dean Palmer, April 29, 2001, off Albie Lopez, Tampa Bay
Dean Palmer, June 9, 2001, off Ben Sheets, Milwaukee

TIGERS WHO HIT
FOUR CONSECUTIVE HOME RUNS

Hank Greenberg, July 26–27, 1938 (2 in each game)
Charlie Maxwell, May 3, 1959 (1 in opening game, 3 in nightcap)
Larry Herndon, May 16 and 18, 1982 (1 in first game, 3 in second)
Bobby Higginson, June 30–July 1, 1997 (3 in first game, 1 in second;
Higginson got walked twice in between his June 30 homers)

TIGERS HITTING
THREE HOME RUNS IN A GAME

Player	Date, Opponent
Ty Cobb	May 25, 1925, vs. St. Louis
Pinky Higgins	May 20, 1940, vs. Boston (consecutive)
Rudy York	September 1, 1941 (first game), vs. St. Louis
Pat Mullin	June 26, 1949 (second game), at New York
Al Kaline	April 17, 1955, vs. Kansas City
Charlie Maxwell	May 3, 1959 (second game), vs. New York (consecutive)
Rocky Colavito	July 5, 1962, at Cleveland (consecutive)
Steve Boros	August 6, 1962, at Cleveland
Willie Horton	June 9, 1970, vs. Milwaukee
Bill Freehan	August 9, 1971, at Boston
Larry Herndon	May 18, 1982, vs. Oakland (consecutive)
Bill Madlock	June 28, 1987 (11 innings), vs. Baltimore
Cecil Fielder	May 6, 1990 (consecutive), at Toronto
	June 6, 1990 (consecutive), at Cleveland
	April 16, 1996 (consecutive), at Toronto
Bobby Higginson	June 30, 1997, vs. New York Mets (consecutive)
	June 24, 2000, at Cleveland (consecutive)

TOP TIGERS HITTING HOME RUNS
TO LEAD OFF A GAME

Player	Years	HR
Lou Whitaker	1982–88	23
Dick McAuliffe	1961–71	19
Tony Phillips	1991–94	13
Eddie Yost	1959–60	8
Luis Polonia	1999–2000	7*
Mickey Stanley	1969–74	7
Roy Johnson	1929–32	7
Jake Wood	1962–65	7
Harvey Kuenn	1954–57	6
Eddie Lake	1946–47	5

*Includes the last game at Tiger Stadium, September 27, 1999.

TIGERS HOME RUNS
IN THE 15TH INNING OR LATER

Player	Versus, Location	Date	On Base	Inning	Score
Billy Rogell	Lefty Gomez, New York, at Detroit	Aug. 15, 1931	0	15	5−7 (16)
Wayne Belardi	Don Mossi, at Cleveland	Aug. 14, 1956	1	15	6−4 (15)
Ray Boone	Don Mossi, at Cleveland	Aug. 14, 1956	0	15	6−4 (15)
Al Kaline	Dick Hall, at Baltimore	May 8, 1965	0	15	4−3 (15)*
Jim Northrup	Lloyd Allen, at California	Aug. 1, 1971	0	16	4−3 (16)*
Lance Parrish	Shane Rawley, at Seattle	May 16, 1978	1	16	4−2 (16)*
Mickey Stanley	Diego Segui, Kansas City, at Detroit	June 17, 1967	0	15	5−6 (19)

*Game winner.

TIGERS ON THE ALL-TIME
PINCH-HOMERS LIST

Rank	Player	Career	As a Tiger
3.*	Gates Brown	16	all

*Tied with Smoky Burgess and Willie McCovey.

CHARLIE MAXWELL'S HOME RUNS
BY DAY OF THE WEEK

Charlie "Paw Paw" Maxwell, who played for the Tigers from 1955 to 1962, was known for hitting home runs on Sundays. Was that reputation justified? Of Maxwell's 133 home runs as a Tiger, here's the day-by-day breakdown. Judge for yourself:

Day of Week	HR
Sunday	35
Monday	7
Tuesday	18
Wednesday	18
Thursday	11
Friday	19
Saturday	25

We can see how he got his reputation. Even noting that the most home runs are hit on Sunday, Maxwell's numbers are noteworthy. Given his high number of Saturday home runs too, it may be surmised that he liked hitting in daylight more than the fact it was Sunday.

TIGERS HITTING BACK-TO-BACK-TO-BACK HOME RUNS

Players	Date	Inning
Roy Cullenbine, Dick Wakefield, Hoot Evers	April 23, 1947	8th inning
Harvey Kuenn, Earl Torgeson, Charley Maxwell	July 7, 1956	7th inning
Norm Cash, Steve Boros, Gates Brown	May 23, 1961	9th inning
Jim Northrup, Norm Cash, Willie Horton	August 17, 1971	7th inning
Aurelio Rodriguez, Al Kaline, Willie Horton	June 27, 1972	1st inning
Al Kaline, Bill Freehan, Mickey Stanley	July 29, 1974*	1st inning
Kirk Gibson, Lance Parrish, Darrell Evans	July 8, 1986	4th inning
Alan Trammell, Kirk Gibson, John Grubb	July 31, 1986	5th inning
John Grubb, Matt Nokes, Bill Madlock	June 28, 1987	9th inning
Alan Trammell, Cecil Fielder, Gary Ward	August 7, 1990	9th inning
Alan Trammell, Cecil Fielder, Mickey Tettleton	April 20, 1992	3rd inning
Robert Fick, Juan Encarnacion, Shane Halter	June 24, 2001	2nd inning

*Second game.

TIGERS WHO GAVE UP SOME OF BABE RUTH'S 60 HOME RUNS IN 1927

#9.   Rip Collins, May 17, at Detroit, 8th inning, 0 on
#17. Earl Whitehill, June 5, at New York, 6th inning, 0 on
#27. Don Hankins, July 8 (2nd game), at Detroit, 2nd inning, 2 on
#28. Ken Holloway, July 9 (1st game), at Detroit, 1st inning, 1 on
#29. Ken Holloway, July 9 (1st game), at Detroit, 4th inning, 2 on
#35. George Smith, Aug. 5, at New York, 8th inning, 0 on
#55. Sam Gibson, September 21, at New York, 9th inning, 0 on
#56. Ken Holloway, September 22, at New York, 9th inning, 1 on

TIGERS WHO GAVE UP SOME OF ROGER MARIS' 61 HOME RUNS IN 1961

#1.   Paul Foytack, April 26, at Detroit, 5th inning, 0 on
#23.   Don Mossi, June 17, at Detroit, 4th inning, 0 on
#24.   Jerry Casale, June 18, at Detroit, 8th inning, 1 on
#31.   Frank Lary, July 4 (2nd game), at New York, 8th inning, 1 on
#52.   Frank Lary, September 2, at New York, 6th inning, 0 on
#53.   Hank Aguirre, September 2, at New York, 8th inning, 1 on
#57.   Frank Lary, September 16, at Detroit, 3rd inning, 1 on
#58.   Terry Fox, September 17, at Detroit, 12th inning, 1 on

TIGERS WHO GAVE UP SOME OF SAMMY SOSA'S 66 HOME RUNS IN 1998

#31.   Seth Greisinger, June 24, at Detroit, 1st inning, 0 on*
#32.   Brian Moehler, June 25, at Detroit, 7th inning, 0 on

* This homer broke Rudy York's record of most home runs in a month; York had hit 18 homers in August, 1937, a 31-day month.

TIGERS WHO GAVE UP SOME OF MARK McGWIRE'S 70 HOME RUNS IN 1998

Trick question; there were none! Tigers hurlers kept McGwire from hitting any in the six interleague games they played. The Tigers were the only team McGwire faced but didn't homer against that year.

MORE HITTING AND OFFENSE

We have been living in an era where offense is paramount in baseball. Hitters haven't had a chance like this to fatten up their stats—and their salaries—since the start of the live-ball era in the 1920s and the Depression years of the 1930s. Sometimes using stats to argue for a player's performance is like trying to clutch a fistful of Jell-O. Still, even impressive numbers may not make much sense unless some context is provided, which is what we attempt here. Notice that relatively early on in this chapter, that we've listed the top Tigers in several offensive categories three ways: career leaders, followed by single-season leaders, followed by their ranking on the major leagues' all-time list. Notice further that, for your ease, we've ordered them to read as you would see them appear in most player tabulations: games played, followed by at-bats, followed by runs scored, and so on. This chapter also includes lists of Tigers who led the American League in their respective categories, and, in an homage to life before the designated hitter, pitchers' hitting. Enjoy!

YEARS THE TIGERS LED THE AMERICAN LEAGUE IN RUNS SCORED

Year	Runs	Games	RS/G	Year	Runs	Games	RS/G
1907	694	153	4.54	1935	919	152	6.05
1908	647	154	4.20	1940	888	155	5.73
1909	660	158	4.22	1955	775	154	5.03
1910	679	155	4.38	1961	841	163	5.16
1915	778	156	4.99	1968	671	164	4.09
1916	670	155	4.32	1980	830	163	5.09
1924	849	156	5.44	1984	829	162	5.12
1925	903	156	5.79	1987	896	162	5.53
1929	926	155	5.97	1992	791	162	4.88
1934	958	154	6.22	1993	899	162	5.55

By contrast, the Tigers have allowed the fewest runs per game in the league only three times.

THE TIGERS' RECORD-SETTING HITTING TEAM OF 1921

Detroit had the highest single-season team batting average, .316, in 1921; the starters' averages, in descending order: Harry Heilmann, RF, .394 (led American League); Ty Cobb, CF-mgr., .389; Bobby Veach, LF, .338; Lu Blue, 1B, .308; Johnny Bassler, C, .307; Ira Flagstead, SS, .305; Bob Jones, 3B, .303; Pep Young, 2B, .299.

THE TIGERS' AL-RECORD RBI OUTFIELD OF 1921

Player, Position	RBI
Harry Heilmann, LF	139
Bobby Veach, RF	128
Ty Cobb, CF	101
Total	**368**

The Tigers' AL-Record RBI Regular Infield of 1934

Player, Position	RBI
Hank Greenberg, 1B	139
Charlie Gehringer, 2B	127
Billy Rogell, SS	100
Marv Owen, 3B	96
Total	**462**

Gehringer, Rogell and Owen played every game in 1934. Hank Greenberg missed only one— when he sat out for Yom Kippur.

Tigers in the .300 Avg., 30 HR, 100 RBI Club

Player	Year	Avg.	HR	RBI
Hank Greenberg	1935	.328	36*	170*
Hank Greenberg	1937	.337	40	183
Rudy York	1937	.307	35	103
Hank Greenberg	1938	.315	58*	146
Hank Greenberg	1939	.312	33	112
Hank Greenberg	1940	.340	41	150
Rudy York	1940	.316	33	134
Norm Cash	1961	.361	41	132
Bobby Higginson	2000	.300	30	102

*Led league.

Tigers in the .300 Avg., 100 R, 40 2B, 30 HR, 100 RBI Club

Player	Year	Avg.	R	2B	HR	RBI
Hank Greenberg	1935	.328	121	63*	36*	170*
Hank Greenberg	1937	.337	137	49	40	183*
Hank Greenberg	1939	.312	112	42	33	112
Hank Greenberg	1940	.340	129	50*	41*	150*
Rudy York	1940	.316	105	46	33	134
Bobby Higginson	2000	.300	104	44	30	102

*Led league.

TIGERS TOP TEN
SINGLE-SEASON CONSECUTIVE-GAME
HITTING STREAKS

Player	Games	Year
Ty Cobb	40	1911
Ty Cobb	35	1917
John Stone	34	1930
Goose Goslin	30	1934
Ron LeFlore	30	1976
Dale Alexander	29	1930
Pete Fox	29	1935
Ron LeFlore	27	1978
Gee Walker	27	1937
Ty Cobb	25*	1906
John Stone	25*	1931

*Tied for 10th.

TIGERS WINNING THE AL
TRIPLE CROWN OF HITTING

Ty Cobb, 1909: .377, 9 HR, 107 RBI

His Triple Crown figures led both major leagues. Cobb also led the majors with 216 hits, .517 slugging percentage, 296 total bases and 76 stolen bases.

TIGERS HITTING FOR THE CYCLE*

Bobby Veach, September 17, 1920, vs. Boston (12 innings)
Bob Fothergill, September 26, 1926, vs. Boston
Gee Walker, April 30, 1937, vs. Cleveland
Charlie Gehringer, May 27, 1939, vs. St. Louis Browns (in single-double-triple-homer order)
Vic Wertz, September 14, 1947, at Washington (game 1)
George Kell, June 2, 1950, at Philadelphia Athletics (game 2)
Hoot Evers, September 7, 1950, vs. Cleveland (10 innings)
Travis Fryman, July 28, 1993, vs. New York
Damion Easley, June 8, 2001, vs. Milwaukee

*Pat McCauley also did it for Detroit's Western League entry August 6, 1897, vs. Kansas City.

TIGERS WITH SIX OR MORE HITS IN A GAME

Doc Nance, July 13, 1901
Bobby Veach, September 17, 1920 (12 innings)
Ty Cobb, May 5, 1925
George Kell, September 20, 1946
Rocky Colavito (7-for-10), June 24, 1962 (22 innings)
Jim Northrup, August 28, 1969 (13 innings)
Cesar Gutierrez (7-for-7), June 21, 1970 (2nd game, 12 innings)
Damion Easley, August 8, 2001

MOST STOLEN BASES IN ONE GAME

Johnny Neun, 5 vs. New York, July 9, 1927. He went 5-for-5 and scored four times in a 14-1 laugher in the second game of a twin bill, called after seven innings due to darkness.

TOP HITS BY TIGERS SWITCH-HITTERS

Player	Hits
Donie Bush	1,745
Billy Rogell	1,210
Lu Blue	1,002
Pep Young	792
Tony Clark	783
Tony Phillips	771
Mickey Tettleton	469
Roy Cullenbine	421

THE TIGERS' ONLY THREE POSITION PLAYERS WHO BATTED RIGHT AND THREW LEFT

Player	Hits
Delos Drake	88
Mark Carreon	78
Pat Meany	0

BEST CAREER BATTING AVERAGE FOR TIGERS PITCHERS (100-AB MINIMUM)

Pitcher	Years	AB	H	Avg.
George Uhle	1929–33	370	105	.284
Schoolboy Rowe	1933–42	551	151	.274
Joe Yeager	1901–03	286	76	.266
Fred Hutchinson	1939–41, 1946–53	642	170	.265
George Mullin	1902–13	1,403	365	.260
Bert Cole	1921–25	174	44	.253
Chief Hogsett	1929–36, 1944	248	61	.246
Sam Gibson	1926–28	180	44	.244
Jean Dubuc	1912–16	557	136	.244
Ed Wells	1923–27	157	36	.229

WORST CAREER BATTING AVERAGE FOR TIGERS PITCHERS (100-AB MINIMUM)

Pitcher	Years	AB	H	Avg.
Dave Wickersham	1964–67	200	12	.060
Mike Kilkenny	1969–72	100	7	.070
Hank Aguirre	1958–67	352	29	.082
Al Benton	1938–42, 1945–48	373	37	.099
Joe H. Coleman*	1971–72	178	18	.101
Mickey Lolich	1963–72	758	83	.109
John Hiller	1965–70, 1972	100	11	.110
George Gill	1937–39	109	13	.119
Duke Maas	1955–57	117	14	.120
Joe Sparma	1964–69	263	32	.122

*Joe's dad, Joe P., has the highest career batting average among Tigers pitchers: .750, although it was on 3-for-4 hitting.

MOST HOME RUNS FOR TIGERS PITCHERS

Pitcher	Years	HR
Dizzy Trout	1939–52	19
Earl Wilson	1966–70	17
Schoolboy Rowe	1933–42	9
Hooks Dauss	1912–26	6
Frank Lary	1954–64	6
Chief Hogsett	1929–36, 1944	5
George Uhle	1929–33	4
Ed Willett	1906–13	4
Jean Dubuc	1912–16	4
Lou Sleater	1957–58	4

THE LONGEST WAIT FOR A PLAYER'S FIRST STOLEN BASE

Slugger Cecil Fielder waited 1,097 games before recording his first stolen base for the Tigers in 1996. In his 10 AL seasons before that, he had only tried five times before—each one unsuccessfully—to steal a base, including as a Blue Jay in Detroit's 1-0 AL East pennant-clinching win October 4, 1987.

TIGERS MASTER BOTH SWINGS OF THE BATTING AVERAGE PENDULUM

1961: Norm Cash led the AL with a .361 average. The next year, he sank to .243; the drop of .118 is the largest recorded single-season drop by a regular.

1995: Bobby Higginson, in his rookie season, hit .224. The next year, he hit .320; the jump of .096 is the largest recorded single-season increase by a regular (100 games minimum).

THE TIGERS' BIGGEST CHEATER?

Norm Cash hit an amazing .361 in 1961, leading the league, and hit 41 home runs in the year Roger Maris broke Babe Ruth's mark with 61. He also had career bests in hits, RBI, runs scored, triples, slugging percentage and on-base percentage. Cash never came close to duplicating those feats. How did he do it in '61? He used a corked bat, in which the bat has been partially hollowed out at the barrel end and filled with cork or a cork-like substance, believed to give the ball more zing once it leaves the bat. Afraid he would be found out, Cash never used a corked bat after that season. Near the end of his career, he said, "I owe my success to expansion pitching, a short right field fence and my hollow bats."

A DISPUTED TY COBB HIT

In a 1922 game against the Yankees, official scorer John Kieran of the *New York Tribune* gave shortstop Everett Scott an error on an infield grounder by Cobb. Detroit writer Frederick Lieb ruled it a hit and sent his notebook to the Associated Press, which credited Cobb with a hit, putting his season-ending average at .401. In his 1946 book *The Detroit Tigers*, Lieb said the controversy would have been buried if AL statistician Irwin Howe "hadn't been so darn honest." Lieb said Howe accepted Lieb's scoring because of "my superior scoring experience." When AL president Ban Johnson learned of the discrepancy, he ruled that Howe's statistics should stand, thus keeping Cobb at .401. Baseball researcher Pete Palmer discovered the discrepancy anew in 1981, but baseball ignored the request to change Cobb's average. Now, stat books are divided on whether to give Cobb a .401 or a .399 average for 1922. Our position: We go with the numbers used by *Total Baseball*, which is the official record of major league baseball. The numbers you'll see in this chapter and elsewhere throughout the book reflect that—even if they vary with earlier historical records.

TIGERS TOP TEN
CAREER GAMES-PLAYED LEADERS

Player	Years	Games
Al Kaline	1953–74	2,834
Ty Cobb	1905–26	2,806
Lou Whitaker	1977–95	2,390
Charlie Gehringer	1924–42	2,323
Alan Trammell	1977–96	2,293
Sam Crawford	1903–17	2,114
Norm Cash	1960–74	2,018
Harry Heilmann	1914, 1916–29	1,989
Donie Bush	1908–21	1,872
Bill Freehan	1961, 1963–76	1,774

TIGERS TOP SINGLE-SEASON
GAMES PLAYED

In 42 of the Tigers' first 100 seasons—but only 12 of the last 40, with the expanded 162-game schedule—some Tiger has played in all the team's games, win, lose or tie. In all, the feat has been accomplished 58 times by 34 players. Those who have done it the most are Charlie Gehringer (six times), Sam Crawford (five), Rudy York (four) and Donie Bush (three).

1903, 137 games: Sam Crawford
1904, 162 games: Jimmy Barrett
1905, 154 games: Sam Crawford
1907, 153 games: Claude Rossman
1913, 153 games: Donie Bush, Sam Crawford
1914, 157 games: Donie Bush, Sam Crawford
1915, 156 games: Sam Crawford, Ty Cobb
1917, 154 games: Bobby Veach
1918, 128 games: Donie Bush
1919, 140 games: Harry Heilmann
1922, 155 games: Topper Rigney, Bobby Veach
1928, 154 games: Charlie Gehringer
1929, 155 games: Dale Alexander, Charlie Gehringer
1930, 154 games: Dale Alexander, Charlie Gehringer
1933, 155 games: Charlie Gehringer, Billy Rogell

46

1934, 154 games: Charlie Gehringer, Marv Owen, Billy Rogell
1935, 152 games: Hank Greenberg
1936, 154 games: Charlie Gehringer, Marv Owen
1938, 155 games: Pete Fox, Hank Greenberg
1940, 155 games: Rudy York
1941, 155 games: Rudy York
1943, 155 games: Dick Wakefield, Rudy York
1945, 155 games: Rudy York
1946, 155 games: Eddie Lake
1947, 158 games: Eddie Lake
1949, 155 games: Vic Wertz
1950, 157 games: Johnny Groth, George Kell, Jerry Priddy
1951, 154 games: Jerry Priddy
1954, 155 games: Harvey Kuenn
1955, 154 games: Bill Tuttle
1958, 154 games: Frank Bolling
1961, 163 games: Rocky Colavito
1962, 161 games: Rocky Colavito
1965, 162 games: Don Wert
1972, 156 games: Ed Brinkman
1973, 162 games: Ed Brinkman
1975, 159 games: Willie Horton
1976, 161 games: Rusty Staub
1978, 162 games: Rusty Staub
1981, 109 games: Lou Whitaker
1991, 162 games: Cecil Fielder
1995, 144 games: Chad Curtis, Travis Fryman
1997, 162 games: Brian Hunter

TIGERS ON THE ALL-TIME GAMES PLAYED LIST

Rank	Player	Games	As a Tiger
4.	Ty Cobb	3,035	2,806
11.	Rusty Staub	2,951	549
14.	Al Kaline	2,834	all
25.	Darrell Evans	2,687	727
37.*	Sam Crawford	2,517	2,254
66.	Eddie Mathews	2,391	67
67.	Lou Whitaker	2,390	all
80.	Charlie Gehringer	2,323	all
86.	Alan Trammell	2,293	all
89.	Goose Goslin	2,287	524

*Tied with Bill Buckner.

TIGERS TOP TEN CAREER AT-BATS LEADERS

Player	At-Bats	Years
Ty Cobb	10,591	1905–26
Al Kaline	10,116	1953–74
Charlie Gehringer	8,860	1924–42
Lou Whitaker	8,570	1977–95
Alan Trammell	8,288	1977–96
Sam Crawford	7,984	1903–17
Harry Heilmann	7,297	1914, 1916–29
Donie Bush	6,970	1908–21
Norm Cash	6,593	1960–74
Bill Freehan	6,073	1961, 1963–76

TIGERS TOP TEN
SINGLE-SEASON AT-BATS

Player	At-Bats	Year
Harvey Kuenn	679	1953
Ron LeFlore	666	1978
Jake Wood	663	1961
Travis Fryman	659	1992
Brian Hunter	658	1997
Harvey Kuenn	656	1954
Ron LeFlore	652	1977
Lou Whitaker	643	1983
Rusty Staub	642	1978
Charlie Gehringer	641*	1936
George Kell	641*	1950

*Tied for 10th.

TIGERS ON THE ALL-TIME
AT-BATS LIST

Rank	Player	Career	As a Tiger
5.	Ty Cobb	11,434	10,591
19.	Al Kaline	10,116	all
27.	Rusty Staub	9,720	2,100
30.	Sam Crawford	9,570	7,984
59.	Darrell Evans	8,973	2,349
61.	Charlie Gehringer	8,860	all
67.	Al Simmons	8,759	568
78.	Lou Whitaker	8,570	all
79.	Eddie Mathews	8,537	160
90.	Alan Trammell	8,288	all

TIGERS TOP TEN
CAREER RUN SCORERS

Player	Runs	Years
Ty Cobb	2,088	1905–26
Charlie Gehringer	1,774	1924–42
Al Kaline	1,622	1953–74
Lou Whitaker	1,386	1977–95
Donie Bush	1,242	1908–21
Alan Trammell	1,231	1977–96
Harry Heilmann	1,209	1914, 1916–29
Sam Crawford	1,115	1903–17
Norm Cash	1,028	1960–74
Hank Greenberg	980	1930, 1933–41, 1945–46

TIGERS TOP TEN
SINGLE-SEASON RUNS SCORED

Player	Runs	Year
Ty Cobb	147*	1911
Ty Cobb	144	1915
Charlie Gehringer	144	1930
Charlie Gehringer	144	1936
Hank Greenberg	144	1938
Hank Greenberg	137	1937
Charlie Gehringer	134	1934
Charlie Gehringer	133	1937
Charlie Gehringer	133	1938
Charlie Gehringer	131**	1929
Lu Blue	131**	1922

* It's the record for most runs in the dead-ball era, before 1921.
** Tied for 10th.

TIGERS ON THE ALL-TIME RUNS SCORED LIST

Rank	Player	Career	As a Tiger
2.	Ty Cobb	2,246*	2,088
16.	Charlie Gehringer	1,774	all
34.**	Al Kaline	1,622	all
53.	Eddie Mathews	1,509	18
54.	Al Simmons	1,507	96
58.	Goose Goslin	1,483	346
71.	Sam Crawford	1,391	1,115
73.	Lou Whitaker	1,386	all
81.	Darrell Evans	1,344	357
96.	Tony Phillips	1,300	502
99.	Harry Heilmann	1,291	1,209

*Cobb broke Honus Wagner's run record of 1,740 May 25, 1923.
**Tied with Fred Clarke.

TIGERS TOP TEN IN CAREER HITS

Player	Hits	Years
Ty Cobb	3,900	1905–26
Al Kaline	3,007	1953–74
Charlie Gehringer	2,839	1924–42
Harry Heilmann	2,499	1914, 1916–29
Sam Crawford	2,466	1903–17
Lou Whitaker	2,369	1977–95
Alan Trammell	2,365	1977–96
Bobby Veach	1,859	1912–23
Norm Cash	1,793	1960–74
Donie Bush	1,745	1908–21

TIGERS TOP TEN
SINGLE-SEASON HITS

Player	Hits	Year
Ty Cobb	248	1911
Harry Heilmann	237	1921
Charlie Gehringer	227	1936
Ty Cobb	226	1912
Ty Cobb	225	1917
Harry Heilmann	225	1925
George Kell	218	1950
Sam Crawford	217	1911
Ty Cobb	216	1909
Dale Alexander	215*	1929
Charlie Gehringer	215*	1929

*Tied for 10th.

TIGERS ON THE ALL-TIME HITS LIST

Rank	Player	Career	As a Tiger
2.	Ty Cobb	4,189*	3,900
22.	Al Kaline	3,007	all
27.	Sam Crawford	2,961	2,466
31.	Al Simmons	2,927	186
40.	Charlie Gehringer	2,839	all
46.	Goose Goslin	2,735	582
49.	Rusty Staub	2,716	582
53.	Doc Cramer	2,705	766
60.	Harry Heilmann	2,660	2,499
74.	Heinie Manush	2,524	674
97.	Lou Whitaker	2,369	all
99.	Alan Trammell	2,365	all

*Cobb broke Honus Wagner's hit record of 3,415 Sept. 20, 1923.

TIGERS TOP TEN
CAREER DOUBLES HITTERS

Player	Doubles	Years
Ty Cobb	665	1905–26
Charlie Gehringer	574	1924–42
Al Kaline	498	1953–74
Harry Heilmann	497	1914, 1916–29
Lou Whitaker	420	1977–95
Alan Trammell	412	1977–96
Sam Crawford	402	1903–17
Hank Greenberg	366	1930, 1933–41, 1945–46
Bobby Veach	345	1912–23
Harvey Kuenn	244	1952–59

TIGERS TOP TEN
IN SINGLE-SEASON DOUBLES

Player	Doubles	Year
Hank Greenberg	63	1934
Charlie Gehringer	60	1936
George Kell	56	1950
Gee Walker	55	1936
Harry Heilmann	50	1927
Charlie Gehringer	50	1934
Hank Greenberg	50	1940
Hank Greenberg	49	1937
Ty Cobb	47*	1911
Charlie Gehringer	47*	1930
Dale Alexander	47*	1930

*Three-way tie for ninth.

TIGERS ON THE ALL-TIME DOUBLES LIST

Rank	Player	Career	As a Tiger
4.	Ty Cobb	724	665
15.	Charlie Gehringer	574	all
17.	Harry Heilmann	542	497
21.	Al Simmons	539	38
36.	Goose Goslin	500	116
37.	Rusty Staub	499	104
38.*	Al Kaline	498	all
41.	Heinie Manush	491	124
58.**	Sam Crawford	458	402
93.	Lou Whitaker	420	all

*Tied with Bill Buckner and Sam Rice.
**Tied with Jimmie Foxx.

TIGERS TOP TEN CAREER TRIPLES HITTERS

Player	Triples	Years
Ty Cobb	284	1905–26
Sam Crawford	249	1903–17
Charlie Gehringer	146	1924–42
Harry Heilmann	145	1914, 1916–29
Bobby Veach	136	1912–23
Al Kaline	75	1953–74
Donie Bush	73	1908–21
Dick McAuliffe	70	1960–73
Hank Greenberg	69	1930, 1933–41, 1945–46
Lu Blue	66	1921–27

TIGERS TOP TEN
SINGLE-SEASON TRIPLES

Player	Triples	Years
Sam Crawford	26	1914
Sam Crawford	25	1903
Ty Cobb	24	1911
Ty Cobb	24	1917
Ty Cobb	23	1912
Sam Crawford	23	1913
Sam Crawford	21	1912
Ty Cobb	20	1908
Sam Crawford	19*	1910
Sam Crawford	19*	1915
Charlie Gehringer	19*	1929
Roy Johnson	19*	1931
Barney McCosky	19*	1940

*Five-way tie for ninth.

TIGERS ON THE
ALL-TIME TRIPLES LIST

Rank	Player	Career	As a Tiger
1.	Sam Crawford	309	249
2.	Ty Cobb	295	284
22.	Goose Goslin	173	22
38.*	Sam Thompson	161	1
40.**	Heinie Manush	160	42
49.***	Harry Heilmann	151	145
51.+	Al Simmons	149	6
53.++	Wally Pipp	148	3
55.	Bobby Veach	147	136
57.	Charlie Gehringer	146	all
83.+++	Earl Averill	128	7

*Tied with George Van Haltren
**Tied with Harry Hooper.
***Tied with Jim Bottomley.
+Tied with Kip Selbach.
++Tied with Enos Slaughter.
+++Tied with Arky Vaughan.

TIGERS TOP TEN
CAREER HOME RUN HITTERS

Player	HR	Years
Al Kaline	399	1953–74
Norm Cash	373	1960–74
Hank Greenberg	306	1930, 1933–41, 1945–46
Willie Horton	262	1963–77
Cecil Fielder	245	1990–96
Lou Whitaker	244	1977–95
Rudy York	239	1934, 1937–45
Lance Parrish	212	1977–86
Bill Freehan	200	1961, 1963–76
Kirk Gibson	195	1979–87, 1993–95

TIGERS TOP TEN
SINGLE-SEASON HOME RUNS

Player	HR	Years
Hank Greenberg	58	1938
Cecil Fielder	51	1990
Rocky Colavito	45	1961
Hank Greenberg	44	1946
Cecil Fielder	44	1991
Hank Greenberg	41	1940
Norm Cash	41	1961
Hank Greenberg	40	1937
Darrell Evans	40	1985*
Norm Cash	39	1962

*Evans is the first player to hit 40–plus homers in a season in each league, 1973 (with Atlanta) and 1985. He's also the oldest to reach 40 homers in a season (age 38 in 1985) and the oldest league home run champion (also 1985).

TIGERS ON THE ALL-TIME HOME RUNS LIST

Rank	Player	Career	As a Tiger
14.*	Eddie Mathews	512	9
32.	Darrell Evans	414	141
34.	Al Kaline	399	all
36.	Juan Gonzalez	397	22
42.**	Frank Howard	382	13
47.***	Norm Cash	377	373
50.	Rocky Colavito	374	139
73.	Hank Greenberg	331	306
74.	Willie Horton	325	258
75.+	Lance Parrish	324	212
77.	Cecil Fielder	319	245
87.++	Al Simmons	307	13
89.	Fred Lynn	306	18
96.	Rusty Staub	292	70

*Tied with Ernie Banks.
**Tied with Jim Rice.
***Tied with Andres Galarraga
+Tied with Gary Carter.
++Tied with Greg Luzinski.

TIGERS TOP TEN IN CAREER RUNS BATTED IN

Player	RBI	Years
Ty Cobb	1,804	1905–26
Al Kaline	1,583	1953–74
Harry Heilmann	1,442	1914, 1916–29
Charlie Gehringer	1,427	1924–42
Sam Crawford	1,264	1903–17
Hank Greenberg	1,202	1930, 1933–41, 1945–46
Norm Cash	1,087	1960–74
Lou Whitaker	1,084	1977–95
Bobby Veach	1,042	1912–23
Alan Trammell	1,003	1977–96

TIGERS TOP TEN
SINGLE-SEASON RUNS BATTED IN

Player	RBI	Years
Hank Greenberg	183	1938
Hank Greenberg	170	1935
Hank Greenberg	150	1940
Hank Greenberg	146	1938
Rocky Colavito	140	1961
Harry Heilmann	139	1921
Hank Greenberg	139	1934
Dale Alexander	137	1929
Dale Alexander	135	1930
Harry Heilmann	134*	1925
Rudy York	134*	1940

*Tied for 10th.

TIGERS ON THE
ALL-TIME RBI LIST

Rank	Player	Career	As a Tiger
5.	Ty Cobb	1,938*	1,804
14.	Al Simmons	1,827	112
22.	Goose Goslin	1,609	369
29.	Al Kaline	1,583	all
34.	Harry Heilmann	1,539	1,442
37.	Sam Crawford	1,525	1,264
42.**	Rusty Staub	1,466	358
44.	Eddie Mathews	1,453	27
49.	Charlie Gehringer	1,427	all
64.	Darrell Evans	1,354	415
80.***	Sam Thompson	1,305	3
89.****	Hank Greenberg	1,276	1,202

*Cobb broke Cap Anson's career RBI record of 1,879 in 1927.
**Tied with Ed Delahanty.
***Tied with Roberto Clemente.
****Tied with Don Baylor.

TIGERS TOP TEN
IN CAREER BATTING AVERAGE
(2,000-AB MINIMUM)

Player	Avg.	Years
Ty Cobb	.368	1905–26
Harry Heilmann	.342	1914, 1916–29
Bob Fothergill	.337	1922–30
George Kell	.325	1946–52
Heinie Manush	.321	1923–27
Charlie Gehringer	.320	1924–42
Hank Greenberg	.319	1930, 1933–41, 1945–46
Gee Walker	.317	1931–37
Harvey Kuenn	.314	1952–59
Barney McCosky	.312	1939–42, 1946

TIGERS TOP TEN
SINGLE-SEASON BATTING AVERAGE

Player	Avg.	Year
Ty Cobb	.420*	1911
Ty Cobb	.410	1912
Harry Heilmann	.403	1923
Ty Cobb	.401	1922
Harry Heilmann	.398	1927
Harry Heilmann	.394	1921
Harry Heilmann	.393	1925
Ty Cobb	.390	1913
Ty Cobb	.389	1921
Ty Cobb	.385	1910

*Cobb's is the highest AL average for an outfielder.

TIGERS ON THE
ALL-TIME BATTING AVERAGE LIST
(1,000-GAME MINIMUM)

Rank	Player	Career	As a Tiger
1.	Ty Cobb	.366	.368
11.	Harry Heilmann	.342	.342
20.	Sam Thompson	.335	.226
21.	Al Simmons	.334	.327
29.	Heinie Manush	.330	.321
34.	Bob Fothergill	.325	.337
38.	Babe Herman	.324	.300
46.	Charlie Gehringer	.320	same
51.	Mickey Cochrane	.320	.313
54.	Earl Averill	.318	.267
64.	Goose Goslin	.316	.297
70.	Hank Greenberg	.313	.319
81.	Barney McCosky	.312	.312
82.	Hughie Jennings	.312	.333
94.	Bobby Veach	.310	.311
98.	Sam Crawford	.309	.309

TIGERS TOP TEN
IN CAREER ON-BASE PERCENTAGE
(2,000-AB MINIMUM)

Player	OBP	Years
Ty Cobb	.434	1905–26
Johnny Bassler	.420	1921–27
Hank Greenberg	.412	1930, 1933–41, 1945–46
Harry Heilmann	.410	1914, 1916–29
Charlie Gehringer	.404	1924–42
Lu Blue	.403	1921–27
Dick Wakefield	.396	1941, 1943–44, 1946–49
Tony Phillips	.395	1990–95
George Kell	.391	1946–52
Topper Rigney	.389	1922–25

TIGERS TOP TEN
SINGLE-SEASON ON-BASE PERCENTAGE

Player	OBP	Year
Norm Cash	.487	1961
Ty Cobb	.486	1915
Harry Heilmann	.481	1923
Harry Heilmann	.475	1927
Ty Cobb	.468	1925
Ty Cobb	.467	1913
Ty Cobb	.467	1911
Ty Cobb	.462	1922
Charlie Gehringer	.458	1937
Ty Cobb	.458	1912

TIGERS ON THE
ALL-TIME ON-BASE PERCENTAGE LIST

Rank	Name	Career	As a Tiger
8.	Ty Cobb	.433	.434
12.	Ferris Fain	.425	.459
20.	Mickey Cochrane	.419	.444
28.	Hank Greenberg	.412	.412
30.	Harry Heilmann	.410	.410
35.	Roy Cullenbine	.408	.412
41.	Charlie Gehringer (career-long Tiger)	.404	.404
66.*	Eddie Yost	.395	.425
67.*	Earl Averill	.395	.342
69.	Johnny Pesky	.394	.367
74.	Wally Schang	.393	.311
90.	Hughie Jennings	.391	.333

Ty Cobb's bat-grip technique permitted him to slap the ball to virtually any spot on the field. He retired with 4,189 hits and the highest batting average in major-league history. (Photo courtesy National Baseball Hall of Fame Library, Cooperstown, N.Y.)

TIGERS TOP TEN
IN CAREER SLUGGING PERCENTAGE
(2,000-AB MINIMUM)

Player	Slg.	Years
Hank Greenberg	.616	1930, 1933–41, 1945–46
Harry Heilmann	.518	1914, 1916–29
Ty Cobb	.517	1905–26
Rudy York	.503	1934, 1937–45
Rocky Colavito	.501	1960–63
Cecil Fielder	.498	1990–96
Norm Cash	.490	1960–74
Bobby Higginson	.489	1995–
Ray Boone	.482	1953–58
Bob Fothergill	.482	1922–30

TIGERS TOP TEN
SINGLE-SEASON SLUGGING PERCENTAGE

Player	Slg.	Year
Hank Greenberg	.683	1938
Hank Greenberg	.670	1940
Hank Greenberg	.668	1937
Norm Cash	.662	1961
Rudy York	.651	1937
Harry Heilmann	.632	1923
Hank Greenberg	.628	1935
Hank Greenberg	.622	1939
Ty Cobb	.621	1911
Harry Heilmann	.616	1927

TIGERS ON THE
ALL-TIME SLUGGING PERCENTAGE LIST
(1,000-GAME MINIMUM)

Rank	Player	Career	As a Tiger
5.	Hank Greenberg	.605	.616
12.	Juan Gonzalez	.568	.505
31.	Al Simmons	.535	.484
33.	Earl Averill	.534	.440
36.	Babe Herman	.532	.450
48.	Harry Heilmann	.520	.518
59.	Ty Cobb	.512	.517
61.	Eddie Mathews	.509	.413
64.	Sam Thompson	.508	.290
76.	Goose Goslin	.500	.456
83.	Frank Howard	.499	.450
99.	Larry Doby	.490	.309

TIGERS TOP TEN
IN CAREER BASES ON BALLS

Player	BB	Years
Al Kaline	1,277	1953–74
Lou Whitaker	1,197	1977–95
Charlie Gehringer	1,186	1924–42
Ty Cobb	1,148	1905–26
Donie Bush	1,125	1908–21
Norm Cash	1,025	1960–74
Alan Trammell	850	1977–96
Dick McAuliffe	842	1960–73
Harry Heilmann	792	1914, 1916–29
Hank Greenberg	748	1930, 1933–41, 1945–46

TIGERS TOP TEN
SINGLE-SEASON BASES ON BALLS

Player	BB	Year
Roy Cullenbine*	137	1947
Eddie Yost	135	1959
Tony Phillips	132	1993
Eddie Yost	125	1960
Norm Cash	124	1961
Mickey Tettleton	122	1992
Eddie Lake	120	1947
Hank Greenberg	119	1938
Donie Bush	118**	1915
Ty Cobb	118**	1915

*Cullenbine had a record 22 straight games getting at least one walk, July 2–24, 1947. His 137 walks in 1947 are the most by a player in his last year. He hit .224, but led the AL in walks and was fourth in homers, and was second on the Tigers in RBI.
**Tied for 10th.

TIGERS ON THE
ALL-TIME BASES ON BALLS LIST

Rank	Player	Career	As a Tiger
9.	Eddie Yost	1,614	260
10.	Darrell Evans	1,605	437
19.	Eddie Mathews	1,444	20
28.	Tony Phillips	1,319	519
32.	Al Kaline	1,277	all
35.	Rusty Staub	1,255	250
36.	Ty Cobb	1,249	1,148
44.*	Lou Whitaker	1,197	all
48.	Charlie Gehringer	1,186	all
49.	Donie Bush	1,158	1,125
60.**	Lu Blue	1,092	589
75.***	Norm Cash	1,043	1,025

*Tied with Brian Downing.
**Tied with Stan Hack.
***Tied with Eddie Joost.

TIGERS TOP TEN
IN CAREER STRIKEOUTS

Player	SO	Years
Lou Whitaker	1,099	1977 – 95
Norm Cash	1,081	1960 – 74
Al Kaline	1,020	1953 – 74
Willie Horton	945	1963 – 77
Dick McAuliffe	932	1960 – 73
Travis Fryman	931	1990 – 97
Kirk Gibson	930	1979 – 87, 1993 – 95
Cecil Fielder	926	1990 – 96
Alan Trammell	874	1977 – 96
Lance Parrish	847	1977 – 86

TIGERS TOP TEN
SINGLE-SEASON STRIKEOUTS

Player	BB	Year
Cecil Fielder	182*	1990
Rob Deer	175	1991
Melvin Nieves	158	1996
Melvin Nieves	157	1997
Dean Palmer	153	1999
Cecil Fielder	151	1991
Cecil Fielder	151	1992
Travis Fryman	149	1991
Travis Fryman	144**	1992
Tony Clark	144	1997

*A record for first basemen.
**A record for shortstops.

TIGERS ON THE
ALL-TIME STRIKEOUTS LIST

Rank	Player	Career	As a Tiger
26.	Lance Parrish	1,527	847
32.	Tony Phillips	1,499	480
34.	Eddie Mathews	1,487	35
35.	Frank Howard	1,460	36
36.	Juan Samuel	1,442	64
45.	Darrell Evans	1,410	433
46.	Rob Deer	1,409	426
48.	Eric Davis	1,398	63
63.	Cecil Fielder	1,316	926
64.	Willie Horton	1,313	945
66.*	Mickey Tettleton	1,307	505
69.	Dean Palmer	1,299	358
71.	Travis Fryman	1,287	931
72.	Kirk Gibson	1,285	930
76.	Pete Incaviglia	1,277	98

*Tied with Tim Wallach.

TIGERS TOP TEN
IN CAREER STOLEN BASES

Player	SB	Years
Ty Cobb	865	1905–26
Donie Bush	400	1908–21
Sam Crawford	317	1903–17
Ron LeFlore	294	1974–79
Alan Trammell	236	1977–96
Kirk Gibson	194	1979–87, 1993–95
George Moriarty	190	1909–15
Bobby Veach	189	1912–23
Charlie Gehringer	181	1924–42
Lou Whitaker	143	1977–95

TIGERS TOP TEN
SINGLE-SEASON STOLEN BASES

Player	SB	Year
Ty Cobb	96	1915
Ty Cobb	83	1911
Ron LeFlore	78	1979
Ty Cobb	76	1909
Brian Hunter	74	1997
Ty Cobb	68	1916
Ron LeFlore	68	1978
Ty Cobb	65	1910
Ty Cobb	61	1912
Ron LeFlore	58	1976

TIGERS ON THE
ALL-TIME STOLEN BASES LIST

Rank	Player	Career	As a Tiger
4.	Ty Cobb	892	865
6.	Vince Coleman	752	0
44.*	Ron LeFlore	455	294
61.	Donie Bush	404	400
65.**	Juan Samuel	396	10
67.+	Dave Collins	395	27
85.	Sam Crawford	366	317
91.++	Hughie Jennings	359	0
93.+++	Gary Pettis	354	100
99.++++	Eric Davis	349	7

*Tied with Ed Delahanty.
**Tied with Sam Mertes.
+Tied with Bill North.
++Tied with Fielder Jones and Barry Larkin.
+++Tied with Buck Ewing.
++++Tied with George Case

TOP TIGERS IN CAREER
STEALS OF HOME

Rank	Player	SB
1.	Ty Cobb	50
26.	Donie Bush	12

Research continues to uncover more steals of home from baseball's early era, and numbers may change over the years.

TIGERS TOP TEN
IN CAREER TOTAL BASES

Player	TB	Years
Ty Cobb	5,466	1905–26
Al Kaline	4,852	1953–74
Charlie Gehringer	4,257	1924–42
Harry Heilmann	3,778	1914, 1916–29
Lou Whitaker	3,651	1977–95
Sam Crawford	3,576	1903–17
Alan Trammell	3,442	1977–96
Norm Cash	3,233	1960–74
Hank Greenberg	2,950	1930, 1933–41, 1945–46
Bobby Veach	2,653	1912–23

TIGERS TOP TEN
SINGLE-SEASON TOTAL BASES

Player	TB	Year
Hank Greenberg	397	1937
Hank Greenberg	389	1935
Hank Greenberg	384	1940
Hank Greenberg	380	1938
Ty Cobb	367*	1911
Harry Heilmann	365	1921
Dale Alexander	362	1929
Hank Greenberg	356	1934
Charlie Gehringer	356	1936
Norm Cash	354	1961

*The record most total bases in dead-ball era, prior to 1921.

TIGERS ON THE
ALL-TIME TOTAL BASES LIST

Rank	Player	Career	As a Tiger
4.	Ty Cobb	5,854	5,466
20.	Al Kaline	4,852	all
26.	Al Simmons	4,685	275
39.	Eddie Mathews	4,349	66
40.	Sam Crawford	4,328	3,576
41.	Goose Goslin	4,325	892
46.	Charlie Gehringer	4,257	all
51.	Rusty Staub	4,185	912
59.	Harry Heilmann	4,053	3,778
73.	Darrell Evans	3,866	1,056
93.	Heinie Manush	3,665	996
96.	Lou Whitaker	3,651	all

TIGERS TOP TEN
SINGLE-SEASON PINCH HITS

Player	PH	Years
Bob Fothergill*	19	1929
Gates Brown	18	1968
Sammy Hale	17	1920
Vic Wertz	17	1962
Gates Brown	16	1974
Gus Zernial	15	1958
Billy Rhiel	13	1932
Pat Mullin	13	1953
Gates Brown	13	1966
Dalton Jones	13	1971

*Fothergill has the highest pinch-hit batting average of anyone with at least 200 at-bats: 60-for-200, a .300 average. Al Kaline is fifth all-time career pinch hitting with at least 100 at-bats. He went 37-for-115 for a .322 average. Kaline and Rod Carew are the only Hall-of-Famers with 100 pinch-hit at-bats.

TIGERS WHO WON
THE AMERICAN LEAGUE BATTING TITLE

Player	Year	Avg.
Ty Cobb	1907	.350*
Ty Cobb	1908	.324*
Ty Cobb	1909	.377
Ty Cobb	1910	.383
Ty Cobb	1911	.420
Ty Cobb	1912	.409
Ty Cobb	1913	.390
Ty Cobb	1914	.368
Ty Cobb	1915	.369
Ty Cobb	1917	.383
Ty Cobb	1918	.382
Ty Cobb	1919	.384
Harry Heilmann	1921	.394
Harry Heilmann	1923	.403
Harry Heilmann	1925	.393
Heinie Manush	1926	.378
Harry Heilmann	1927	.398
Charlie Gehringer**	1937	.371
George Kell	1949	.343
Al Kaline	1955	.340
Harvey Kuenn	1959	.353
Norm Cash	1961	.361

*Cobb and Ted Williams are the only two players to have won two batting titles with averages below their career averages.

**At age 34, Gehringer is the oldest AL player to win his first batting title.

TIGERS WHO WON
THE AMERICAN LEAGUE HOME RUN TITLE

Player	Year	HR
Sam Crawford	1908	7*
Ty Cobb	1909	9**
Hank Greenberg	1935	36***
Hank Greenberg	1938	58
Hank Greenberg	1940	41
Rudy York	1943	34
Hank Greenberg	1946	44
Darrell Evans	1985	40
Cecil Fielder	1990	51
Cecil Fielder	1991	44***

*Crawford shares the record for fewest home runs an
AL home run leader.
**Cobb missed two Triple Crowns due to home runs;
he tied for second in 1907, and was one home run
short in 1911.
***Tied.

TIGERS WHO WON
THE AMERICAN LEAGUE RBI TITLE

Player	Year	RBI
Ty Cobb	1907	119
Ty Cobb	1908	108
Ty Cobb	1909	107
Sam Crawford	1910	120
Ty Cobb	1911	127
Sam Crawford	1914	104
Sam Crawford	1915	112*
Bobby Veach	1915	112*
Bobby Veach	1917	103
Bobby Veach	1918	78
Hank Greenberg	1935	170
Hank Greenberg	1937	183
Hank Greenberg	1940	150
Rudy York	1943	118
Hank Greenberg	1946	127
Ray Boone	1955	116*
Cecil Fielder	1990	132
Cecil Fielder	1991	133
Cecil Fielder**	1992	124

*Tied.
**Fielder's three straight RBI titles were equaled only
by Babe Ruth.

TIGERS WHO LED THE AMERICAN LEAGUE IN ON-BASE PERCENTAGE

Player	Year	OBP
Jimmy Barrett	1901	.401
Ty Cobb	1909	.431
Ty Cobb	1910	.456
Ty Cobb	1913	.467
Ty Cobb	1915	.486
Ty Cobb	1917	.444
Ty Cobb	1918	.440
Eddie Yost	1959	.435
Eddie Yost	1960	.414
Norm Cash	1961	.488

TIGERS WHO LED THE AMERICAN LEAGUE IN SLUGGING PERCENTAGE

Player	Year	Slg.
Ty Cobb	1907	.468
Ty Cobb	1908	.475
Ty Cobb	1909	.517
Ty Cobb	1910	.551
Ty Cobb	1911	.621
Ty Cobb	1912	.584
Ty Cobb	1914	.513
Ty Cobb	1917	.570
Hank Greenberg	1940	.670
Rudy York	1943	.527
Al Kaline	1959	.530
Cecil Fielder	1990	.592

TIGERS WHO LED THE AMERICAN LEAGUE IN RUNS SCORED

Player	Year	Runs
Ty Cobb	1909	116
Ty Cobb	1910	106
Ty Cobb	1911	147
Ty Cobb	1915	144
Ty Cobb	1916	113
Charlie Gehringer	1929	131
Charlie Gehringer	1934	134
Hank Greenberg	1938	144
Eddie Yost	1959	115
Dick McAuliffe	1968	95
Ron LeFlore	1978	126
Tony Phillips	1992	114

TIGERS WHO LED
THE AMERICAN LEAGUE IN HITS

Player	Year	Hits
Ty Cobb	1907	212
Ty Cobb	1908	188
Ty Cobb	1909	216
Ty Cobb	1911	248
Ty Cobb	1912	226
Ty Cobb	1915	208
Ty Cobb	1917	225
Ty Cobb	1919	191*
Bobby Veach	1919	191*
Dale Alexander	1929	215*
Charlie Gehringer	1929	215*
Charlie Gehringer	1934	214
Barney McCosky	1940	200*
Dick Wakefield	1943	200
George Kell	1950	218
George Kell	1951	191
Harvey Kuenn**	1953	209
Harvey Kuenn	1954	201*
Al Kaline	1955	200
Harvey Kuenn	1956	196
Harvey Kuenn	1959	198
Norm Cash	1961	193

*Tied.
**Kuenn also set a rookie mark for singles in a season with 167.

TIGERS WHO LED
THE AMERICAN LEAGUE IN DOUBLES

Player	Year	2B
Ty Cobb	1908	36
Sam Crawford	1909	35
Ty Cobb	1911	47
Bobby Veach	1915	40
Ty Cobb	1917	44
Bobby Veach	1919	45
Harry Heilmann	1924	45*
Roy Johnson	1929	45*
Charlie Gehringer	1929	45*
Hank Greenberg	1934	63
Charlie Gehringer	1936	60
Hank Greenberg	1940	50
Dick Wakefield	1943	38
George Kell	1950	56
George Kell	1951	36*
Harvey Kuenn	1955	38
Harvey Kuenn	1958	39
Harvey Kuenn	1959	42
Al Kaline	1961	41

*Tied.

TIGERS WHO LED
THE AMERICAN LEAGUE IN TRIPLES

Player	Year	3B
Sam Crawford	1903	25
Ty Cobb	1908	20
Sam Crawford	1910	19
Ty Cobb	1911	24
Sam Crawford	1913	23
Sam Crawford	1914	26*
Sam Crawford	1915	19
Ty Cobb	1917	24
Ty Cobb	1918	14
Bobby Veach	1919	17
Charlie Gehringer	1929	19
Roy Johnson	1931	19
Barney McCosky	1940	19
Hoot Evers	1950	11**
Jake Wood	1961	14

*Tied for most triples by an AL outfielder.
**Tied.

TIGERS WHO LED
THE AMERICAN LEAGUE IN TOTAL BASES

Player	Year	TB
Ty Cobb	1907	283
Ty Cobb	1908	276
Ty Cobb	1909	296
Ty Cobb	1911	367
Sam Crawford	1913	298
Ty Cobb	1915	284
Ty Cobb	1917	335
Hank Greenberg	1935	389
Hank Greenberg	1940	384
Rudy York	1943	301
Al Kaline	1955	321
Rocky Colavito	1962	309
Cecil Fielder	1990	339

TIGERS WHO LED
THE AMERICAN LEAGUE IN
BASES ON BALLS

Player	Year	BB
Donie Bush	1909	88
Donie Bush	1910	78
Donie Bush	1911	98
Donie Bush	1912	117
Donie Bush	1914	112
Hank Greenberg	1938	119*
Eddie Yost	1959	135
Eddie Yost	1960	125
Mickey Tettleton	1992	122*
Tony Phillips	1993	132

*Tied.

TIGERS WHO LED
THE AMERICAN LEAGUE IN
STRIKEOUTS

Player	Year	SO
Hank Greenberg	1939	95
Jake Wood	1961	141
Cecil Fielder	1990	182
Rob Deer	1991	175
Travis Fryman	1994	128

TIGERS WHO LED THE AMERICAN LEAGUE IN STOLEN BASES

Player	Year	SB
Ty Cobb	1907	49
Ty Cobb	1909	76
Ty Cobb	1911	83
Ty Cobb	1915	96
Ty Cobb	1916	68
Ty Cobb	1917	55
Charlie Gehringer	1929	27
Marty McManus	1930	23
Ron LeFlore	1978	68
Brian Hunter	1997	74

TIGERS WHO LED THE AMERICAN LEAGUE IN RUNS CREATED

Player	Year	RC
Ty Cobb	1907	133
Ty Cobb	1908	113
Ty Cobb	1909	138
Ty Cobb	1910	138
Ty Cobb	1911	172
Ty Cobb	1915	154
Ty Cobb	1917	144
Ty Cobb	1918	90
Hank Greenberg	1935	156
Hank Greenberg	1940	152
Eddie Yost	1959	112
Norm Cash	1961	158

TIGERS WHO LED AMERICAN LEAGUE CATCHERS IN RUNS CREATED/GAME*

Player	Year	RC/G
Oscar Stanage	1911	3.4
Mickey Cochrane	1934	7.5
Mickey Cochrane	1935	8.3
Bill Freehan	1966	3.4
Bill Freehan	1967	6.4
Bill Freehan	1968	6.3
Bill Freehan	1969	5.0
Bill Freehan	1971	5.3
Lance Parrish	1982	6.2
Lance Parrish	1984	4.1
Matt Nokes	1987	6.2
Mickey Tettleton	1991	7.1
Mickey Tettleton	1992	6.0

*Runs Created Per Game is a statistic invented by Bill James. It estimates the number of runs per game a team made up of entirely that player would score. For example, a team made up entirely of 1934 Mickey Cochranes would have scored 7.5 runs per game.

TIGERS WHO LED AMERICAN LEAGUE FIRST BASEMEN IN RUNS CREATED/GAME

Player	Year	RC/G
Claude Rossman	1908	5.2
Jim Delahanty	1911	7.4
Rudy York	1940	8.6
Rudy York	1943	6.6
Hank Greenberg	1946	7.8
Gail Harris	1958	5.4
Norm Cash	1961	11.6
Norm Cash	1963	6.6
Norm Cash	1965	7.0
Norm Cash	1971	7.0
Cecil Fielder	1990	7.5

TIGERS WHO LED
AMERICAN LEAGUE SECOND BASEMEN IN
RUNS CREATED/GAME

Player	Year	RC/G
Charlie Gehringer	1927	6.4
Charlie Gehringer	1930	7.7
Charlie Gehringer	1934	9.5
Charlie Gehringer	1936	9.3
Charlie Gehringer	1937	9.4
Charlie Gehringer	1938	8.4
Charlie Gehringer	1939	8.7
Charlie Gehringer	1940	7.6
Dick McAuliffe	1967	5.7
Dick McAuliffe	1968	5.5
Lou Whitaker	1983	6.4
Lou Whitaker	1984	5.2
Lou Whitaker	1991	7.5

TIGERS WHO LED
AMERICAN LEAGUE SHORTSTOPS IN
RUNS CREATED/GAME

Player	Year	RC/G
Kid Elberfeld	1901	7.8
Donie Bush	1909	5.0
Donie Bush	1910	5.1
Donie Bush	1914	4.1
Topper Rigney	1924	5.9
Harvey Kuenn	1955	5.8
Dick McAuliffe	1966	6.6
Alan Trammell	1987	8.4
Alan Trammell	1988	5.9
Alan Trammell	1990	6.9
Travis Fryman	1993	7.3

TIGERS WHO LED
AMERICAN LEAGUE THIRD BASEMEN IN
RUNS CREATED/GAME

Player	Year	RC/G
Marty McManus	1929	5.5
Pinky Higgins	1943	4.7
Pinky Higgins	1944	6.1
George Kell	1947	5.6
George Kell	1949	7.3
Ray Boone	1956	7.2
Eddie Yost	1959	7.7
Eddie Yost	1960	6.4

TIGERS WHO LED
AMERICAN LEAGUE OUTFIELDERS IN
RUNS CREATED/GAME

Player	Year	RC/G
Ty Cobb	1907	8.5
Ty Cobb	1909	9.3
Ty Cobb	1910	10.8
Ty Cobb	1911	12.4
Ty Cobb	1913	9.2
Ty Cobb	1915	10.2
Ty Cobb	1917	9.9
Ty Cobb	1918	8.7
Ty Cobb	1925	10.7
Hank Greenberg	1940	10.2
Al Kaline	1959	7.9

TIGERS TOP TEN
IN CAREER RUNS CREATED

Player	RC	Years
Ty Cobb	2,406	1905–26
Al Kaline	1,794	1953–74
Charlie Gehringer	1,766	1924–42
Harry Heilmann	1,502	1914, 1916–29
Lou Whitaker	1,398	1977–95
Sam Crawford	1,392	1903–17
Alan Trammell	1,248	1977–96
Norm Cash	1,218	1960–74
Hank Greenberg	1,180	1930, 1933–41, 1945–46
Bobby Veach	966	1912–23

TIGERS TOP TEN
IN CAREER RUNS CREATED PER GAME
(2,000-AB MINIMUM)

Player	RC/G	Years
Hank Greenberg	9.2	1930, 1933–41, 1945–46
Ty Cobb	8.8	1905–26
Harry Heilmann	7.7	1914, 1916–29
Charlie Gehringer	7.4	1924–42
Mickey Tettleton	6.8	1991–94
Dick Wakefield	6.6	1941, 1943–44, 1946–49
Goose Goslin	6.6	1934–37
Norm Cash	6.6	1960–74
Rudy York	6.5	1934, 1937–45
Bob Fothergill	6.5	1922–30

TIGERS TOP TEN
SINGLE-SEASON RUNS CREATED

Player	Year	RC
Ty Cobb	1911	172
Hank Greenberg	1938	163
Hank Greenberg	1937	160
Norm Cash	1961	158
Hank Greenberg	1935	156
Ty Cobb	1915	154
Hank Greenberg	1940	152
Charlie Gehringer	1936	149
Ty Cobb	1912	148
Charlie Gehringer	1934	145

TIGERS TOP TEN
SINGLE-SEASON RUNS CREATED
PER GAME

Player	Year	RC/G
Ty Cobb	1911	12.4
Norm Cash	1961	11.6
Harry Heilmann	1927	11.4
Ty Cobb	1912	11.3
Harry Heilmann	1923	11.0
Ty Cobb	1910	10.8
Hank Greenberg	1938	10.8
Ty Cobb	1925	10.7
Hank Greenberg	1937	10.4
Hank Greenberg	1940	10.2

Pitching and Defense

Despite Tiger Stadium's reputation as a hitter's park, good pitchers have flourished within its confines. It's just that bad pitchers can't be disguised as being better than they really are in such cozy quarters. Detroit's mound mastery began with the likes of Roscoe Miller, Wild Bill Donovan and George Mullin, continued through the heydays of Hooks Dauss, Earl Whitehill, Tommy Bridges, Schoolboy Rowe, Hal Newhouser, Dizzy Trout and Virgil Trucks in the first half of the twentieth century, and prospered anew when Jim Bunning, Frank Lary, Denny McLain, Mickey Lolich, Mark Fidrych, Jack Morris and Dan Petry toed the slab. Despite the fact that Newhouser is the only pitcher in the Hall of Fame with the Old English "D" on his cap, Tigers pitchers truly have been kings of the hill. See for yourself.

Years the Tigers Led the League in Fewest Runs Allowed

Year	Runs	Games
1944	581	156
1968	492	164
1984	645	162

TIGERS WHO PITCHED NO-HITTERS

George Mullin, July 4, 1912, vs. St. Louis at Navin Field, 7-0
Virgil Trucks, May 15, 1952, vs. Washington at Briggs Stadium, 1-0
Virgil Trucks*, August 25, 1952, vs. New York at Yankee Stadium, 1-0
Jim Bunning, July 20, 1958, vs. Boston at Fenway Park, 3-0
Jack Morris, April 9, 1984, vs. Chicago at Comiskey Park, 4-0

*Trucks' no-hitters came in 1952, when the club's offense was so miserable—note that both games were 1-0—it was joked that Trucks had to pitch a no-hitter to win. Trucks himself went 5-19 for Detroit that year. See also the August 25, 1952, entry in "Let's Go to the Highlights!" for more on Trucks' second no-hitter.

WINNERS OF BOTH ENDS OF A DOUBLEHEADER

George Mullin, September 22, 1906, vs. Washington. Two complete games, winning 5-3 and 4-3. His pitching lines:

Game	IP	H	R	ER	BB	SO
Opener	9	8	3	3	3	4
Nightcap	9	9	3	3	2	5
Total	**18**	**17**	**6**	**6**	**5**	**9**

Ed Summers, September 25, 1908, vs. Philadelphia. Two complete games, winning 7-2 and 1-0. His pitching lines:

Game	IP	H	R	ER	BB	SO
Opener	9	6	3	3	3	1
Nightcap	10	2	0	0	0	6
Total	**19**	**8**	**3**	**3**	**3**	**7**

Bobo Newsom, September 25, 1940, vs. Chicago. Two innings pitched in relief in the 10-9 (10 innings) opener and a complete game in the 3-2 nightcap. His pitching lines:

Game	IP	H	R	ER	BB	SO
Opener	2	1	0	0	0	1
Nightcap	9	8	2	2	2	7
Total	**11**	**9**	**2**	**2**	**2**	**8**

John Hiller, June 1, 1976, vs. Milwaukee. The only Tiger whose two same-doubleheader wins both came in relief, winning 8-7 and 6-5. His pitching lines:

Game	IP	H	R	ER	BB	SO
Opener	0.1	0	0	0	0	1
Nightcap	2.1	1	2	0	3	3
Total	2.2	1	2	0	3	4

The back-to-back victories came in the heat of pennant races the Tigers would ultimately win.

TWO TIGERS PITCHERS WITH NEAR-PERFECT GAMES

Tommy Bridges, August 5, 1932, vs. Washington, 8.2 innings, broken up on a first-pitch single by pinch hitter Dave Harris. The Tigers won 13-0.

Milt Wilcox, April 15, 1983, vs. Chicago, 8.2 innings, broken up on a first-pitch single by pinch hitter Jerry Hairston. The Tigers won 6-0.

TIGERS WINNING THE AL TRIPLE CROWN OF PITCHING

Hal Newhouser, 1945: 25 wins, 212 strikeouts, 1.81 ERA

His Triple Crown figures led both major leagues. Newhouser also led the majors with 313.1 innings, 29 complete games and 8 shutouts. He also won his second AL Most Valuable Player award in 1945, becoming the only pitcher to be MVP in consecutive years.

TIGERS WHO GAVE UP HITS DURING JOE DiMAGGIO'S 56-GAME STREAK IN 1941

Game #7:   Schoolboy Rowe, 1 hit, May 21
            Al Benton, 1 hit, May 21
Game #8:   Archie McKain, 1 hit, May 22
Game #20: Dizzy Trout, 1 hit, June 3
Game #21: Hal Newhouser, 1 hit, June 5
Game #33: Bobo Newsom, 2 hits, June 20
Game #34: Archie McKain, 2 hits, June 20
Game #35: Dizzy Trout, 1 hit, June 21

ONE TIME WHEN DENNY MCLAIN WAS A NICE GUY

On September 19, 1968, McLain, who already had 30 wins and was cruising toward his 31st, faced aging New York Yankees slugger Mickey Mantle, in his last season and making his last appearance in Detroit. McLain served up soft, slow pitches that were easy to hit. Once Mantle realized what McLain was doing, he swung at one and pounded it deep into the upper deck of Tiger Stadium for his 535th career homer, topping Jimmie Foxx on the all-time list. He would hit only one more home run that season before retiring.

WHAT MADE FRANK LARY "THE YANKEE KILLER"

In the midst of the New York Yankees' incredible run of eight pennants during the 10 seasons Lary pitched against them as a Tiger, Lary had the answer to the Bronx Bombers' seeming invincibility. Note the 12-2 record over 1958–59, and his 21-4 mark during 1956–59, that cemented his reputation. Lary pitched in an era when starters pitched more innings than today; nearly half of his starts were complete games. This meant he had to solve hitters at least four times a game. Moreover, clubs faced each other 22 times a season before the American League expansion in 1961, and 18 times a season thereafter, meaning more opportunities for hitters to figure out a pitcher.

Year	G	GS	CG	W-L	IP	H	R	ER	BB	SO	HR	ERA
1954	1	0	0	0-0	1	2	0	0	1	0	0	0.00
1955	4	4	3	2-1	33.1	29	8	8	17	20	2	2.18
1956	8	7	5	5-1	56	50	20	18	16	30	6	2.89
1957	7	5	1	2-2	36	42	17	13	14	20	4	3.25
1958	8	8	6	7-1	67.2	49	16	14	15	35	2	1.85
1959	7	7	4	5-1	51.1	50	25	18	12	39	9	3.18
1960	5	5	2	2-2	38.1	40	18	18	11	21	6	4.26
1961	6	6	3	4-2	45.2	50	24	22	15	23	8	4.30
1962	5	5	0	1-1	25	33	13	12	12	13	5	4.70
1963	2	2	0	0-2	12	16	10	10	4	3	3	7.50
Tot.	53	49	24	28-13	366.1	361	151	133	117	204	45	3.19

DENNY McLAIN GAME BY GAME IN 1968

Date	Opponent	Score	IP	H	R	ER	BB	SO	W/L	Rec.
April 11	Boston	4-3	7	6	3	3	3	6	-	0-0
April 17	Cleveland	4-3(10)	7	6	2	2	2	9	-	0-0
April 21	@Chicago	4-2	9	7	2	2	1	8	W	1-0
April 27	@New York	7-0	9	5	0	0	2	6	W	2-0
May 1	Minnesota	3-2	9	6	2	2	0	9	W	3-0
May 5	California	5-2	9	7	2	2	1	7	W	4-0
May 10	@Washington	12-1	9	7	1	1	0	7	W	5-0
May 15	Baltimore	8-10	2	4	4	4	1	0	L	5-1
May 20	@Minnesota	4-3(10)	10	7	3	3	0	7	W	6-1
May 25	@Oakland	7-1	9	6	1	0	1	8	W	7-1
May 29	@California	3-0	9	4	0	0	1	13	W	8-1
June 2	New York	3-4	8	9	3	3	1	4	-	8-1
June 5	@Boston	5-4	6	5	4	3	0	1	W	9-1
June 9	Cleveland	0-2	8	3	2	2	0	4	L	9-2
June 13	Minnesota	3-1	9	6	1	1	1	6	W	10-2
June 16	@Chicago	6-1	7	3	1	1	2	5	W	11-2
June 20	Boston	5-1	9	3	1	1	2	10	W	12-2
June 24	@Cleveland	14-3	9	9	3	3	0	8	W	13-2
June 29	Chicago	5-2	9	8	2	2	2	5	W	14-2
July 3	California	5-2	9	4	2	1	2	10	W	15-2
July 7	Oakland	5-4	9	5	4	4	1	9	W	16-2
July 12	@Minnesota	5-1	9	3	1	0	4	5	W	17-2
July 16	@Oakland	4-0	9	8	0	0	0	8	W	18-2
July 20	Baltimore	3-5	4.1	6	5	5	3	4	L	18-3
July 23	@Washington	6-4	7	8	4	4	4	7	W	19-3
July 27	@Baltimore	9-0	9	3	0	0	2	7	W	20-3
July 31	Washington	4-0	9	4	0	0	1	9	W	21-3
August 4	@Minnesota	2-1	9	5	1	0	4	4	W	22-3
August 8	Cleveland	13-1	9	6	1	1	3	2	W	23-3
August 12	@Cleveland	6-3	9	5	3	3	1	5	W	24-3
August 15	@Boston	4-0	9	7	0	0	1	9	W	25-3
August 20	Chicago	2-10	5.2	9	9	2	2	3	L	25-4
August 24	@New York	1-2	7	5	2	2	0	6	L	25-5
August 28	California	6-1	9	6	1	1	2	11	W	26-5
September 1	Baltimore	7-3	9	7	3	3	2	9	W	27-5
September 6	Minnesota	8-3	9	9	3	3	1	12	W	28-5
Sept. 10	@California	7-2	9	9	2	2	1	12	W	29-5
Sept. 14	Oakland	5-4	9	6	4	4	1	10	W	30-5
Sept. 19	New York	6-2	9	8	2	2	3	7	W	31-5
Sept. 23	@Baltimore	1-2	7	5	2	1	5	4	L	31-6
Sept. 28	Washington	1-2	7	2	0	0	0	4	-	31-6
Totals		**(1.96 ERA)**	**336**	**241**	**86**	**73**	**63**	**280**		**31-6**

Mark Fidrych captivated Detroit and the nation not only with his personality and mound antics, but with talent that won him American League Rookie of the Year honors with a 19-9 record and 2.34 ERA in 1976. (Photo courtesy National Baseball Hall of Fame and Museum Library, Cooperstown, N.Y.)

MARK FIDRYCH GAME BY GAME IN HIS MAGICAL 1976 SEASON

Date	Opponent	Score	IP	H	R	ER	BB	SO	W/L	Record	Time*	Att.
April 20	Oakland	5-6	0**	1	0	0	0	0	-	0-0	2:47	3,080
May 5	Minnesota	2-8	1**	2	0	0	0	0	-	0-0	2:20	8,317
May 15	Cleveland	2-1	9	2***	1	1	1	5	W	1-0	1:57	14,583
May 25	@Boston	0-2	8	6	2	2	2	1	L	1-1	1:57	21,033
May 31	Milwaukee	5-4	11	11	4	4	4	8	W	2-1	3:04	17,894
June 5	@Texas	3-2	11	7	2	2	1	8	W	3-1	2:42	32,678
June 11	California	4-3	9	9	3	1	0	4	W	4-1	2:28	36,377
June 16	Kansas City	4-3	9	5	3	2	2	2	W	5-1	2:08	21,659
June 20	@Minnesota	7-3	7.1	9	3	3	6	2	W	6-1	2:40	11,916
June 24	@Boston	6-3	9	7	3	3	2	4	W	7-1	2:31	26,293
June 28	New York	5-1	9	7	1	1	0	2	W	8-1	1:51	47,855
July 3	Baltimore	4-0	9	4	0	0	3	4	W	9-1	1:54	51,032
July 9	Kansas City	0-1	9	9	1	1	1	2	L	9-2	2:03	51,041
July 16	Oakland	1-0	11	7	0	0	4	6	W	10-2	2:26	45,905
July 20	@Minnesota	8-3	9	10	3	3	2	2	W	11-2	2:39	30,425
July 24	@Cleveland	5-4	9	6	1	1	1	3	-	11-2	2:10	35,395

Date	Opponent	Score	IP	H	R	ER	BB	SO	W/L	Record	Time*	Att.
July 29	Baltimore	0-1	9	6	1	0	1	8	L	11-3	1:52	44,068
August 3	@New York	3-4	7	8	4	4	1	3	L	11-4	2:21	44,909
August 7	Cleveland	6-1	9	6	1	1	1	3	W	12-4	2:10	35,395
August 11	Texas	4-3	9	9	3	3	1	5	W	13-4	2:22	36,523
August 17	California	3-2	9	9	3	3	1	2	W	14-4	2:08	51,822
August 21	Minnesota	3-7	10	12	7	7	2	1	L	14-5	2:45	34,760
August 25	Chicago	3-1	9	5	1	0	1	1	W	15-5	1:48	39,884
August 29	@Oakland	1-2	11.1	7	2	2	3	1	L	15-6	2:42	25,659
Sept. 3	Milwaukee	2-11	3.2	8	9	7	3	3	L	15-7	2:21	32,951
Sept. 7	Baltimore	3-5	9	11	5	2	3	2	L	15-8	2:19	16,410
Sept. 12	@New York	6-0	9	9	0	0	1	5	W	16-8	2:15	52,707
Sept. 17	Boston	3-8	2.2	7	7	6	2	1	L	16-9	2:09	20,371
Sept. 21	Cleveland	5-3	9	9	3	3	2	2	W	17-9	2:00	7,147
Sept. 28	@Cleveland	4-0	9	5	0	0	1	3	W	18-9	1:48	3,394
October 2	@Milwaukee	4-1	9	5	1	1	1	4	W	19-9	1:46	9,044
Totals	**(2.34 ERA)**		**250.1**	**217**	**76**	**65**	**53**	**97**			**2:16 avg.**	**912,636 (29,440 avg.)**

*Tigers games averaged 2:18 for 1976, fastest in the American League, and Fidrych was the team's quickest worker; note that he pitched into extra innings in five of his starts. To compare, the average major-league game in 2000 hit an all-time high of 2:58.
**Pitched in relief.
***No-hitter through 6.2 innings.

ONE UNFORTUNATE PITCHING CATEGORY LEADER

In 1922, Howard Ehmke hit batters with a pitched ball 23 times, leading the majors that year and still the Detroit record. But if you're thinking about "unfortunate," consider the batter!

TIGERS TOP TEN
IN CAREER WINS

Player	Wins	Years
Hooks Dauss	223	1912–26
George Mullin	209	1902–13
Mickey Lolich	207	1963–75
Hal Newhouser*	200	1939–53
Jack Morris	198	1977–90
Tommy Bridges	194	1930–43, 1945–46
Dizzy Trout	162	1939–52
Wild Bill Donovan	141	1903–12, 1918
Earl Whitehill	133	1923–32
Frank Lary	123	1954–64

*The last pitcher to win 25–plus games three years in a row (1944–46).

TIGERS TOP TEN
SINGLE-SEASON WINS

Player	Wins	Years
Denny McLain	31	1968
George Mullin	29	1909
Hal Newhouser	29	1944
Dizzy Trout	27	1944
Hal Newhouser	26	1946
Hal Newhouser	25	1945
Wild Bill Donovan	25	1907
Ed Killian	25	1907
Mickey Lolich*	25	1971
Ed Summers	24**	1908
Hooks Dauss	24**	1915
Schoolboy Rowe	24**	1934
Denny McLain	24**	1969

*The only pitcher to win 25 games but lose that year's Cy Young Award to a pitcher with under 25 wins (Vida Blue, Oakland, 24).
**Four-way tie for 10th.

TIGERS ON THE ALL-TIME WINS LIST

Rank	Name	Career	As a Tiger
37.*	Jack Morris	254	198
49.	Frank Tanana	240	96
58.	George Mullin	228	209
59.**	Jim Bunning	224	118
62.+	Hooks Dauss	223	all
66.	Joe Niekro	221	21
68.++	Earl Whitehill	218	133
70.+++	Mickey Lolich	217	207
74.^	Jim Perry	215	14
78.^^	Billy Pierce	211	3
78.^^	Bobo Newsom	211	50
82.^^^	Ed Cicotte	209	1
87.#	Hal Newhouser	207	200
96.##	George Uhle	200	44

*Tied with Red Faber.
**Tied with Catfish Hunter and Tom Glavine.
+Tied with Paul Derringer and Mel Harder.
++Tied with Bob Caruthers.
+++Tied with Freddie Fitzsimmons.
^Tied with Stan Coveleski.
^^Tied with Bob Welch.
^^^Tied with Vida Blue, Don Drysdale and Milt Pappas.
#Tied with Bob Lemon.
##Tied with Randy Johnson.

TIGERS TOP TEN
IN CAREER LOSSES

Player	L	Years
Hooks Dauss	182	1912–26
George Mullin	179	1902–13
Mickey Lolich	175	1963–75
Dizzy Trout	153	1939–52
Jack Morris	150	1977–90
Hal Newhouser	148	1939–53
Tommy Bridges	138	1930–43, 1945–46
Earl Whitehill	119	1923–32
Frank Lary	110	1954–64
Vic Sorrell	101	1928–37

TIGERS TOP TEN
SINGLE-SEASON LOSSES

Player	L	Year
George Mullin	23	1904
George Mullin	21	1905
Hooks Dauss	21	1920
Mickey Lolich	21	1974
Ed Killian	20	1904
George Mullin	20	1907
Bobo Newsom	20	1941
Art Houtteman	20	1952
Herman Pilette*	19**	1923
Virgil Trucks	19**	1952
Mickey Lolich	19**	1970
Lerrin LaGrow	19**	1974

*Herman Pilette led the AL in losses in 1923; his son, Duane, tied for the AL losses lead with 14 for the Browns in 1951, thus becoming the only father and son to lead a league in losses.
**Four-way tie for ninth.

TIGERS ON THE ALL-TIME
LOSSES LIST

Rank	Name	Career	As a Tiger
16.	Frank Tanana	236	82
24.	Bobo Newsom	222	35
40.*	Joe Niekro	204	22
42.**	George Mullin	196	179
48.***	Mickey Lolich	191	175
54.+	Jack Morris	186	150
56.++	Earl Whitehill	185	119
58.+++	Jim Bunning	184	87
62.^	Hooks Dauss	182	all
62.^	Waite Hoyt	182	16
75.	Mike Moore	175	34
77.^^	Doyle Alexander	174	29
77.^^	Jim Perry	174	13
87.	Billy Pierce	169	0
92.^^^	Howard Ehmke	166	75
92.^^^	George Uhle	166	41

*Tied with Jim Whitney.
**Tied with Adonis Troy.
***Tied with Rick Reuschel, Jerry Reuss and Tom Zachary.
+Tied with Mel Harder.
++Tied with Mike Morgan.
+++Tied with Joe Bush.
^Tied with Danny Darwin.
^^Tied with Bob Gibson, Tom Hughes and Amos Rusie.
^^^Tied with Don Drysdale, Catfish Hunter and Will White.

TIGERS TOP TEN
IN CAREER EARNED RUN AVERAGE
(1,000-INNING MINIMUM)

Player	ERA	Years
Harry Coveleski	2.34	1914–18
Ed Killian	2.38	1904–10
Wild Bill Donovan	2.49	1903–12, 1918
Ed Siever	2.61	1901–02, 1906–08
George Mullin	2.76	1902–13
John Hiller	2.83	1965–70, 1972–80
Ed Willett	2.89	1906–13
Jean Dubuc	3.06	1912–16
Hal Newhouser	3.07	1939–53
Bernie Boland	3.09	1915–20

TIGERS TOP TEN
SINGLE-SEASON EARNED RUN AVERAGE
(1 INNING PITCHED PER TEAM GAME MINIMUM)

Player	ERA	Year
Ed Summers	1.64	1908
Ed Killian	1.71	1909
Ed Killian	1.78	1907
Hal Newhouser	1.81	1945
Ed Siever	1.91	1902
Hal Newhouser	1.94	1946
Denny McLain	1.96	1968
Harry Coveleski	1.97	1916
Al Benton	2.02	1945
Wild Bill Donovan	2.08	1908

TIGERS ON THE ALL-TIME
ERA LIST (1,500-INNING MINIMUM)

Rank	Name	Career	As a Tiger
15.*	Ed Cicotte	2.38	3.50
15.*	Ed Killian	2.38	2.38
36.	Ed Siever	2.60	2.61
54.**	Wild Bill Donovan	2.69	2.49
72.+	George Mullin	2.82	2.76
90.++	Dean Chance	2.92	3.50

*Tied with George McQuillian.
**Tied with Fred Toney.
+Tied with Ray Fisher, Ed Morris and Tully Sparks.
++Tied with Harry Brecheen, Doc Crandall and Carl Mays.

TIGERS TOP TEN
IN CAREER GAMES PITCHED

Player	GP	Years
John Hiller	545	1965–70, 1972–80
Hooks Dauss	538	1912–26
Mickey Lolich	508	1963–75
Dizzy Trout	493	1939–52
Mike Henneman	491	1987–95
Hal Newhouser	460	1939–53
George Mullin	435	1902–13
Jack Morris*	430	1977–90
Tommy Bridges	424	1930–43, 1945–46
Guillermo Hernandez**	358	1984–89

*Holds the AL record of 515 consecutive starts (September 30, 1978–end of career, 1994).
**You will see Hernandez listed in this book both as "Willie" and "Guillermo." During the 1987 season, Hernandez asked to be referred to by his birth name rather than his Americanized nickname in order that his son appreciate his Hispanic heritage. Achievements by Hernandez before 1987 will carry the "Willie" appellation—just as Kareem Abdul-Jabbar's feats at UCLA are recorded by his name at the time, Lew Alcindor— but achievements from 1987 to 1989 and career accomplishments will be accompanied by "Guillermo."

TIGERS TOP
SINGLE-SEASON GAMES PITCHED

Pitcher	GP	Year
Sean Runyan*	88	1998
Mike Myers*	88	1997
Mike Myers*	83	1996
Willie Hernandez*	80	1984
Willie Hernandez*	74	1985
Richie Lewis*	72	1996
Aurelio Lopez	71	1984
Dan Miceli	71	1997
Doug Brocail	70	1999
Mike Henneman	69	1990
Fred Scherman*	69	1971

*Left-handed.

TIGERS ON THE ALL-TIME
GAMES PITCHED LIST

Rank	Name	Career	As a Tiger
18.	Don McMahon	874	54
37.	Guillermo Hernandez	744	358
39.	Ron Perranoski	737	28
45.*	Mike Marshall	723	37
50.	Johnny Klippstein	711	5
54.	Joe Niekro	702	87
55.**	Bill Campbell	700	34
71.+	Waite Hoyt	674	42
90.	Frank Tanana	638	250
96.++	Jim Perry	630	35

*Tied with Roger McDowell.
**Tied with Jeff Montgomery.
+Tied with Dan Quisenberry.
++Tied with Greg Swindell.

TIGERS TOP TEN
IN CAREER GAMES STARTED

Player	GS	Years
Mickey Lolich	459	1963–75
Jack Morris	408	1977–90
George Mullin	395	1902–13
Hooks Dauss	388	1912–26
Hal Newhouser	373	1939–53
Tommy Bridges	362	1930–43, 1945–46
Dizzy Trout	305	1939–52
Earl Whitehill	287	1923–32
Frank Lary	274	1954–64
Dan Petry	274	1979–87, 1990–91

TIGERS TOP TEN
SINGLE-SEASON GAMES STARTED

Player	GP	Year
Mickey Lolich	45	1971
George Mullin	44	1904
George Mullin	42	1907
Mickey Lolich	42	1973
George Mullin	41	1905
Denny McLain	41	1968
Denny McLain	41	1969
Mickey Lolich	41	1972
Mickey Lolich	41	1974
Joe H. Coleman	41	1974

TIGERS ON THE ALL-TIME GAMES STARTED LIST

Rank	Name	Career	As a Tiger
14.	Frank Tanana	616	243
30.*	Jack Morris	527	408
33.	Jim Bunning	519	251
40.	Joe Niekro	500	56
43.	Mickey Lolich	496	459
50.**	Bobo Newsom	483	101
54.***	Earl Whitehill	473	287
61.	Doyle Alexander	464	78
68.	Jim Perry	447	34
71.+	Mike Moore	440	86
77.	Billy Pierce	432	5
79.++	George Mullin	428	395
82.+++	Waite Hoyt	425	32

*Tied with Jerry Koosman.
**Tied with Red Faber.
***Tied with Vida Blue.
+Tied with Charlie Hough.
++Tied with Mark Langston.
+++Tied with Freddie Fitzsimmons.

TIGERS TOP TEN IN COMPLETE GAMES

Pitcher	CG	Years
George Mullin	336	1902–13
Hooks Dauss	245	1912–26
Wild Bill Donovan	213	1903–12, 1918
Hal Newhowser	212	1939–52
Tommy Bridges	200	1930–42, 1945–46
Mickey Lolich	190	1963–75
Dizzy Trout	156	1939–52
Jack Morris	154	1977–90
Earl Whitehill	148	1923–32
Ed Killian	142	1904–10

TIGERS TOP TEN
SINGLE-SEASON COMPLETE GAMES

Player	CG	Year
George Mullin	42	1904
Roscoe Miller	35	1901
George Mullin	35	1905
George Mullin	35	1906
George Mullin	35	1907
Wild Bill Donovan	34	1903
Ed Killian	33	1905
Dizzy Trout	33	1944
Ed Killian	32	1904
George Mullin	31	1903

TIGERS ON THE ALL-TIME
COMPLETE GAMES LIST

Rank	Name	Career	As a Tiger
23.	George Mullin	353	336
48.*	Wild Bill Donovan	289	213
79.**	Ed Cicotte	249	1
82.	Bobo Newsom	246	41
83.***	Hooks Dauss	245	all
96.	George Uhle	232	62

*Tied with Bobby Matthews.
**Tied with Stump Wiedman.
***Tied with George Bradley, Phil Niekro and John Ward.

TIGERS TOP TEN
IN CAREER SAVES

Player	Saves	Years
Mike Henneman	154	1987–95
Todd Jones	142	1997–2001
John Hiller	125	1965–70, 1972–80
Guillermo Hernandez	120	1984–89
Aurelio Lopez	85	1979–85
Terry Fox	55	1961–66
Al Benton	45	1938–42, 1945–48
Hooks Dauss	40	1912–26
Larry Sherry	37	1964–67
Fred Scherman	34*	1969–73
Dizzy Trout	34*	1939–52

*Tied for 10th.

TIGERS TOP TEN
SINGLE-SEASON SAVES

Player	Saves	Year
Todd Jones	42	2000
John Hiller	38	1973
Willie Hernandez	32	1984
Willie Hernandez	31	1985
Todd Jones	31	1997
Todd Jones	30	1999
Todd Jones	28	1998
Tom Timmerman	27	1970
Willie Hernandez	24*	1986
Mike Henneman	24*	1992
Mike Henneman	24*	1993

*Three-way tie for ninth.

TIGERS ON THE ALL-TIME SAVES LIST

Rank	Name	Career	As a Tiger
24.	Gregg Olson	217	8
30.*	Mike Henneman	193	154
30.*	Roy Face	193	0
33.	Mike Marshall	188	10
37.	Todd Jones	183	142
40.	Ron Perranoski	179	2
48.	Don McMahon	153	2
51.	Guillermo Hernandez	147	120
67.**	Bill Campbell	126	3
67.**	Mel Rojas	126	0
70.	John Hiller	125	all
72.	Dick Radatz	122	0
80.	Fred Gladding	109	33
85.+	John Wyatt	103	2
91.++	Firpo Marberry	101	5

*Tied with each other.
**Tied with Dave LaRoche.
+Tied with Ron Reed.
++Tied with Craig Lefferts.

TIGERS TOP TEN IN CAREER INNINGS PITCHED

Player	IP	Years
George Mullin	3,394.0	1902–13
Hooks Dauss	3,390.2	1912–26
Mickey Lolich	3,361.2	1963–75
Jack Morris	3,042.2	1977–90
Hal Newhouser	2,944.0	1939–53
Tommy Bridges	2,826.1	1930–43, 1945–46
Dizzy Trout	2,591.2	1939–52
Earl Whitehill	2,171.1	1923–32
Wild Bill Donovan	2,137.0	1903–12, 1918
Frank Lary	2,008.2	1954–64

TIGERS TOP TEN
SINGLE-SEASON INNINGS PITCHED

Player	IP	Year
George Mullin	382.1	1904
Mickey Lolich	376.0	1971
George Mullin	357.1	1907
Dizzy Trout	352.1	1944
George Mullin	347.2	1905
Denny McLain	336.0	1968
Roscoe Miller	332.0	1901
Ed Killian	331.2	1904
George Mullin	330.0	1906
Mickey Lolich	327.1	1972

TIGERS ON THE ALL-TIME
INNINGS PITCHED LIST

Rank	Name	Career	As a Tiger
31.	Frank Tanana	4,188.1	1,551.1
45.	Jack Morris	3,824.0	3,042.2
48.	Waite Hoyt	3,762.1	227.2
49.	Jim Bunning	3,760.1	1,867.1
50.	Bobo Newsom	3,759.1	760.1
51.	George Mullin	3,686.2	3,394.0
54.	Mickey Lolich	3,638.1	3,361.2
57.	Joe Niekro	3,584.0	382.1
59.	Earl Whitehill	3,564.2	2,171.1
74.	Hooks Dauss	3,390.2	all
76.	Doyle Alexander	3,367.2	540.1
81.*	Billy Pierce	3,306.2	65.1
83.**	Jim Perry	3,285.2	203.0
86.	Ed Cicotte	3,226.0	18.0

*Tied with Rube Marquard.
**Tied with Dennis Eckersley.

TIGERS TOP TEN
IN CAREER HITS ALLOWED

Player	Hits	Years
Hooks Dauss	3,407	1912–26
George Mullin	3,206	1902–13
Mickey Lolich	3,093	1963–75
Jack Morris	2,767	1977–90
Tommy Bridges	2,675	1930–43, 1945–46
Hal Newhouser	2,639	1939–53
Dizzy Trout	2,504	1939–52
Earl Whitehill	2,329	1923–32
Frank Lary	1,975	1954–64
Wild Bill Donovan	1,862	1903–12, 1918

TIGERS TOP TEN
IN SINGLE-SEASON HITS ALLOWED

Pitcher	Hits	Year
George Mullin	346	1907
George Mullin	345	1904
Roscoe Miller	339	1901
Mickey Lolich	336	1971
Ed Siever	334	1901
Hooks Dauss	331	1923
George Mullin	315	1906
Mickey Lolich	315	1973
Dizzy Trout	314	1944
Mickey Lolich	310	1974

TIGERS ON THE ALL-TIME
HITS ALLOWED LIST

Rank	Name	Career	As a Tiger
32.	Frank Tanana	4,063	1,578
33.	Waite Hoyt	4,037	300
38.	Earl Whitehill	3,917	2,329
44.	Bobo Newsom	3,769	722
53.	Jack Morris	3,567	2,767
56.	George Mullin	3,518	3,206
63.	Jim Bunning	3,433	1,692
64.	George Uhle	3,417	866
66.	Hooks Dauss	3,407	all
68*	Doyle Alexander	3,376	568
71.	Mickey Lolich	3,366	3,093
96.	Jim Perry	3,127	225

*Tied with Red Donahue.

TIGERS TOP TEN
IN CAREER WALKS ALLOWED

Player	BB	Years
Hal Newhouser	1,227	1939–53
Tommy Bridges	1,192	1930–43, 1945–46
George Mullin	1,106	1902–13
Jack Morris	1,086	1977–90
Hooks Dauss	1,067	1912–26
Mickey Lolich	1,014	1963–75
Dizzy Trout	978	1939–52
Earl Whitehill	831	1923–32
Dan Petry	744	1979–87, 1990–91
Virgil Trucks	732	1941–43, 1945–52, 1956

TIGERS TOP TEN
SINGLE-SEASON WALKS ALLOWED

Player	BB	Year
Joe H. Coleman	158	1974
Paul Foytack	142	1956
George Mullin	138	1905
Hal Newhouser	137	1941
George Mullin	131	1904
Howard Ehmke	124	1920
Virgil Trucks	124	1949
Mickey Lolich	122	1969
Tommy Bridges	119	1932
Earl Whitehill	118*	1931
Bobo Newsom	118*	1941

*Tied.

TIGERS ON THE ALL-TIME
WALKS ALLOWED LIST

Rank	Name	Career	As a Tiger
6.	Bobo Newsom	1,732	322
13.	Earl Whitehill	1,431	831
16.*	Jack Morris	1,390	1,086
35.	Joe Niekro	1,262	129
39.	Frank Tanana	1,255	527
42.	Hal Newhouser	1,249	1,227
43.	George Mullin	1,238	1,106
51.	Tommy Bridges	1,192	all
55.	Billy Pierce	1,178	61
58.	Mike Moore	1,156	246
71.	Mickey Lolich	1,099	1,014
73.	Virgil Trucks	1,088	732
81.	Hooks Dauss	1,067	all
86.	Wild Bill Donovan	1,059	685
90.	Dizzy Trout	1,046	978
91.	Howard Ehmke	1,042	516

*Tied with Tom Seaver.

TIGERS TOP TEN
IN CAREER STRIKEOUTS

Player	SO	Years
Mickey Lolich	2,679	1963–75
Jack Morris	1,980	1977–90
Hal Newhouser	1,770	1939–53
Tommy Bridges	1,674	1930–43, 1945–46
Jim Bunning	1,406	1955–63
George Mullin	1,380	1902–13
Hooks Dauss	1,201	1912–26
Dizzy Trout	1,199	1939–52
Denny McLain	1,150	1963–70
Wild Bill Donovan	1,079	1903–12, 1918

TIGERS TOP TEN
SINGLE-SEASON STRIKEOUTS

Pitcher	SO	Year
Mickey Lolich	308	1971
Denny McLain	280	1968
Hal Newhowser	275	1946
Mickey Lolich	271	1969
Mickey Lolich	250	1972
Joe H. Coleman	236	1971
Jack Morris	232	1983
Mickey Lolich	230	1970
Mickey Lolich	226	1965
Jack Morris	223	1986

TIGERS ON THE ALL-TIME STRIKEOUTS LIST

Rank	Name	Career	As a Tiger
13.	Jim Bunning	2,855	1,406
14.	Mickey Lolich	2,832	2,679
16.	Frank Tanana	2,773	958
25.	Jack Morris	2,478	1,980
48.	Bobo Newsom	2,082	503
56.	Billy Pierce	1,999	46
75.	Hal Newhouser	1,796	1,770
79.	Joe Niekro	1,747	168
85.*	Joe H. Coleman	1,728	1,000
100.	Tommy Bridges	1,674	all

*Tied with Milt Pappas.

TIGERS LEADING THE AMERICAN LEAGUE IN WINS

Player	Year	Wins
George Mullin	1909	29
Tommy Bridges	1936	23
Dizzy Trout	1943	20*
Hal Newhouser	1944	29
Hal Newhouser	1945	25*
Hal Newhouser	1946	26
Hal Newhouser	1948	21
Frank Lary	1956	21
Jim Bunning	1957	20*
Earl Wilson	1967	22*
Denny McLain	1968	31
Denny McLain	1969	24
Mickey Lolich	1971	25
Jack Morris	1981	14*
Bill Gullickson	1991	20*

*Tied.

TIGERS LEADING
THE AMERICAN LEAGUE IN ERA

Player	Year	ERA
Ed Siever	1902	1.91
Dizzy Trout	1944	2.12
Hal Newhouser	1945	1.81
Hal Newhouser	1946	1.94
Hank Aguirre	1962	2.21
Mark Fidrych	1976	2.34

TIGERS PITCHERS LEADING THE
AMERICAN LEAGUE IN STRIKEOUTS

Player	Year	SO
Tommy Bridges	1935	163
Tommy Bridges	1936	175
Hal Newhouser	1944	187
Hal Newhouser	1945	212
Virgil Trucks	1949	153
Jim Bunning	1959	201
Jim Bunning	1960	201
Mickey Lolich	1971	308
Jack Morris	1983	232

TIGERS LEADING THE AMERICAN LEAGUE
IN WINNING PERCENTAGE

Player	Year	Pct. W-L
Wild Bill Donovan	1907	.862, 25-4
George Mullin	1909	.784, 29-8
Elden Auker	1935	.720, 18-7
Schoolboy Rowe	1940	.842, 16-3
Hal Newhouser	1945	.735, 25-9
Denny McLain	1968	.838, 31-6

TIGERS LEADING THE AMERICAN LEAGUE IN SHUTOUTS

Player	Year	Shutouts
Ed Killian	1905	8
Ed Wells	1926	4
Tommy Bridges	1932	4
Schoolboy Rowe	1935	6
Dizzy Trout	1943	5*
Dizzy Trout	1944	7
Hal Newhouser	1945	8
Virgil Trucks	1949	6*
Art Houtteman	1950	4
Billy Hoeft	1955	7
Mickey Lolich	1967	6*
Denny McLain	1969	9
Jack Morris	1986	6

*Tied.

TIGERS LEADING THE AMERICAN LEAGUE IN SAVES*

Player	Year	Saves
George Mullin	1903	2**
Hooks Dauss	1914	4**
Jim Middleton	1921	7**
Al Benton	1940	17
John Hiller	1974	38
Todd Jones	2000	42**

*All save figures prior to 1969, when it became an official statistic, were figured retroactively.
**Tied.

DETROIT'S ONLY
UNASSISTED TRIPLE PLAY

Tigers first baseman Johnny Neun pulled off an unassisted triple play in the ninth inning to win a 1-0 game against Cleveland May 31, 1927. Neun caught Homer Summa's line drive, touched Charlie Jamieson in the base line and got to second base before runner Glenn Myatt could return. Neun reportedly ran off the field yelling, "Triple play unassisted! Triple play unassisted!" and "I'm running into the Hall of Fame!" Note that there was no Hall of Fame back in 1927; the phrase was used to mark a one-game achievement that would make a player famous forever. Cooperstown merely put bricks and mortar to the abstract notion—and Neun never made it into the Hall.

TRULY A GAME-DECIDING CATCH

On July 24, 1983, the Tigers were playing the Angels in Anaheim. The game went into extra innings, and the Tigers went ahead 4-3 in the top of the 12th. In the bottom of the 12th, the Angels got a runner on, and with two out, Rod Carew came up. He hit a deep fly to center field. Chet Lemon, playing relatively shallow, went back and leaped for the ball heading over the fence. If the ball goes over, the Angels win; if the ball is caught, the Tigers win. Lemon reached over the wall and literally took the home run and the game away from California. While it was hardly the first time anybody got his glove over the fence to make a catch, coming as it did with the profusion of sports on television, Lemon's catch set the standard for other over-the-wall catches in highlight films.

PENNANTS
AND POSTSEASON PLAY

In most baseball cities across the land, the cry is "Wait until next year!" Tigers fans may be getting hoarse; Detroit's postseason drought (no pennants or wild-card appearances since 1987) is exceeded only by Anaheim and Kansas City in the American League, and Milwaukee and Montreal in the National League. Still, when the pennant does come to Motown, it's cause for fans rejoicing in the streets, writers and broadcasters hopping on the Tigers bandwagon and, in the era of day games, teachers letting students watch the Tigers on TV in school. We've packed as many facts as these pages can hold, giving special emphasis to Detroit's 1968, 1984, and 1987 teams.

THE TIGERS-CUBS
WORLD SERIES OF 1907

Game One, October 8 in Chicago: Detroit 3, Chicago 3, tie (12 innings, darkness)
The Tigers were close to celebrating a 3-2 win. The Cubs had a runner on third with two out in the ninth inning and a 2-2 count

on the hitter. On the next pitch, Tigers catcher Boss Schmidt missed the strike-three ball, which skipped all the way back to the screen. The runner from third scored, and three scoreless extra innings followed before the 3-3 game was declared a tie on account of darkness.

Game Two, October 9 in Chicago: Chicago 3, Detroit 1

Cubs pitcher Jack "The Giant Killer" Pfiester subdued the Tigers 3-1, scattering nine hits. Meanwhile, the Cubs bunched six of their nine hits into two innings to account for all of their runs.

Game Three, October 10 in Chicago: Chicago 5, Detroit 1

Cubs second baseman Johnny Evers paced the Cubs' attack with three hits, including two doubles, while the Tigers could manage only six hits against Chicago's Ed Reulbach.

Game Four, October 11 in Detroit: Chicago 5, Detroit 1

The Tigers' offense continued to move in reverse, scratching out only five hits against Orval Overall in a 5-1 loss in the first World Series game played in Detroit.

Game Five, October 12 in Detroit: Chicago 2, Detroit 0

Under overcast skies, a howling wind and temperatures in the low 40s, Mordecai "Three Finger" Brown wrapped up the series for the Cubs, blanking the Tigers on seven hits. Adding insult to injury, the Cubs stole four bases during the game and 18 overall.

THE TIGERS-CUBS WORLD SERIES OF 1908

Game One, October 10 in Detroit: Chicago 10, Detroit 6

A steady rain in Detroit made conditions tough for both teams. Ed Summers, in his seventh inning of relief for starter Ed Killian, had a 6-5 lead going into the ninth inning but five Cubs scored in the final frame on the strength of six straight singles and a double steal, giving Chicago a 10-6 win.

Game Two, October 11 in Chicago: Chicago 6, Detroit 1

Back in Chicago, the Cubs continued to have the Tigers' number, scoring six times in the eighth inning—after being held to one hit in the first seven—to defeat the Tigers, with Joe Tinker's two-run blast opening the floodgates.

Game Three, October 12 in Chicago: Detroit 8, Chicago 3

The Tigers fell behind early, 3-1, but came back behind a seven-hit, complete-game win from George Mullin (and four hits by Ty Cobb) to beat the Cubs, Detroit's first ever World Series game victory, featuring a five-run sixth inning.

Game Four, October 13 in Detroit: Chicago 3, Detroit 0

Returning to the Motor City, Three-Finger Brown shut out Detroit on four hits at Bennett Park as the Cubs regained momentum.

Game Five, October 14 in Detroit: Chicago 2, Detroit 0

Orval Overall blanked the Tigers on two hits—and retired the last 11 batters—in a 2-0 shutout win to give the Cubs their second consecutive World Series. They haven't won another since. Overall also struck out four Tigers in the first inning, thanks to a passed ball by Cubs catcher Johnny Kling. This game had a lowest-ever World Series attendance of 6,210.

THE TIGERS-PIRATES WORLD SERIES OF 1909

Game One, October 8 in Pittsburgh: Pittsburgh 4, Detroit 1

In the Pirates' new ballpark, Forbes Field, Ty Cobb told Pirates pitcher Babe Adams that he would steal a base on him. Instead, shortstop Honus Wagner tagged him out, slapping his balled glove against Cobb's jaw, cutting Ty's lip and loosening two of his teeth. Four Tigers errors led to three unearned Pittsburgh runs in the fifth and sixth innings.

Game Two, October 9 in Pittsburgh: Detroit 7, Pittsburgh 2
Cobb stole home to lead the Tigers to their win. Detroit's Wild
Bill Donovan held Pittsburgh to five hits.

Game Three, October 11 in Detroit: Pittsburgh 8, Detroit 6
Honus Wagner one-upped Cobb by stealing three bases, along
with hitting three singles and scoring three runs, in an 8-6
Pirates victory. Sloppy play was the watchword, as only two
Pittsburgh runs, and just one of Detroit's, were earned.

Game Four, October 12 in Detroit: Detroit 5, Pittsburgh 0
On a 32-degree day with a biting wind in the Iron City, George
Mullin struck out 10 Bucs as the Tigers blanked Pittsburgh. The
Pirates committed six errors in this game but none of them
caused any additional damage. It was the first Fall Classic match
to have more than two umpires. Bill Klem was at home, Billy
Evans worked the bases, and Silk O'Loughlin and Jimmy
Johnstone worked the foul lines after a Game Three dispute over
a fair/foul ball.

Game Five, October 13 in Pittsburgh: Pittsburgh 8, Detroit 4
The seesaw nature of the Series continued as the Pirates, behind
Babe Adams, won despite Sam Crawford's 3-for-4 (single, double, home run) performance. Davy Jones led off the game with a
homer, which, like Crawford's, carried into the temporary stands
set up in center field.

Game Six, October 14 in Detroit: Detroit 5, Pittsburgh 4
The Tigers evened the series yet again with a 5-4 win, but paid a
heavy price for doing so. Catcher Boss Schmidt and third baseman George Moriarty were spiked trying to tag out Pirates runners, and first baseman Tom Jones was knocked unconscious
when he ran over the Bucs' Owen Wilson while chasing a ball. A
ninth-inning Pirates rally was cut short by a runner being
thrown out at home followed by a double play.

Game Seven, October 16 in Detroit: Pittsburgh 8, Detroit 0
The 27-year-old rookie hurler Adams won his third game of the Series, shutting out the Tigers on six hits. For the series, the Pirates stole 18 bases, tying the Cubs' record.

THE TIGERS-CARDINALS WORLD SERIES OF 1934

Game One, October 3 in Detroit: St. Louis 8, Detroit 3
Hank Greenberg hit a home run in front of the home fans, but the infield committed five errors, all in the first three innings. Meanwhile, Ducky Medwick got four hits, including a home run, as the Tigers went down to defeat.

Game Two, October 4 in Detroit: Detroit 3, St. Louis 2 (12 innings)
Defeat stared the Tigers in the face again. Down 2-1 in the bottom of the ninth, Gee Walker hit a pop foul that dropped between the catcher and the first baseman. Still alive, Walker hit the next pitch for a single to tie the game. In the bottom of the 12th inning, Goose Goslin singled to left, scoring Charlie Gehringer to give the Tigers a 3-2 win. Schoolboy Rowe went all the way for Detroit, letting only one runner on base between the fourth and ninth innings to get the Tigers back into the game.

Game Three, October 5 in St. Louis: St. Louis 4, Detroit 1
Daffy Dean gave up nine hits, but the Tigers stranded 13 runners. Pepper Martin hit a couple of extra-base hits off Tommy Bridges to pace the Cards.

Game Four, October 6 in St. Louis: Detroit 10, St. Louis 4
Rookie Elden Auker went the distance for the Tigers as Greenberg and Billy Rogell combined for seven RBI as the Tigers routed the Redbirds. Dizzy Dean was inserted as a pinch-runner in the seventh inning when the score was still 5-4. On a double-play ball, Rogell took the throw from Charlie Gehringer to force

Schoolboy Rowe, seemingly able to defy the laws of gravity and physics in this photo, led the Tigers to victories during the 1934 and 1935 World Series. (Photo courtesy Associated Press and the National Baseball Hall of Fame Library, Cooperstown, N.Y.)

Dean at second, but his relay to first hit Diz between the eyes. While the incident looked scary, Dean was not hurt badly, leading to the urban-legend headline: "X-Rays Of Dean's Head Show Nothing."

Game Five, October 7 in St. Louis: Detroit 3, St. Louis 1
Gehringer's sixth-inning homer gave the Tigers a lead they would not relinquish, as Bridges outdueled a recovered Dizzy Dean.

Game Six, October 8 in Detroit: St. Louis 4, Detroit 3
Back in Detroit, Daffy Dean battled Schoolboy Rowe, and helped his own cause by driving in the game-winning run with a seventh-inning single to knot the series at three games each. But the die for defeat was cast in the bottom of the sixth inning, with the Tigers down 3-1, when third base umpire Bill Delancey called Mickey Cochrane out on Goose Goslin's attempted sacrifice. Photographs in the pre-replay era clearly showed Cochrane had slid in safely. The Tigers managed to tie the game, but a lead in a World Series-clinching game would have prompted a pinch-hitter for Daffy Dean—and a lot of what-ifs.

Game Seven, October 9 in Detroit: St. Louis 11, Detroit 0
Disaster struck the Tigers as the pitching collapsed. The lasting memory from this game will be the hard slide by Ducky Medwick into Tigers third baseman Marv Owen in the sixth inning, which precipitated a scuffle between the two. When Medwick took his place in left field in the Tigers' half of the sixth, fans pelted him with anything they could lay their hands on, halting the game for twenty minutes. Commissioner Kenesaw Mountain Landis ordered Cards manager Frankie Frisch to remove Medwick from the game for his own safety.

THE TIGERS-CUBS WORLD SERIES OF 1935

Game One, October 2 in Detroit: Chicago 3, Detroit 0
Cubs hurler Lon Warneke shut the Tigers out on four hits as Chicago took the opener over Schoolboy Rowe.

Game Two, October 3 in Detroit: Detroit 8, Chicago 3
A Hank Greenberg home run put the exclamation point on a four-run first inning, and Tommy Bridges easily put away the Cubs. But Greenberg was sidelined for the rest of the series when he broke two bones in his left wrist colliding with Chicago catcher Gabby Hartnett on a play at the plate.

Game Three, October 4 in Chicago: Detroit 6, Chicago 5 (11 innings)
Umpire (and ex-Tigers third baseman and manager) George Moriarty ejected Cubs manager Charlie Grimm and two players for bench jockeying; Moriarty was especially incensed at the anti-Semitic slurs directed at the injured Greenberg. Billy Rogell highlighted a four-run eighth inning by turning a foiled steal into a rundown that lasted long enough for that fourth run to cross the plate. Detroit would need it, as Chicago scored twice in the bottom of the ninth inning to tie the game. The Tigers won in 11 as Jo-Jo White singled home Marv Owen, who shifted from third base to first after Greenberg's injury.

Game Four, October 5 in Chicago: Detroit 2, Chicago 1
Pitcher Alvin "General" Crowder picked up the win for the Bengals with the help of a sixth-inning unearned run.

Game Five, October 6 in Chicago: Chicago 3, Detroit 1
Schoolboy Rowe, who won Game Three in relief, was not so lucky as Chuck Klein homered for the Cubs and Lon Warneke pitched six shutout innings to stave off a Series defeat.

Game Six, October 7 in Detroit: Detroit 4, Chicago 3
With the game tied at three going into the ninth inning, Bridges allowed an inning-opening triple to Stan Hack, but he retired the next three Cubs in order. Mickey Cochrane hit a one-out single

past second base, advancing to second on a slow roller by Charlie Gehringer. Goose Goslin drilled the first pitch coming to him into left field to score Cochrane, giving the Tigers the win and their first World Series championship. In the clubhouse afterward, Cochrane praised that "little giant, Tommy Bridges," who pitched his second complete-game Series win that day, adding, "This is the happiest day of my life. . . . My greatest thrill in baseball was scoring that winning run." Crowds snake-danced through Cadillac Square (now Kennedy Square) and Grand Circus Park well past midnight exulting in their first World Series win.

THE TIGERS-REDS WORLD SERIES OF 1940

Game One, October 2 in Cincinnati: Detroit 7, Cincinnati 2
Bobo Newsom benefited from five Tigers runs in the second inning, and a two-run homer from Detroit's Bruce Campbell, as Detroit cruised to victory. Newsom's father, who was in the stands that day, died of a heart attack after the game.

Game Two, October 3 in Cincinnati: Cincinnati 5, Detroit 3
Bucky Walters held the Tigers to three hits as he evened up the series for the Reds.

Game Three, October 4 in Detroit: Detroit 7, Cincinnati 4
The Tigers won on the strength of seventh-inning two-run homers by first baseman Rudy York and third baseman Pinky Higgins.

Game Four, October 5 in Detroit: Cincinnati 5, Detroit 2
Cincinnati pitcher Paul Derringer, knocked from the box early in Game One, reverted to his typical form with a complete-game win for the Reds, again tying the series.

Game Five, October 6 in Detroit: Detroit 8, Cincinnati 0
Newsom, coming back after the death of his father, tossed a three-hitter, and Hank Greenberg smashed a three-run homer

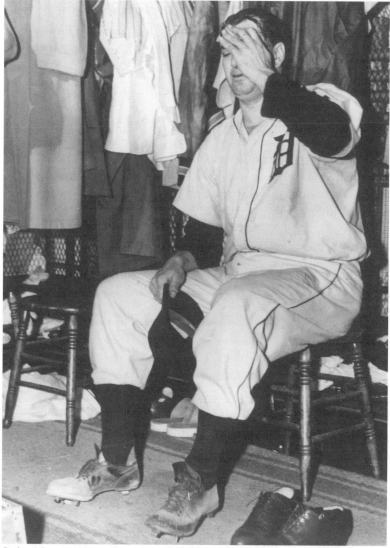

Bobo Newsom weeps in the clubhouse after leading the Tigers to a win in the fifth game of the 1940 World Series. Newsom's father had watched him win the first game of the series, and died of a heart attack that evening. (Photo courtesy of Associated Press and the National Baseball Hall of Fame Library, Cooperstown, N.Y.)

in the third inning, as the Tigers whitewashed the Reds.

Game Six, October 7 in Cincinnati: Cincinnati 4, Detroit 0

The Reds came back yet again, as Bucky Walters tossed a shutout and hit a solo home run to boot.

Game Seven, October 8 in Cincinnati: Cincinnati 2, Detroit 1

The Tigers scored one run in the third inning without a ball being hit out of the infield. But Cincinnati responded in the seventh inning with a Frank McCormick double off Bobo Newsom, followed by a Jim Ripple double, then a sacrifice bunt and a sacrifice fly to score the deciding run in the 2-1 game—and win the World Series for the Reds.

THE TIGERS-CUBS WORLD SERIES OF 1945

Game One, October 3 in Detroit: Chicago 9, Detroit 0

The Tigers, on a chilly October afternoon, froze up at home as Hank Borowy shut them out. Losing the game was the Tigers' own "Prince Hal" Newhouser, who gave up seven runs in less than three innings.

Game Two, October 4 in Detroit: Detroit 4, Chicago 1

Hank Greenberg hit a three-run homer in the fifth inning and Virgil Trucks—who had just been discharged from the Navy less than a week before—went the distance, spreading out seven hits on his way to victory. Detroit's offense consisted of a two-out RBI single by Doc Cramer followed by Greenberg's three-run blast.

Game Three, October 5 in Detroit: Chicago 3, Detroit 0

Cubs pitcher Claude Passeau stymied the Tigers on one hit, while Stubby Overmire's game couldn't match up. The Cubs won with players and fans dodging pregame raindrops. In anticipation of continued wartime travel restrictions, the first three games were played in Detroit, with the rest in Chicago.

Game Four, October 6 in Chicago: Detroit 4, Chicago 1
Dizzy Trout pitched a five-hitter as Detroit got all of its runs in the fourth inning.

Game Five, October 7 in Chicago: Detroit 8, Chicago 4
Greenberg hit three doubles to pace the Tiger attack, and Newhouser shut down the Cubbies, striking out nine of them.

Game Six, October 8 in Chicago: Chicago 8, Detroit 7 (12 innings)
The Tigers came back from a 7-3 deficit with a Greenberg homer tying the score at 7 in the eighth inning. In the 12th inning, with a runner on first, Stan Hack hit a lazy single to left field. Greenberg played the ball with the intent of nailing the runner at third, but the ball inexplicably hopped over his shoulder and rolled all the way to the wall. The runner scored and the Cubs won, knotting the series at three games each. An error on Greenberg was originally charged on the play, but it was changed the next day to a double for Hack.

Game Seven, October 10 in Chicago: Detroit 9, Chicago 3
Borowy, starting for the Cubs on one day's rest, gave up hits to the only three Tigers he faced. The Tigers pummeled Cubs pitching for five runs in the first inning, and Newhouser struck out 10 Cubs to claim a World Series championship for Detroit.

INTERESTING FACTS ABOUT THE 1968 TIGERS

- Going into the 1968 season, this was the Tigers' rotation, in order of perceived quality: Earl Wilson, Mickey Lolich, Joe Sparma, and Denny McLain. Incredibly, McLain was considered to be the fourth starter. In fact, he was almost traded to Baltimore before the 1968 season. McLain had gone 17-16 with a 3.76 ERA in 1967, the lowest winning percentage and highest ERA in the rotation. Wilson had gone 22-9, 3.27, in 1967; Lolich, 14-13, 3.04; and Sparma, 16-9, 3.76.

- The Tigers lost on Opening Day to the Red Sox 7-3 before winning their next nine games.

- Detroit went into first place for good on May 10 after beating the Senators 12-1.

- Jim Northrup hit five grand slams in 1968. The first one happened May 17. He then bunched together three in one week—two of them in one game June 24, and another June 29. Northrup hit the fifth in Game 6 of the World Series.

- Four players represented the Tigers in the All-Star Game: Denny McLain, Bill Freehan, Northrup, and Don Wert (who was hitting .220 at the break).

- The Tigers suffered one losing streak of four games, August 23-26, all against New York (plus a tie). All of the losses were by one run and all occurred while Dick McAuliffe was suspended for charging the mound after being hit by the White Sox's Tommy John.

- Denny McLain won 13 of his 31 games following a Tigers loss.

- Two of the most historic games in Tigers history came within a week of each other that season. On Saturday, September 14, 1968, in front of an NBC "Game of the Week" national audience, Denny McLain won his 30th game, 5-4. On Tuesday, September 17, 1968, the Tigers won their eighth American League pennant with a 2-1 win over the Yankees. The Tigers won both games in the bottom of the ninth.

- The Tigers had 12 straight complete games from September 6-19. This stretch included McLain's 30th victory and the pennant clincher. The Tigers went 10-2 over this stretch.

- Detroit led the majors in home runs with 185, leading the American League by 53. Who hit the most home runs per at-bat? Pitcher Earl Wilson, with seven home runs in 88 at-bats, hit home runs in 8.0 percent of his at-bats. Willie Horton, with 36 home runs in 512 at-bats, was a distant second at 7.0 percent.

- Detroit tallied 40 wins after being tied or trailing from the seventh inning on.

- The Tigers played more official games in 1968 than in any other season—164. They had two tie games, which don't count in the standings but do in the statistics. They tied Oakland 2-2 in seven innings on May 24 and the Yankees 3-3 in 19 on August 23.

- St. Louis, the 1964 and 1967 World Series champions, were heavily favored to beat Detroit in the 1968 World Series, with 10-17 odds, but looking at the stats, it's hard to see why. Compare these numbers:

Team	Record	GA	RS/G	RA/G
Detroit	103-59	12	4.1	3.0
St. Louis	97-65	9	3.6	2.9

The Tigers had a better record, won by more games, scored a half-run more per game and allowed about the same number of runs per game (the American League and National League both averaged 3.4 runs per game). The Tigers scored the most runs per game in the American League; the Cards were third in the National League (both teams allowed the fewest runs per game in the league). In addition, the Tigers had an 11-game winning streak in September while the Cards went 11-14 in the last month of the season.

- Mickey Stanley was moved from center field to shortstop in the Series to get Al Kaline's bat in the Series. With four top outfielders (Willie Horton and Jim Northrup, too) and no DH, it was the only way to get them all in the lineup at the same time. Stanley got nine games at shortstop to prepare for his Series role, his first nine games there as a major leaguer. Ray Oyler, the Tigers' regular shortstop, hit .135, low even in the Year of the Pitcher.

- Mayo Smith used the same starting eight in the same lineup order for each Series game:

  Dick McAuliffe, 2B
  Mickey Stanley, SS
  Al Kaline, RF
  Norm Cash, 1B
  Willie Horton, LF
  Jim Northrup, CF
  Bill Freehan, C
  Don Wert, 3B

- In the Tigers' World Series wins in Games 2, 5, 6 and 7, late in the game, Oyler came in at shortstop for defensive purposes, moving Stanley to center field, Northrup to left field and Horton to the bench.

- Initially, manager Mayo Smith planned on starting righthander Earl Wilson in Game 2 in St. Louis and southpaw Mickey Lolich in Game 3 in Detroit because of the short right-field fence in Detroit. However, he switched them because he wanted Wilson's home run bat in the lineup in Detroit (by contrast, Lolich hit .114 in 1968 and had never hit a home run in the majors). What happened? Lolich hit the only home run in his big-league career in Game 2 in St. Louis and Wilson went 0-for-1 and was hit hard in Game 3 in Detroit. Smith let Lolich hit for himself in a key situation in the seventh inning of Game 5 with one out and none on and the Tigers down 3-2. Lolich blooped a single to right to start a game-winning three-run rally.

1968 Tigers from Michigan

Bill Freehan
Lenny Green
Willie Horton
Jim Northrup
Dennis Ribant
Mickey Stanley

THE TIGERS-CARDINALS WORLD SERIES OF 1968

Game One, October 2 in St. Louis: St. Louis 4, Detroit 0
Cards ace Bob Gibson, who had a 1.12 ERA for the season and was never removed from a game during the middle of an inning that year, struck out a record 17 Tigers in a shutout win over 31-game winner Denny McLain.

Game Two, October 3 in St. Louis: Detroit 8, St. Louis 1
The Tigers went for the long ball to even up the series, with circuit clouts by Willie Horton, Norm Cash, and even pitcher Mickey Lolich. Al Kaline, whose bat prompted the shift of Mickey Stanley to shortstop, chipped in on defense by snaring two Cardinals fly balls.

Game Three, October 5 in Detroit: St. Louis 7, Detroit 3
A two-run homer by Kaline and a solo shot by Dick McAuliffe accounted for all of the Tigers' scoring, but Tim McCarver and Orlando Cepeda each hit three-run blasts for the Redbirds, and Lou Brock stole three bases to go up 2-1 in the Series.

Game Four, October 6 in Detroit: St. Louis 10, Detroit 1
Under wet and rainy conditions—the game was delayed for 74 minutes in the third inning—the Tigers, behind 4-0, stalled, hoping for another rain delay and possible postponement. The Cardinals intentionally made outs to speed the game along. Commissioner William Eckert told both clubs to end the horse-play. Brock led off the game with a home run, and Gibson got one himself before the day was over, triumphing again over McLain.

Game Five, October 7 in Detroit: Detroit 5, St. Louis 3
In a season full of come-from-behind victories, this one may have been the sweetest of all. One game from elimination, things looked particularly grim about 10 minutes into the game, as three Cards scored to put the Tigers down 3-0 right away. Later, down 3-2 in the fifth inning, Brock tried to score from second standing up on Julian Javier's single to left field. Horton,

129

the weakest defensively of the Tigers' four primary outfielders, threw a one-hop strike to Bill Freehan, who nailed Brock. In the seventh inning, Kaline laced a single into center field scoring Lolich and McAuliffe to put the Tigers ahead for good in the game.

Game Six, October 9 in St. Louis: Detroit 13, St. Louis 1
In the most lopsided Tigers World Series win ever, 10 Bengals crossed the plate in the third inning, setting an array of World Series records that still stand and hushing the St. Louis crowd. The inning was highlighted by yet another Jim Northrup grand slam. McLain, pitching on two days' rest, breezed to the win.

Game Seven, October 10 in St. Louis: Detroit 4, St. Louis 1
In a pitchers' showdown, Lolich (2-0) pitched on two days' rest against Gibson (2-0). The game was scoreless through six innings. In the seventh, with two runners on base, Northrup hit a line drive to center field that Curt Flood misjudged. The ball got over his head and rolled all the way to the wall for a triple. That was all the runs the Tigers would need, but they scored a couple more to win the game handily, 4-1.

THE GREATEST INNING IN TIGERS WORLD SERIES HISTORY

It was the third inning of Game Six of the 1968 Series. The Tigers scored 10 runs in the inning and in the process set or tied a number of records that still stand to this day. Here's what happened, batter by batter:

Dick McAuliffe was walked on four straight pitches by St. Louis Cardinals starter Ray Washburn.

Mickey Stanley hit a single to left field, sending McAuliffe to second base.

Al Kaline hit a line single to center field; McAuliffe scored and Stanley took third base. Cards manager Red Schoendienst brought in Larry Jaster to relieve Washburn.

Norm Cash hit a first-pitch single to center; Stanley scored and Kaline took third base.

Jaster walked Willie Horton to load the bases, Cash moving to second.

Jim Northrup hit a grand slam home run—the 11th in World Series history, and Northrup's fifth of 1968—into the right-field seats in Busch Stadium, driving in four runs. Schoendinst pulled Jaster in favor of Ron Willis.

Bill Freehan was walked by Willis.

Willis hit Don Wert with a pitch, moving Freehan to second.

Denny McLain laid a bunt down the third base line, sacrificing Freehan to third and Wert to second. McLain, the ninth Tigers batter, was the first out of the inning.

McAuliffe, up for the second time in the inning, was walked intentionally to load the bases.

Stanley, in his second at-bat of the third, grounded to first baseman Orlando Cepeda, who forced Freehan at home for the second out. Stanley was safe at first; Wert took third base and McAuliffe second.

Kaline then hit his second single of the inning, driving in Wert and McAuliffe and sending Stanley to third. Schoendinst then brought in Dick Hughes to relieve Willis.

Cash, next up, hit his second single of the inning as well, scoring Stanley as before and moving Kaline to third base.

Horton lined a pitch off Hughes' glove which landed safely for a single, scoring Kaline and moving Cash to second.

Northrup made the third out of the inning with a fly out to left fielder Lou Brock.

The totals: 10 runs, seven hits, no errors, two men left on base, and as the game headed into the bottom of the third inning it was Detroit 12, St. Louis 0.

THE TIGERS-A'S AL CHAMPIONSHIP SERIES OF 1972

Game One, October 7 in Oakland: Oakland 3, Detroit 2 (11 innings)

Al Kaline put the Tigers ahead in the 11th inning with a solo home run, but after fielding a game-tying single in the bottom half of the inning, his throw to gun down a runner approaching third base hit the runner as he was sliding, and Oakland came back to win.

Game Two, October 8 in Oakland: Oakland 5, Detroit 0

John "Blue Moon" Odom threw a three-hit shutout to put the A's within one game of going to the World Series. But the game will best be remembered for Tigers pitcher Lerrin LaGrow throwing—on manager Billy Martin's orders—at the feet of Oakland shortstop Bert Campaneris. Campy didn't even take time to dust himself off before he threw his bat at LaGrow and charged the mound, resulting in his suspension for the remainder of the ALCS for triggering the bench-clearing brawl that ensued.

Game Three, October 10 in Detroit: Detroit 3, Oakland 0

Tigers hurler Joe Coleman was in peak form, striking out 14 Oakland hitters in a shutout of the A's, as catcher Bill Freehan hit a home run before the home-town fans.

Game Four, October 11 in Detroit: Detroit 4, Oakland 3 (10 innings)

In the highest-scoring contest of the series, Dick McAuliffe hit a homer and the Tigers answered two A's runs in the top of the 10th inning with three of their own in the bottom half. They loaded the bases with none out. Catcher Gene Tenace, forced to play second base, dropped a double-play ball to let one run in. A bases-loaded walk to Norm Cash tied the score, and Jim Northrup singled Kaline home for the win and Game Five showdown.

Game Five, October 12 in Detroit: Oakland 2, Detroit 1

Woodie Fryman, who went 10-3 after being acquired by the Tigers for the stretch drive, surrendered single runs in the second inning on a delayed steal of home by Reggie Jackson—who pulled a hamstring on the play, prematurely ending his season— and the fourth inning, and that was enough for Oakland as Vida Blue overcame a first-inning Tigers marker to win the game and the series. This was the start of Oakland's dynasty, as they would go on to win the World Series in 1972 (even without Jackson), '73 and '74.

INTERESTING FACTS
ABOUT THE 1984 TIGERS

- When Sparky Anderson became the manager of the Tigers during the 1979 season, he promised a World Series in five years. The 1984 season was the fifth year.

- The Tigers finished second in 1983 with a 92-70 record, staying in the race into September. They made two critical personnel moves before the 1984 season: Signing their first substantial free agent, Darrell Evans (see "The 1980s"), and trading for Willie Hernandez and Dave Bergman the week before the season began (see "The Five Best Trades in Tigers History").

- The Tigers won their first nine games, including a no-hitter in the fifth game against the White Sox.

- The Tigers had the best 40-game start in major league history, 35-5. However, they had not lapped the field in the American League East with that start. The second-best record in baseball, 26-14, belonged to their division rival, the Toronto Blue Jays. After losing two out of three to Toronto soon after that, the Tigers' 39-13 record put them only 3-1/2 games ahead of the Jays on June 6.

- The Tigers won the Hall of Fame Game in Cooperstown over the Braves. Interestingly enough, the Tigers also won the Hall of Fame Game in the 1968 championship season. Only the

1942 Cardinals and 1991 Twins also won the Hall of Fame Game and the World Series in the same season.

- Making up rainouts, the Tigers played doubleheaders on three consecutive days August 5-7, one against Kansas City and two against Boston. They went 2-4 in the games. Carl Willis, called up for Rusty Kuntz to start the fourth game, lasted one-third of an inning, allowing five hits and four runs. In the fifth game, Jack Morris was bombed. He was upset over an umpire's call and allowed two grand slams in the first two innings.

- The Tigers won all three clinchers at Tiger Stadium: the division on September 18 against Milwaukee, the pennant against the Royals, and the Series against the Padres. Willie Hernandez got the save in each of those games.

- Despite a starting staff of Jack Morris, Dan Petry, Milt Wilcox, Dave Rozema, and Juan Berenguer, none of them started and won the division clincher. Rookie Randy O'Neal pitched seven shutout innings to win the clincher. O'Neal pitched for the Tigers until 1986 and later the Braves, Cardinals, Phillies, and Giants in a big-league career that lasted until 1990. The night before, rookie pitcher Roger Mason won the game that clinched the tie. Mason pitched for the Tigers, Giants, Astros, Pirates, Padres, Phillies, and Mets and lasted until 1994. Both O'Neal and Mason later pitched for Tiger pitching coach Roger Craig when Craig managed the Giants.

- Willie Hernandez was the American League MVP and Cy Young Award winner. Six Tigers made the All-Star team: Hernandez, Chet Lemon, Jack Morris, Lance Parrish, Alan Trammell, and Lou Whitaker.

- The 1984 Tigers are the only World Championship team to not have a start from a left-hander. The 1932 Cubs are the only other such team to have even won a pennant.

- The Tigers swept the Royals 3-0 in the playoffs and beat the San Diego Padres in the Series 4-1. The 7-1 postseason record, for an .875 winning percentage, matched exactly the percentage of their 35-5 start.

- Howard Johnson was the Tigers' third baseman in the regular season, but by season's end Sparky Anderson had lost confidence in him and started Marty Castillo, Tom Brookens and Darrell Evans in the postseason, limiting Johnson to one at-bat. After the season, Johnson was dealt to the Mets for Walt Terrell.

THE TIGERS' RECORD-SETTING 35-5 START IN 1984

Game	Date	Opponent	Result	Rec.	GA*	Winning Pitcher
1	April 3	@Minnesota	W, 8-1	1-0	—	Morris, 1-0
2	April 5	@Minnesota	W, 7-3	2-0	—	Petry, 1-0
3	April 5	@Chicago	W, 3-2	3-0	—	Wilcox, 1-0
4	April 7	@Chicago	W, 4-0	4-0	1/2	Morris, 2-0**
5	April 8	@Chicago	W, 7-3	5-0	11/2	Lopez, 1-0
6	April 10	Texas	W, 5-1	6-0	2-1/2	Petry, 2-0
7	April 12	Texas	W, 9-4	7-0	3	Morris, 3-0
8	April 13	Boston	W, 13-9	8-0	3	Bair, 1-0
9	April 18	Kansas City	W, 4-3(10)	9-0	3	Hernandez, 1-0
10	April 19	Kansas City	L, 5-2	9-1	1-1/2	Petry+, 2-1
11	April 20	Chicago	W, 3-2	10-1	2-1/2	Lopez, 2-0
12	April 21	Chicago	W, 4-1	11-1	3-1/2	Rozema, 1-0
13	April 22	Chicago	W, 9-1	12-1	4-1/2	Berenguer, 1-0
14	April 24	Minnesota	W, 6-5	13-1	5	Morris, 4-0
15	April 24	Minnesota	W, 4-3	14-1	5-1/2	Abbott, 1-0
16	April 25	@Texas	W, 9-4	15-1	6	Wilcox, 2-0
17	April 26	@Texas	W, 7-5	16-1	6	Bair, 2-0
18	April 27	Cleveland	L, 8-4(18)	16-2	5	Abbott+, 1-1
19	April 28	Cleveland	W, 6-2	17-2	5-1/2	Morris, 5-0
20	April 29	Cleveland	W, 6-1	18-2	6	Petry, 3-1
21	April 30	Boston	W, 11-2	19-2	6-1/2	Wilcox, 3-0
22	May 2	Boston	L, 5-4	19-3	6-1/2	Berenguer+, 1-1
23	May 3	Boston	L, 1-0	19-4	5	Morris+, 5-1
24	May 4	@Cleveland	W, 9-2	20-4	5	Petry, 4-1
25	May 5	@Cleveland	W, 6-5	21-4	5	Abbott, 2-1
26	May 6	@Cleveland	W, 6-5(12)	22-4	5	Lopez, 3-0
27	May 7	@Kansas City	W, 10-3	23-4	5-1/2	Berenguer, 2-1
28	May 8	@Kansas City	W, 5-2	24-4	6	Morris, 6-1
29	May 9	@Kansas City	W, 3-1	25-4	7	Petry, 5-1
30	May 11	California	W, 8-2	26-4	7-1/2	Wilcox, 4-0

Game	Date	Opponent	Result	Rec.	GA*	Winning Pitcher
31	May 12	California	L, 4-2	26-5	7-1/2	Berenguer+, 2-2
32	May 14	Seattle	W, 7-5	27-5	8	Lopez, 4-0
33	May 15	Seattle	W, 6-4	28-5	8	Morris, 7-1
34	May 16	Seattle	W, 10-1	29-5	8	Wilcox, 5-0
35	May 18	Oakland	W, 8-4++	30-5	7-1/2	Petry, 6-1
36	May 19	Oakland	W, 5-4	31-5	8	Morris, 8-1
37	May 20	Oakland	W, 4-3	32-5	8	Wilcox, 6-0
38	May 22	@California	W, 3-1	33-5	8	Berenguer, 3-2
39	May 23	@California	W, 4-2	34-5	8	Petry, 7-1
40	May 24	@California	W, 5-1	35-5	8-1/2	Morris, 9-1

*Games ahead.
**No-hitter.
+Losing pitcher.
++5.1 innings, rain.

THE TIGERS-ROYALS AL CHAMPIONSHIP SERIES OF 1984

Game One, October 2 in Kansas City: Detroit 8, Kansas City 1
Larry Herndon, Lance Parrish and Alan Trammell all hit home runs on the road, Jack Morris pitched a five-hitter, and Kirk Gibson made a terrific snag of a George Brett liner with the bases loaded to give the Tigers the advantage.

Game Two, October 3 in Kansas City: Detroit 5, Kansas City 3 (11 innings)
 A Gibson home run was not enough to get the Tigers over the top, but as play continued into extra innings, reserve outfielder John Grubb hit a two-run double to give the Tigers a 5-3 win in 11 innings and a 2-0 series lead.

Game Three, October 5 in Detroit: Detroit 1, Kansas City 0
Milt Wilcox, who didn't pitch a complete game all season, got help from Willie Hernandez to preserve a three-hit shutout in Detroit to propel the Tigers into the World Series. The only run came in the second inning, when Chet Lemon scored on a broken double play.

THE TIGERS-PADRES WORLD SERIES OF 1984

Game One, October 9 in San Diego: Detroit 3, San Diego 2
Larry Herndon hit a two-run homer in the fifth inning to give
the Tigers the road win. Padres fans had heckled the Tigers during pregame introductions by shouting out after each name,
"Who's he?" Jack Morris answered with a complete-game win,
and the Tigers executed a perfect 9-to-4-to-5 sequence of relays
to cut down San Diego's Kurt Bevacqua, who tried to stretch a
double into a triple.

Game Two, October 10 in San Diego: San Diego 5, Detroit 3
Bevacqua avoided the need for relay throws by hitting one out
of the park. He blew kisses to the fans as he circled the bases as
San Diego overcame a 3-0 deficit after the Tigers' first inning.
For the Tigers, who had led the AL East wire to wire, it was the
only time all year a loss had dropped them into any kind of tie.

Game Three, October 12 in Detroit: Detroit 5, San Diego 2
When San Diego's pitchers weren't walking Tigers—11 in all—
third baseman Marty Castillo hit a two-run homer as part of a
four-run second inning to chase Padres starter Tim Lollar and
keep Detroit ahead for good. Milt Wilcox, with help from Bill
Scherrer and Willie Hernandez, got the win.

Game Four, October 13 in Detroit: Detroit 4, San Diego 2
On a drizzly afternoon at Tiger Stadium, Alan Trammell
smacked a pair of two-run homers to account for all of Detroit's
runs, and Jack Morris pitched a five-hit complete game to put
the Tigers in the driver's seat.

Game Five, October 14 in Detroit: Detroit 8, San Diego 4
In a late-afternoon contest, Kirk Gibson hit a two-run homer
in the first inning to highlight an early Detroit 3-0 lead. The
Padres came back with one run in the third and two in the
fourth to tie it. In the fifth, Gibson alertly tagged from third on
Rusty Kuntz' sacrifice pop-up behind second base; San Diego
second sacker Alan Wiggins may have been in position to make

137

the catch, but not to make a strong enough throw to retire Gibson at the plate. In the seventh inning, Lance Parrish hit a solo home run to give the Tigers a two-run cushion, but the Padres answered with a homer of their own by Bevacqua in the top half of the eighth. In the bottom of the eighth, with two Tigers on base, San Diego reliever Goose Gossage talked manager Dick Williams out of walking Gibson. Gibby answered with his second homer of the game to put the Padres away, 8-4, giving the Tigers a world championship. The postgame cheer was marred by a riotous celebration outside the stadium, marked by thrown beer bottles and a torched police car. One person was killed and scores were injured. It made the media more vigilant in ensuing years about destructive and violent victory celebrations.

THE 1987 SHOWDOWN SERIES: DETROIT VERSUS TORONTO

In 1987, the Detroit Tigers and the Toronto Blue Jays faced off in seven games over the last two weekends of the 1987 season to determine who would win the American League East Division. With no wild card at the time, the division winner would go to the playoff while the other team would watch on television. The Showdown Series started with four games in Toronto on September 24-27. The Tigers then faced the Baltimore Orioles in four games while the Jays played the Milwaukee Brewers in a three-game set before the two teams reconvened in Detroit for the final three games of the regular season.

Things did not look good for the Tigers as the 1987 season started. Tiger fans assumed that after the great 1984 season that a dynasty was in the making, which was reinforced by a 6-0 start to the 1985 season. However, the Tigers stumbled the rest of the year, finishing a disappointing 84-77, in third place, 15 games behind the Blue Jays. The 1986 season was more of the same; they actually spent 25 days in last or tied for last. After a dreadful

9-20 spring training, it seemed that the '84 Tigers had been just a one-year wonder. The opening month of the Tigers' 1987 season made it clear the party was over. The team endured a 3-12 stretch in a 11-19 start, leaving them in sixth place, 9-1/2 games out.

However, the 1987 Tigers were not through. They won 13 of the next 15 to make their record a respectable 24-21, but they were still in fourth place, five games behind in the toughest division in baseball. An 11-game winning streak by the Blue Jays pushed the Tigers 7-1/2 games back in mid-June, but Detroit kept on winning and closed to within a half-game by July 27. The Jays kept just ahead of the Tigers, but on August 19, a Tigers victory over the Twins finally gave the Tigers first place in the East. From August 15 until the start of the first series in Toronto on September 24, the two teams stayed within 1-1/2 games of each other, and for only four days during that span were they ever that far apart. Everyone knew the seven-game Showdown Series would decide who won the East.

Game 1: Thursday, September 24, 1987, at Toronto
Toronto in first by 1/2-game
Pitchers: Jack Morris (18-9, 3.40) vs. Mike Flanagan (5-7, 4.28)
The intensity of the series became apparent in the top of the third. Bill Madlock led off the inning with a single. Kirk Gibson, up next, hit a ground ball to second. Damaso Garcia threw the ball to Tony Fernandez covering second base. Madlock slid hard into Fernandez, who went into the air and landed on his elbow on the piece of wood at the divider separating the artificial turf and the dirt cutout at Exhibition Stadium. Fernandez' elbow was broken and his season was over. Toronto thought Madlock had gone out of the line to upend Fernandez; the Tigers contended it was a clean slide. In that inning, the Tigers drew first blood with two runs on three singles, a throwing error by George Bell and a wild pitch by Flanagan. The Jays came back in the bottom of the inning with four runs, the last run coming on a wild pitch from one of Morris' many balls in the dirt. The Tigers got one more in the

seventh but a great diving catch by Fernandez' replacement, Manny Lee, on a popup behind him may have saved the Jays, as they won 4-3. After the loss, the Tigers were 1-1/2 games out, the farthest behind they had been since August 14.

Game 2: Friday, September 25, 1987, at Toronto
Toronto in first by 1-1/2 games
Pitchers: Frank Tanana (13-10, 4.35) vs. Jimmy Key (17-6, 2.78)
This was a game the Tigers should have won but did not. The Tigers scored single runs off Key in the second and sixth, with the second run assisted by Key's throwing error. Tanana pitched seven innings of scoreless ball and Dickie Noles pitched a scoreless eighth. Noles started the ninth, but after an out and a single, he was replaced by Guillermo Hernandez. Hernandez had been the American League MVP in 1984, but 1987 had been a rough year for the former relief ace. He had only eight saves in 11 opportunities coming into the game, and the team saves leader was actually Eric King. Hernandez allowed a double and a triple. Sparky Anderson replaced him with rookie Mike Henneman with the game tied 2-2. Henneman intentionally walked the bases loaded, hoping for the double-play ball. He got it, a bouncer to Lou Whitaker, who threw home for the force—but in the dirt. The runner from third scored, and the Jays won 3-2.

Game 3: Saturday, September 26, 1987, at Toronto
Toronto in first by 2-1/2 games
Pitchers: Walt Terrell (16-10, 3.90) vs. Dave Stieb (13-8, 3.79)
The Tigers had to win this game to have a decent chance to win the East. Things looked good with three runs in the first but the Jays countered with three in the bottom of the inning. The Tigers got four back in the third to go up 7-3, and later made the lead 9-4 in the fifth. Sparky pinch-hit for first baseman Dave Bergman in the fifth, and later ran for his replacement, Dwight Lowry, in the seventh. DH Darrell Evans was

the only first baseman left. Evans went to play first, meaning that the pitcher had to enter the lineup, hitting in the sixth spot in the batting order. That spot, filled by Mike Henneman, came up in the ninth inning with runners at first and second and one out. Sparky left him in because he wanted Henneman to pitch the ninth and the Tigers led by two. The runners stole second and third on the first pitch, but Anderson had Henneman bunt anyway. However, he struck out bunting on an 0-2 pitch. Henneman allowed the first three men to get on via a bloop hit, a weak grounder, and a hit batsman. Noles came in and Juan Beniquez hit a ball to the wall to score all three runners and give Toronto its third straight one-run win, 10-9. After the game, outfielder Kirk Gibson, refusing to accept defeat, suggested, "Maybe we're setting the biggest bear trap of all time."

Game 4: Sunday, September 27, 1987, at Toronto
Toronto in first by 3-1/2 games
Pitchers: Doyle Alexander (8-0, 1.40) vs. Jim Clancy (15-10, 3.60)
The Tigers had to win this game to have any chance to win the East. Doyle Alexander allowed one run in the first when George Bell knocked in Nelson Liriano, but that seemed enough for the Jays. Entering the bottom of the ninth, with American League save leader Tom Henke on the mound, Toronto was three outs away from all but finishing off the Tigers. Kirk Gibson strode to the plate to lead off the ninth and promptly saved the season with a game-tying home run, the first Tiger to even reach third base. Darrell Evans hit a home run in the 11th to put the Tigers up 2-1, but an unearned run off Alexander and the shaky Tigers bullpen tied the game 2-2. In the 13th, Jim Walewander led off with a walk and took second on Whitaker's sacrifice bunt. After Evans was intentionally passed, Gibson won it on a bloop hit that bounced off the turf and over center fielder Lloyd Moseby's head. Final score: 3-2—the fourth straight one-run game.

141

Now, Toronto could not clinch the East by sweeping the Brewers. If the Tigers held their own against the woeful Orioles, the Tigers would be able to win it in Detroit the next weekend. The Tigers hosted Baltimore for four games while Toronto hosted Milwaukee for three. Neither played well in their midweek series. The Tigers split with the hapless Orioles: loss, win, loss, win. The Jays were swept by the Brewers to stretch their losing streak to four, getting only 17 hits in the three games against Milwaukee. Even worse, their starting catcher, Ernie Whitt, broke two ribs sliding into second in the middle game, meaning the Jays would be missing two starters the rest of the way.

Game 5: Friday, October 2, 1987, at Detroit
Toronto in first by 1 game
Pitchers: Doyle Alexander (8-0, 1.33) vs. Jim Clancy (15-10, 3.50)
A win would tie up the race; a loss would mean the Tigers would have to win Saturday, Sunday, and a Monday playoff. Things did not start well. Alexander gave up a three-run homer to Manny Lee in the third, but the Tigers came back with two in the bottom of the inning on a Scott Lusader home run. Trammell's solo shot to lead off the third tied the game. After Evans walked, Blue Jays rookie sensation David Wells relieved Clancy and the Tigers got the game-winning run on a single, Rance Mulliniks' second error of the game at third, and a double-play grounder. The Tigers' defense helped make sure the Jays were done scoring. In the fifth, with runners on first and third, one out, and George Bell on deck, Mulliniks hit a grounder up the middle. Trammell caught it, flipped it backhand to Whitaker, who threw to first for the double play. In the seventh, Lusader made a diving catch on a ball in the right-field corner that could have been a triple. Unlike in two of the games in Toronto, the bullpen did the job; Henneman pitched two scoreless innings to clinch the race-tying victory, in yet another one-run game, 4-3.

Game 6: Saturday, October 3, 1987 at Detroit
Detroit and Toronto tied for first
Pitchers: Jack Morris (18-11, 3.43) vs. Mike Flanagan (6-8, 4.33)
This was the game that broke the Blue Jays' backs. Toronto actually drew first blood, but since the team scoring first was 1-4 so far in the Showdown Series, that did not mean much. The Tigers tied it in the third and each team scored in the fifth, and the game went into extra innings tied 2-2. Henneman came in to pitch the 10th (and pitched the last three innings), but Flanagan stayed out there through 11. Toronto manager Jimy Williams did not put in ace Tom Henke in the 12th but middle reliever Jeff Musselman instead. Had Flanagan or Henke gotten through the 12th, the Tigers were in trouble because their choices were Mark Thurmond or Dickie Noles with Guillermo Hernandez out sick, but Williams was saving Henke for when he got a lead. It never happened. Musselman got the first out but two singles and a walk loaded the bases. Mark Eichhorn came in to face Alan Trammell in a big-at-bat for the MVP candidate shortstop. The Jays played the infield in and Trammell lined the ball through the legs of shortstop Manny Lee to win the game for the Tigers, 4-3. Now, either a win Sunday or in a playoff on Monday would win the East for the Tigers.

Game 7: Sunday, October 4, 1987, at Detroit
Detroit in first by 1 game
Pitchers: Frank Tanana (14-10, 4.08) vs. Jimmy Key (17-7, 2.81)
This was it. A win and the Tigers would be champions of the AL East. Detroit native and Catholic Central High School graduate Frank Tanana pitched the game of his life for his home-town team. He did not have his curve ball working, but he made up for it with his screwball, or as he put it afterward, "slop here, slop there, and every once in a while, one in the 80s to keep them honest." The Jays got six hits and three walks but went 0-for-8 with runners in scoring position. The Tigers hit just one fly ball to the outfield that day. It came off the bat of Larry

Herndon, who parked it a few rows beyond the left field fence with one out in the second, and it was the only run of the day. In the fourth, Toronto had its best chance to score, but a baserunning blunder stopped them. Rookie Cecil Fielder was on first with Manny Lee at the plate. Manager Williams put the hit-and-run sign on but Lee missed it. The manager then took the sign off, but Fielder missed that and was thrown out at second trying to steal. Lee than tripled, but Fielder was not on base to score and the Tigers still led 1-0. Toronto's last real chance to score was in the eighth with Lloyd Moseby at third with two out, but Tanana threw out Juan Beniquez on a slow high-hop ball over the middle to end the threat. In the ninth, Fielder struck out on a full-count delivery, Lee hit a grounder to third that Jim Walewander played fine but threw into the dirt, with Evans scooping it out successfully for out number two. The last hitter, Garth Iorg, hit the first pitch back to Tanana on one hop. He tossed the ball to Evans, and it was over. The Tigers had done it. The auxiliary scoreboard in left field said it all: 1-0. After losing the first three games in the Showdown Series each by one run, the Tigers won the final four games, all by one run.

As Lou Whitaker left the field, he took second base with him. He presented it to his keystone partner, Alan Trammell, with the inscription "To Alan Trammell, MVP, 1987. Congratulations, Louis Rodman Whitaker." Trammell played great down the stretch, hitting .416 with six home runs over the last four weeks of the season and .381 with a .500 on-base percentage in the last 11 games of the season. His main MVP competition, George Bell, by contrast, ended up the season in a 2-for-26 slump. However, Bell had more RBI and won the MVP award in a travesty of a vote.

The Showdown Series is not as well remembered today as it should be. That is probably because the Tigers, mentally whipped after such a great finish to the regular season, lost the AL playoffs to the Minnesota Twins four games to one and therefore did not make the World Series. The 1987 Tigers, whose 98-64 mark—87-45 after the 11-19 low point—was the best record in baseball, were a great team, a tough team that did not give up. In a 1996 interview, Sparky Anderson said, "My favorite team was '87, because they should have been a fourth- or fifth-place club. That's what we were. And they went out and proved that if you do all the things right, and pull together, you can win. And they won 98 games, which I to this day cannot believe. . . . I never believed that we could win that many games. In fact, I picked us fourth. Boy, they really played. They're my favorites because they did that." They deserve much credit for a wonderful season and one of the most exciting weeks Detroit baseball fans have ever seen.

The Tigers-Twins AL Championship Series of 1987

Game One, October 7 in Minnesota: Minnesota 8, Detroit 5
Detroit finished with the majors' best won-lost record, thanks in part to late-season acquisition Doyle Alexander's sterling 9-0 mark as a starter. But his luck ran out on him as he was pounded for six runs in seven-plus innings by the Twins in Minnesota.

Game Two, October 8 in Minnesota: Minnesota 6, Detroit 3
Jack Morris, who had an 11-game winning streak in his native Minnesota, got roughed up for three runs in the second after the Tigers had scored two in the top half of the frame. Twins fans, their "Homer Hankies" in hand, witnessed a trouncing of Detroit.

Game Three, October 10 in Detroit: Detroit 7, Minnesota 6
Back in Detroit, The Tigers escaped going into a 3-0 series hole on the strength of Pat Sheridan's two-run homer in the eighth inning as Detroit pulled out the victory.

Game Four, October 11 in Detroit: Minnesota 5, Detroit 3
The Twins scored one run in five different innings and took the lead for good on Greg Gagne's fourth-inning homer to give Minnesota a near-invincible ALCS edge.

Game Five, October 12 in Detroit: Minnesota 9, Detroit 5
More bad luck for Alexander as he was chased during a four-run Twins second inning. The Tigers tried to come back but Minnesota kept on scoring, including three ninth-inning runs off Mike Henneman, for a 9-5 victory.

ONCE-AND-FUTURE TIGERS FACING THE TIGERS IN THE POSTSEASON

Name	Year	Team	When a Tiger
Roy Henshaw	1935	Chicago	1942–44
Frank Secory	1945	Chicago	1940
Hank Borowy	1945	Chicago	1950–51
Lynn Jones	1984	Kansas City	1979–83
Pat Sheridan	1984	Kansas City	1986–88
Luis Salazar	1984	San Diego	1988
Champ Summers	1984	San Diego	1979–81
Mark Thurmond	1984	San Diego	1986–87
Juan Berenguer	1987	Minnesota	1982–85
Dan Gladden	1987	Minnesota	1992–93

OUTSTANDING IN THEIR FIELD

It's one of those paradoxes: Ballplayers tell reporters they're playing for the team, and they'd gladly give up individual glory to get a pennant or a World Series. But it's the ballplayer's individual accomplishments that help propel the team to contention, if not an outright title. Whether judged by their peers on the field, the bosses in the executive suite, the reporters from the media, or the fans in the stands, the Tigers have not lacked for recognition at the end of the season. If there's no championship to be had that year, the honors make for a nice consolation prize—not to mention a bargaining chip at contract time. And if there is a pennant in the midst of a player's spectacular achievement, it's more icing on the cake.

TIGERS IN THE ALL-STAR GAME

Hank Aguirre: 1962 (game 1)#, 1962 (game 2)
Doyle Alexander: 1988
Brad Ausmus: 1999
Al Benton: 1941#, 1942
Ray Boone: 1954*, 1956
Tommy Bridges: 1934–36#, 1937, 1939*, 1940#

Ed Brinkman: 1973

Jim Bunning: 1957*, 1959 (game 1), 1961–1962 (game 1), 1962 (game 2)#, 1963

Norm Cash: 1961*, 1966, 1971–72

Tony Clark: 2001

Mickey Cochrane: 1934, 1935#

Rocky Colavito: 1961*, 1962

Damion Easley: 1998

Hoot Evers: 1948*, 1950*

Mark Fidrych: 1976, 1977+

Cecil Fielder: 1990, 1991*, 1993

Bill Freehan: 1964#, 1965, 1966–72*, 1973#, 1975#

Travis Fryman: 1992–94, 1996

Charlie Gehringer: 1933–38*

Goose Goslin: 1936

Ted Gray: 1950

Hank Greenberg: 1937–38, 1939–40*, 1945 (no game; teams chosen)

Mike Henneman: 1989#

Willie Hernandez: 1985#

Pinky Higgins: 1944

John Hiller: 1974#

Billy Hoeft: 1955#

Willie Horton: 1965*, 1968*, 1970, 1973

Art Houtteman: 1950

Fred Hutchinson: 1951

Todd Jones: 2000

Al Kaline: 1955–57*, 1958, 1959–61, 1962 (game 2), 1963*, 1964+, 1965–66, 1967+, 1971, 1974

George Kell: 1947*, 1948#, 1949–51*

Steve Kemp: 1979

Vern Kennedy: 1938#

Harvey Kuenn: 1953, 1954#, 1955–58, 1959+

Frank Lary: 1960–1961 (game 1)

Ron LeFlore: 1976*

Chet Lemon: 1984

Mickey Lolich: 1969#, 1971–72

Aurelio Lopez: 1983

Jerry Lumpe: 1964#

Charlie Maxwell: 1956#, 1957

Dick McAuliffe: 1965–66*, 1967

Denny McLain: 1966, 1968–69
Jack Morris: 1981*, 1984–87
Pat Mullin: 1947#, 1948*
Hal Newhouser: 1942#, 1943–44, 1946, 1947*, 1948
Bobo Newsom: 1939#, 1940
Matt Nokes: 1987
Lance Parrish: 1980, 1982–83, 1984*, 1985*+, 1986
Dan Petry: 1985
Schoolboy Rowe: 1935#, 1936
Rusty Staub: 1976*
Birdie Tebbetts: 1941#, 1942*
Mickey Tettleton: 1994
Jason Thompson: 1977#, 1978
Justin Thompson: 1997
Alan Trammell: 1980, 1984+, 1985, 1987, 1988*+, 1990
Dizzy Trout: 1944#, 1947#
Virgil Trucks: 1949
Dick Wakefield: 1943*
Gee Walker: 1937#
David Wells: 1995
Don Wert: 1968
Vic Wertz: 1949, 1951*, 1952#
Lou Whitaker: 1983, 1984*, 1985, 1986*, 1987+
Rudy York: 1938, 1941–42*, 1943, 1944#

#Did not appear in game.
*Voted starter or started.
+Selected but unable to play.
Note: Two All-Star Games were played 1959–62. Designations apply for both games that year unless noted otherwise.

All-Star Games in Detroit

1941: AL 7, NL 5. Arky Vaughan of Pittsburgh became the first player to hit two homers in an All-Star game, but Ted Williams' three-run homer capped a four-run bottom-of-the-ninth AL comeback.

1951: NL 8, AL 3. The game was held in Detroit to celebrate the city's 250th anniversary. Tigers Vic Wertz and George Kell homered. The Yanks' Ed Lopat told Brooklyn's Preacher Roe he had found out a way to pitch to the Cardinals' Stan Musial. In the fourth inning, Musial lined Lopat's first pitch into the right-field seats. Roe shouted to Lopat, "I see what you mean, but I found that way to pitch to him a long time ago, all by myself." The White Sox's Chico Carrasquel became the first Latin-American ballplayer in an All-Star tilt.

1971: AL 6, NL 4. This game featured not only the first all-black starters (Vida Blue vs. Dock Ellis) but a record-setting six home runs, highlighted by Reggie Jackson's spectacular shot off a light tower in right field.

MAJOR AWARDS WON BY THE TIGERS (EXCLUDING HITTING AND ERA TITLES)

Player	Award	Year(s)
Sparky Anderson	AL Manager of the Year	1984, 1987
Frank Bolling	Gold Glove (second base)	1958
Ed Brinkman	Gold Glove (shortstop)	1972
Norm Cash	AL Comeback Player of the Year	1965, 1971
Ty Cobb	Chalmers Award (MVP)	1911
Mickey Cochrane*	AL Most Valuable Player	1934
Damion Easley	Silver Slugger (second base)	1998
Mark Fidrych	AL Rookie of the Year	1976
Cecil Fielder	Silver Slugger (first base)	1990–91
Bill Freehan	Gold Glove (catcher)	1965–69
Travis Fryman	Silver Slugger (shortstop)	1992
Charlie Gehringer	AL Most Valuable Player	1937
Hank Greenberg**	AL Most Valuable Player	1935>,1940
Willie Hernandez	AL Most Valuable Player	1984
Willie Hernandez	AL Cy Young Award	1984
John Hiller	AL Comeback Player of the Year	1973
Todd Jones	Rolaids Relief Man Award	2000
Al Kaline	Sporting News Player of the Year	1955, 1963
Al Kaline	Gold Glove (outfield)	1957–59, 1961–67
Harvey Kuenn	AL Rookie of the Year	1953
Frank Lary	Gold Glove (pitcher)	1961
Mickey Lolich	World Series MVP	1968
Denny McLain	AL Most Valuable Player	1968>
Denny McLain+	AL Cy Young Award	1968>, 1969^
Hal Newhouser	AL Most Valuable Player	1944–45
Matt Nokes	Silver Slugger (catcher)	1987

OUTSTANDING IN THEIR FIELD

Player	Award	Year(s)
Dean Palmer	Silver Slugger (third base)	1999
Lance Parrish	Silver Slugger (catcher)	1980,1982–84,1986
Lance Parrish	Gold Glove (catcher)	1983–85
Gary Pettis	Gold Glove (outfield)	1988–89
Aurelio Rodriguez	Gold Glove (third base)	1976
Mickey Stanley	Gold Glove (outfield)	1968–70, 1973
Mickey Tettleton	Silver Slugger (catcher)	1991–92
Alan Trammell	Gold Glove (shortstop)	1980–81, 1983–84
Alan Trammell	AL Comeback Player of the Year	1983
Alan Trammell	World Series MVP	1984
Alan Trammell	Silver Slugger (shortstop)	1987–88, 1990
Lou Whitaker	AL Rookie of the Year	1978
Lou Whitaker	Gold Glove (second base)	1982, 1984
Lou Whitaker	Silver Slugger (second base)	1982–85, 1987

*The first catcher to win MVP.
**Greenberg is the first player to have won the MVP playing two different positions—first base (1935) and left field (1940).
>Unanimous.
+The first pitcher to win the MVP and Cy Young in the same year.
^Tie.

AMERICAN LEAGUE PLAYER OF THE MONTH WINNERS

Al Kaline, September 1974
Willie Horton, April 1976
Ron LeFlore, May 1976
Alan Trammell, April 1984, September 1987
Cecil Fielder, August 1990

AMERICAN LEAGUE PITCHER OF THE MONTH WINNERS

Mark Fidrych, June 1976
Jack Morris, August 1983, April 1984
Willie Hernandez, June 1984
Doyle Alexander, September 1987
Bill Gullickson, August 1993
Steve Sparks, August 2000

AMERICAN LEAGUE PLAYER
OF THE WEEK WINNERS

Willie Horton: week beginning Aug. 3, 1975; April 25, 1976
Ron LeFlore: May 9, 1976
Ben Oglivie: June 6, 1976
Jason Thompson: June 25, 1978
Lance Parrish: May 29, 1979; June 18, 1984
Alan Trammell: May 12, 1980
Tom Brookens: August 18, 1980
Steve Kemp: September 14, 1980
Kirk Gibson: August 24, 1981; September 28, 1981; June 3, 1985; April 7,
     1986; June 23, 1986; July 14, 1986; May 28, 1995
Larry Herndon: May 17, 1982
Milt Wilcox: April 11, 1983
Lou Whitaker: June 6, 1983
Jack Morris: April 2, 1984; July 7, 1986; September 22, 1986
Darrell Evans: May 13, 1985
John Grubb: July 21, 1986
Pat Sheridan: June 27, 1988
Chet Lemon: September 26, 1988
Cecil Fielder: May 7, 1990; August 13, 1990; June 20, 1993
Tony Phillips: May 26, 1991
Walt Terrell: August 25, 1991
Rob Deer: September 21, 1992
Travis Fryman: April 18, 1993
Dan Gladden: August 15, 1993
Tony Clark: September 29, 1996; April 20, 1997; June 19, 2000
Brian Hunter: July 6, 1997
Damion Easley: May 24, 1998
Joe Randa: September 13, 1998
Bobby Higginson: June 12, 2000; July 10, 2000; September 25, 2000; July
     15, 2001

TIGER OF THE YEAR WINNERS

Don Wert, 1965
Denny McLain, 1966, 1968, 1969
Bill Freehan, 1967
Tom Timmerman, 1970
Mickey Lolich, 1971
Ed Brinkman, 1972
John Hiller, 1973
Al Kaline, 1974
Willie Horton, 1975
Mark Fidrych, 1976
Ron LeFlore, 1977, 1978
Steve Kemp, 1979
Alan Trammell, 1980, 1987, 1988
Kirk Gibson, 1981, 1994
Lance Parrish, 1982
Lou Whitaker, 1983, 1989
Willie Hernandez, 1984
Darrell Evans, 1985
Jack Morris, 1986
Cecil Fielder, 1990, 1991, 1992
Tony Phillips, 1993
Travis Fryman, 1995, 1996
Tony Clark, 1997*
Bobby Higginson, 1997*, 2000
Damion Easley, 1998
Dean Palmer, 1999
Steve Sparks, 2001

*Tie.

TIGER ROOKIE OF THE YEAR WINNERS

Mike Kilkenny, 1969
Elliott Maddox, 1970
Chuck Seelbach, 1972
Dick Sharon, 1973
Ron LeFlore, 1974
Vern Ruhle, 1975
Mark Fidrych, 1976

Dave Rozema, 1977
Lou Whitaker, 1978
Lynn Jones, 1979
Rick Peters, 1980
Glenn Wilson, 1982
Dave Gumpert, 1983
Barbaro Garbey, 1984
Nelson Simmons, 1985
Eric King, 1986
Matt Nokes, 1987
Paul Gibson, 1988
Kevin Ritz, 1989
Travis Fryman, 1990
Milt Cuyler, 1991
Scott Livingstone, 1992
Chris Gomez, 1993, 1994*
Bobby Higginson, 1995
Tony Clark, 1996
Deivi Cruz, 1997
Matt Anderson, 1998
Gabe Kapler, 1999
Jose Macias, 2000
Victor Samos, 2001

No award was given in 1971 and 1981.
*Gomez qualified as a rookie under major league rules each year he won, according to association secretary George Eichorn.

American Amateur Baseball Congress Graduate of the Year

Joe Sparma, 1967
Lou Whitaker, 1978

Two ex-Tigers farmhands also won: Dick Drago in 1971 and John Smoltz in 1992.

TIGERS IN THE NATIONAL BASEBALL HALL OF FAME, COOPERSTOWN, N.Y.

Name, Position	In Detroit	Inducted
Sparky Anderson, manager	1979–95	2000
Earl Averill, CF	1939–40	1975
Ed Barrow, executive	1903–04 (manager)	1953
Dan Brouthers, 1B	1886–88*	1945
Jim Bunning, P	1955–63	1996
Ty Cobb, CF-manager	1905–26	1935
Mickey Cochrane, C-manager	1934–38	1947
Sam Crawford, RF	1903–17	1957
Ray Dandridge, 3B	1933**	1987
Larry Doby, OF	1959	1998
Billy Evans, umpire	1947–51 (general manager)	1973
++Joe Falls, writer	1953–	2002
Rick Ferrell, C	1950–92 (gen. mgr./scout)	1984
Charlie Gehringer, 2B-coach-GM	1924–42, 1951–53	1949
Goose Goslin, LF	1934–37	1968
Hank Greenberg, 1B-LF	1930, 1933–41, 1945–46	1956
Ned Hanlon, manager	1881–88*	1996
Bucky Harris, manager	1929–33, 1955–56	1975
+Ernie Harwell, broadcaster	1960–91, 1993–	1981
Harry Heilmann, RF-broadcaster	1914, 1916–29, 1934–50	1952
Waite Hoyt, P	1930–31	1969
Hughie Jennings, SS-manager	1907–20	1945
Al Kaline, RF-broadcaster	1953–74, 1976–	1980
George Kell, 3B-broadcaster	1946–52, 1959–63, 1965–96	1983
Heinie Manush, LF	1923–27	1964
Eddie Mathews, 3B	1967–68	1978
++H.G. Salsinger, writer	1907–58	1968
Al Simmons, LF	1936	1953
Turkey Stearnes, CF	1923–31**	2000
Sam Thompson, RF	1885–88*, 1906	1974

*Detroit Wolverines of National League.
**Detroit Stars of Negro National League.
+Ford C. Frick Award for excellence in broadcasting.
++J. G. Taylor Spink Award for excellence in writing.

INSCRIPTIONS ON THE PLAQUES OF SELECTED DETROIT HALL OF FAMERS

GEORGE LEE ANDERSON, "SPARKY"
CINCINNATI, N.L. 1970–1978, DETROIT, A.L. 1979–1995

One of the game's most successful and colorful managers, his 2,194 wins rank third in history behind Connie Mack and John McGraw. The crank that turned the Big Red Machine, his skillful leadership helped those Cincinnati teams dominate in the 1970s. Revered and treasured by his players for his humility, eternal optimism and knowledge of the game. Baseball's only manager to win a World Series in both leagues and lead two franchises in victories. His teams won three World Series, seven division titles and five pennants, compiling a .619 post-season winning percentage.

TYRUS RAYMOND COBB
DETROIT AND PHILADELPHIA, A.L. 1905–1928

Led American League in batting twelve times and created or equalled more major league records than any other player. Retired with 4,191 major league hits.

GORDON "MICKEY" COCHRANE
PHILADELPHIA A.L. 1925–1933, DETROIT A.L. 1934–1937

Fiery catcher compiled a notable record both as a player and manager. The spark of the Athletics' championship teams of 1929–30–31, had an average batting mark of .346 in those three years. Led Detroit to two league championships and a World Series title in 1935.

SAMUEL EARL CRAWFORD, "WAHOO SAM"
CINCINNATI N.L., 1899–1902, DETROIT A.L. 1903–1917

Had lifetime record of 2,964 hits, batting average of .308. Played 2,505 games, holds major league record for most triples, 312. League leader one or more seasons in doubles, triples, runs batted in, runs scored, chances accepted, home runs (N.L., 1901, A.L., 1908) and total bases (N.L., 1902, A.L., 1913).

156

CHARLES L. GEHRINGER

Second baseman with Detroit A.L. from 1925 to 1941 and coach in 1942. Compiled lifetime batting average of .321. In 2,323 games, collected 2,839 hits. Named Most Valuable Player in A.L. in 1937. Batted .321 in World Series competition and had a .500 average for six All-Star Games.

HENRY BENJAMIN GREENBERG
DETROIT A.L. 1933–1946, PITTSBURGH N.L. 1947

One of baseball's greatest right-handed batters. Tied for most home runs by a right-handed batter in 1938 totalling 58. Most runs batted in 1935–37–40–46, and home runs 1938–40–46. Won 1945 pennant on last day of season with grand slam home run in 9th inning. Played in 4 World Series, 2 All-Star Games. Most valuable A.L. player twice, 1935 and 1940. Lifetime batting average .313.

HARRY EDWIN HEILMANN
DETROIT A.L. CINCINNATI N.L. 1916–1932

Right-handed hitting outfielder and first baseman, won American League batting championship four times, 1921, '23, '25 and '27. In 1923, batted .403. Collected 2,660 hits and 183 home runs in 2,146 major league games. Had lifetime batting average of .342 and fielding mark of .975.

ALBERT WILLIAM KALINE
DETROIT A.L. 1953–1974

Twelfth player to reach elite 3,000-hit plateau. Socked 399 home runs and attained .297 career average, with nine years in .300 class. Finished in all-time top 15 with 2,834 games, 3,007 hits, 1,585 runs batted in and 4,852 total bases. Played 100 or more games 20 years and had 242 consecutive errorless games in outfield, 1970–1972, for A.L. records. Led in hits and won A.L. batting title in 1955 at age 20.

Jack Morris pumps his fist in triumph as he records a strikeout cementing his 1984 no-hitter against the White Sox. Morris was a 2001 inductee into the Michigan Sports Hall of Fame. (Photo courtesy Ron Vesely and the National Baseball Hall of Fame Library, Cooperstown, N.Y.)

GEORGE CLYDE KELL
PHILADELPHIA A.L. 1941–1946, DETROIT A.L. 1946–1952, BOSTON A.L. 1952–1954, CHICAGO A.L. 1954–1956, BALTIMORE A.L. 1956–1957

Premier A.L. third baseman of 1940s and 1950s. Solid hitter and sure-handed fielder with strong accurate arm. Batted over .300 9 times, leading league with .343 in 1949. Led A.L. third baseman in fielding pct. 7 times, assists 4 times, and putouts and double plays twice.

HAROLD NEWHOUSER, "PRINCE HAL"
DETROIT A.L. 1939–1953, CLEVELAND A.L. 1954–1955

Only pitcher in major league history to win back-to-back MVP awards (1944–1945). Strikeout king with blazing fastball. 207-150 over 17 campaigns. Consecutive seasons of 29-9, 25-9, and 26-9 with corresponding ERA's of 2.22, 1.81, and 1.94 from 1944–1946. Hurled pennant-clincher in 1945 followed by 2 World Series victories over Cubs.

NORMAN THOMAS STEARNES, "TURKEY"
NEGRO LEAGUES, 1923–1941

One of the Negro Leagues' most feared hitters, he hit better than .300 in 14 of 19 seasons, collected six home run titles and led the league in triples four times. A graceful center fielder as well, he played in four East-West All-Star Games. Played 11 seasons for the Detroit Stars, also excelling with the New York Lincolns, Kansas City Monarchs, Chicago American Giants and Philadelphia Stars.

TIGERS IN THE MICHIGAN SPORTS HALL OF FAME, DETROIT

Name, Role	In Detroit	Inducted
Hank Aguirre, P	1958–67	1997*
Sparky Anderson, manager	1979–95	1992
Tommy Bridges, P	1930–43, 1945–46	1963
Walter O. Briggs Sr., owner	1920–52	1969
Jim Bunning, P	1955–63	1981
James A. Campbell, GM-president	1949–92	1985
Paul Carey, broadcaster	1973–91	1992
Norm Cash, 1B	1960–74	1984
Ty Cobb, CF-manager	1905–26	1955
Mickey Cochrane, C-manager	1934–38	1957
Gates Brown, OF-coach	1963-75, 1978-84	2002
Sam Crawford, RF	1903–17	1958
Wish Egan, P-scout	1902, 1913–51	1960
John E. Fetzer, owner	1956–83	1984
Bill Freehan, C	1961, 1963–76	1982
Charlie Gehringer, 2B-coach-GM	1924–42, 1951–53	1956
Kirk Gibson, RF-broadcaster	1979–87, 1993–95, 2000–	1999
Goose Goslin, CF	1934–37	1965
Hank Greenberg, 1B-LF	1930, 1933–41, 1945–46	1958
Ernie Harwell. broadcaster	1960–91, 1993–	1989
Harry Heilmann, RF-broadcaster	1914, 1916–29, 1934–50	1956
John Hiller, P	1964–70, 1972–80	1989
Willie Horton, LF-DH	1963–77	1987
Mike and Marian Ilitch, owners	1992–	1999*
Hughie Jennings, SS-manager	1907–20	1958
Al Kaline, RF-broadcaster	1953–74, 1976–	1978
George Kell, 3B-broadcaster	1946–52, 1959–63, 1965–96	1969
Harvey Kuenn, SS-CF	1952–59	1993
Ray Lane, broadcaster	1962–72, 1995–	1997
Mickey Lolich, P	1963–75	1982
Don Lund, OF-scout-coach-farm dir.	1949, 1952–59, 1963–70	1987
Heinie Manush, LF	1923–27	1964
Charlie Maxwell, LF	1955–62	1997
Dick McAuliffe, SS-2B	1960–73	1986
Barney McCosky, CF	1939–42, 1946	1995
Denny McLain, P	1963–70	1991
Jack Morris, P	1977–90	2001
George Mullin, P	1902–13	1962
Frank Navin, owner	1902–35	1976
Hal Newhouser, P	1939–53	1962
Jim Northrup, OF	1964–74	1995
Lance Parrish, C-coach-broadcaster	1977–86, 1999–	2002
Van Patrick, broadcaster	1952–58	1991
Billy Rogell, SS	1930–39	1970
Schoolboy Rowe, P	1933–42	1961
Mickey Stanley, CF-SS	1964–78	1994

160

OUTSTANDING IN THEIR FIELD

Name, Role	In Detroit	Inducted
Alan Trammell, SS-coach	1977–96, 1999	2000
Virgil Trucks, P	1941–43, 1945–52, 1956	1985
Ty Tyson, broadcaster	1927–42, 1947–52	1996
Vic Wertz, LF	1947–52, 1961–63	1983
Lou Whitaker, 2B	1977–95	2000
Rudy York, C-1B	1934, 1937–45	1972

*Won the Michigan Sports Hall of Fame's Gerald R. Ford Award.

TIGERS IN THE POLISH-AMERICAN SPORTS HALL OF FAME, ORCHARD LAKE, MICHIGAN

Name, Position	In Detroit	Inducted
Steve Gromek, P	1953–57	1981
Barney McCosky, CF	1939–42, 1946	1995
Joe Niekro, P	1970–72	1992
Ron Perranoski, P	1971–72	1983
Al Simmons, CF	1936	1975
Frank Tanana, P	1985–92	1996
Alan Trammell, SS-coach	1977–96, 1999	1998

TIGERS IN HALLS OF FAME IN OTHER STATES

Name, Position	In Detroit	State/Hall of Fame
Sparky Anderson, manager	1979–95	Texas Baseball
Elden Auker, P	1933–38	Kansas Sports
Buddy Bell, manager	1996–98	Texas Baseball
Red Borom, 2B	1944–45	Texas Baseball
Tommy Bridges, P	1930–43, 1945–46	Tennessee Sports
Donie Bush, SS	1908–21	Indiana Baseball
Ty Cobb, CF-manager	1905–26	Georgia Sports
Jack Coombs, P-coach	1920	Maine Sports
Larry Doby, OF	1959	Sports HOF of New Jersey
Walt Dropo, 1B	1952–54	Connecticut Sports
Goose Goslin, CF	1934–37	Sports HOF of New Jersey
Hank Greenberg, 1B-LF	1930, 1933–41, 1945–46	Texas Baseball
Tommy Henrich, coach	1959	New York Sports
Whitey Herzog, OF-IF	1963	Missouri Sports
Whitey Herzog, OF-IF	1963	Texas Baseball
Pinky Higgins, 3B	1939–44, 1946	Texas Sports
Ralph Houk, manager	1974–78	Kansas Sports
Frank Howard, OF-DH	1972–73	Ohio State Sports

OUTSTANDING IN THEIR FIELD

Name, Position	In Detroit	State/Hall of Fame
Frank Howard, OF-DH	1972–73	Texas Baseball
Fred Hutchinson, P-manager	1939–41, 1951–54	Florida Sports
Deacon Jones, P	1916–18	Florida Sports
Al Kaline, RF-broadcaster	1953–74, 1976–	Maryland Sports
George Kell, 3B	1946–62, '59–'63, '65–96	Arkansas State
Mickey Lolich, P	1963–75	Oregon Sports
Jerry Lumpe, 2B	1964–67	Missouri Sports
Firpo Marberry, P	1933–35	Texas Sports
Eric McNair, IF	1941–42	Mississippi Sports
Willie Mitchell, P	1916–19	Mississippi Sports
Johnny Neun, 1B	1925–28	Maryland Sports
Mel Ott, broadcaster	1956–58	Louisiana Sports
Mel Ott, broadcaster	1956–58	New York Sports
Johnny Pesky, SS	1952–54	Oregon Sports
Bubba Phillips, 3B-OF	1955, 1963–64	Mississippi Sports
Paul Richards, C	1943–46	Texas Sports
Schoolboy Rowe, P	1933–43	Arkansas State
Johnny Sain, coach	1967–69	Arkansas State
Rip Sewell, P	1932	Florida Sports
Rusty Staub, RF-DH	1976–79	Louisiana Sports
Sam Thompson, RF	1885–88*, 1906	Indiana Baseball
Dizzy Trout, P	1939–52	Indiana Baseball
Skeeter Webb, SS-2B	1945–48	Mississippi Sports
John Wockenfuss, C-1B-DH	1974–83	Delaware Sports

*Detroit Wolverines of National League.

TIGERS IN OTHER NATIONS' HALLS OF FAME

Name, Position	In Detroit	Nation/Hall of Fame
Reno Bertoia, 3B-2B-OF	1953–58, 1961–62	Canadian Baseball
Hank Greenberg, 1B-LF	1930, 1933–41, 1945–46	Intl. Jewish Sports, Israel
John Hiller, P	1964–70, 1972–80	Canadian Baseball
Aurelio Lopez, P	1979–85	Mexican Baseball
John McHale Sr., 1B	1954–45, 1947–48	Canadian Baseball
Jerry Morales, OF	1979	Puerto Rico Sports
Frank O'Rourke, 2B-3B	1924–26	Canadian Baseball
Orlando Peña, P	1965–67	Cuban Baseball
Aurelio Rodriguez, 3B	1971–79	Mexican Baseball
Tony Taylor, 2B	1971–73	Cuban Baseball
Ozzie Virgil Sr., IF-OF-C	1958, 1960–61	Dominican Rep. Sports

TIGERS IN CITY/REGIONAL HALLS OF FAME

Name, Position	In Detroit	City/Region/Hall of Fame
Howard Bailey, P	1981–83	Muskegon Area Sports
Dick Bartell, SS	1940–41	San Fran Bay Area Sports
Babe Birrer, P	1955	Buffalo Baseball
Steve Boros, 3B	1957–58, 1961–62	Greater Flint Sports
Ralph Branca, P	1953–54	Westchester (N.Y.)Sports
Dan Brouthers, 1B	1886–88*	Buffalo Baseball
Dave Campbell, IF	1967–68	Greater Lansing Sports
Rocky Colavito, LF	1960–63	Reading (Pa.) Baseball
Ed Farmer, P	1973	Chicagoland Sports
Ed Farmer, P	1973	Chicago Catholic League
Cecil Fielder, 1B-DH	1990–96	Kinston (N.C.) Baseball
Ira Flagstead, OF-SS	1917, 1919–23	Muskegon Area Sports
Charlie Gehringer, 2b-coach-GM	1924–42, 1951–53	Greater Lansing Sports
Dick Gernert, 1B-OF	1960–61	Reading (Pa.) Baseball
Johnny Groth, CF	1946–52, 1957–60	Buffalo Baseball
Luke Hamlin, P	1933–34	Greater Lansing Sports
Harry Heilmann, RF-broadcaster	1914, 1916–29, 1934–50	San Fran Bay Area Sports
Guillermo Hernandez, P	1984–89	Reading (Pa.) Baseball
Frank Howard, OF-DH	1972–73	D.C. Hall of Stars
Fred Hutchinson, P-manager	1939–41, 1951–54	Buffalo Baseball
Charlie Keller, OF	1950–51	Kinston (N.C.) Baseball
Billy Martin, SS-manager	1958, 1971–73	San Fran Bay Area Sports
Benny McCoy, 2B-SS	1936–39	Grand Rapids Sports
Keith Moreland, DH-C-IF	1989	Reading (Pa.) Baseball
Stubby Overmire, P-coach	1943–49, 1963–66	Grand Rapids Sports
Jim Perry, P	1973	Reading (Pa.) Baseball
Billy Pierce, P	1945, 1948	Chicagoland Sports
Vada Pinson, coach	1985–91	San Fran Bay Area Sports
Wally Pipp, 1B	1913	Grand Rapids Sports
Jim Price, C-broadcaster	1967–71, 1993–	Kinston (N.C.) Baseball
Phil Regan, P	1960–65	Grand Rapids Sports
Frank Secory, OF	1940	Muskegon Area Sports
Mayo Smith, manager	1967–70	Buffalo Baseball
Mickey Stanley, OF	1964–78	Grand Rapids Sports
Jim Stump, P	1957–59	Lansing Area Sports
Jack Tighe, mgr.-coach-scout	1935–1958, 1963–92	Muskegon Area Sports
Alan Trammell, SS-coach	1977–96, 1999	Breitbard/San Diego
Vic Wertz, RF	1947–52, 1961–63	Reading (Pa.) Baseball
Deacon White, 3B	1886–88*	Buffalo Baseball
Hal White, P	1941–43, 1946–52	Buffalo Baseball
Eddie Yost, 3B	1959–60	D.C. Hall of Stars

*Detroit Wolverines of National League.

163

TIGERS IN STILL OTHER HALLS OF FAME

Name, Position	In Detroit	Hall of Fame
Doug Bair, P	1983–85	Bowling Green State U.
Sean Bergman, P	1993–95	Southern Illinois Univ.
Steve Boros, 3B	1957–58, 1961–62	U-Michigan Hall of Honor
Hank Borowy, P	1950–51	Fordham University
Jim Bunning, P	1955–63	Xavier University
Norm Cash, 1B	1960–74	NAIA, Tulsa
Rocky Colavito, LF	1960–63	Natl. Ital.-Amer. Sports
Rip Collins, P	1923–27	International League
Jack Coombs, P-coach	1920	Duke University Sports
Tony Cuccinello, coach	1967–68	Natl. Ital.-Amer. Sports
Jack Dittmer, 3B	1957	Natl. Iowa Varsity Club
Duffy Dyer, C	1980–81	Ariz. State U. Sports
John Flaherty, C	1996–98	G. Washington U. Athl'c.
Kirk Gibson, CF-broadcaster	1979–87, 1993–95, 2000–	Michigan State Univ.
Luis Gonzalez, LF	1998	Univ. of South Alabama
Alex Grammas, coach	1980–91	AHEPA Hellenic Athletic
Alex Grammas, coach	1980–91	Athletic Hellenic, D.C.
Alex Grammas, coach	1980–91	Sports HOF, Miss. St. U.
Hank Greenberg, 1B-LF	1930, 1933–41, 1945–46	New York Jewish Sports
Dave Gumpert, P	1982–83	NAIA, Tulsa
Luke Hamlin, P	1933–34	International League
Ernie Harwell, broadcaster	1960–91, 1993–	Am. Sportscasters Assn.
Ernie Harwell, broadcaster	1960–91, 1993–	National Sportscasters
Ernie Harwell, broadcaster	1960–91, 1993–	Radio
Whitey Herzog, OF-IF	1963	Natl. Baseball Congress
Ralph Houk, manager	1974–78	Natl. Baseball Congress
Frank Howard, OF-DH	1972–73	U-Texas Longhorns Base.
Fred Hutchinson, P-manager	1939–41, 1951–54	International League
Riccardo Ingram, OF	1994	Ga. Tech Yellow Jackets
Ron Jackson, 1B	1981	Western Michigan Univ.
Jeff Kaiser, P	1991	Western Michigan Univ.
Charlie Keller, OF	1950–51	International League
Wayne Krenchicki, 3B	1983	University of Miami
Lerrin LaGrow, P	1970, 1972–75	Ariz. State U. Sports
William Lajoie, GM	1984–90	Mid-American Conference
William Lajoie, GM	1984–90	Western Michigan Univ.
Jack Lazorko, P	1986	Sports HOF, Miss. St. U.
Don Lee, P	1957–58	Univ. of Arizona Sports
Mickey Lolich, P	1963–75	Babe Ruth League
Torey Lovullo, IF	1988–89	UCLA Bruins Athletic
Billy Martin, SS-manager	1958, 1971–73	Natl. Baseball Congress
Billy Martin, SS-manager	1958, 1971–73	Natl. Ital.-Amer. Sports
Joe Niekro, P	1970–72	NAIA, Tulsa

Name, Position	In Detroit	Hall of Fame
Jim Northrup, OF	1964–74	NAIA, Tulsa
Steve O'Neill, coach-manager	1941, 1943–48	International League
Eddie Onslow, 1B	1912–13	International League
Jimmy Outlaw, OF-3B	1943–49	P&C Stadium, Syracuse
Stubby Overmire, P	1943–49	Western Michigan Univ.
Vada Pinson, coach	1985–91	Babe Ruth League
Jack Russell, P	1937	NAIA, Tulsa
A.J. Sager, P	1996–98	U. of Toledo Rockets
Frank Secory, OF	1940	Western Michigan Univ.
George Stallings, manager	1901	International League
Dave Stegman, OF	1978–80	Univ. of Arizona Sports
Franklin Stubbs, 1B-OF	1995	Virginia Tech Sports
Billy Sullivan Jr., C	1940–41	University of Portland
Jason Thompson, 1B	1976–80	CSU-Northridge Sports
Tom Tresh, SS-OF	1969	Central Michigan Univ.
Gus Triandos, C	1963	AHEPA Hellenic Athletic
Gus Triandos, C	1963	Athletic Hellenic, D.C.
John Tsitouris, P	1957	Athletic Hellenic, D.C.
Dixie Walker, LF	1936–39	International League
Kip Young, P	1978–79	Bowling Green State U.

THE TY COBB PLAQUE UNVEILED JULY 17, 1963, AT TIGER STADIUM

TYRUS RAYMOND COBB
1886–1961
Greatest Tiger of All
A Genius in Spikes

THE INSCRIPTIONS ON THE STATUES AT COMERICA PARK

When Comerica Park debuted in 2000, one of the features designed to set it apart from the spate of other "nouveau-retro" ballparks was to acknowledge the Tigers' glorious history. For the first-ever ballgame that April, five statues were unveiled, with word that a sixth would join them shortly. At midseason, it was announced the Detroit-raised Willie Horton would join Ty Cobb, Charlie Gehringer, Hank Greenberg, Al Kaline and Hal Newhouser behind left field. Despite some unclear and inaccurate information on the accompanying plaques, which we have indicated and corrected here, the statues are a wonder to behold. Look at the sculpted dirt from Cobb's slide and the hidden face by the base. Observe the spike in Kaline's glove; if a home run makes it that far, there's a decent chance the ball will stick in his mitt! Here are the texts from the plaques, going from left field to right.

WILLIE HORTON
"WILLIE THE WONDER"
Born October 18, 1942 Arno, Virginia

Detroit Tigers OF, DH 1963–77 Texas Rangers*, Cleveland Indians & Toronto Blue Jays DH, OF 1978 Seattle Mariners DH 1979–80
A HOMETOWN HERO WHOSE ACCOMPLISHMENTS ON AND OFF THE FIELD ARE A CREDIT TO THE CITY OF DETROIT
ACHIEVEMENTS AND HONORS
Raised in a Detroit housing project and overcame adversity
to become a Tiger home town hero
Was a baseball star for Detroit's Northwestern High School
and played Detroit sandlot baseball
Was instrumental in helping crush the violence that erupted
during the 1967 riots in Detroit
Batted .326 his first season with the Tigers
Had 100 or more RBI in 1965 104 and 1966 100
Threw out Lou Brock at home plate in the pivotal Game Five
of the 1968 World Series
Led the team in home runs 1968 36, 1969 28 and 1975 25
Was elected to four All-Star teams as a Tiger
Had his uniform number 23 retired July 15, 2000

Sculptors: Julie and Omri R. Amrany   Co-sculptor: Gary Tillery
Dedicated July 15, 2000

---

*Horton played for both Detroit and Texas in 1977, and in 1978 with Cleveland, the Oakland A's and Toronto.

TY COBB
"THE GEORGIA PEACH"
Born: December 18, 1886 Narrows, Georgia
Died: July 17, 1961 Atlanta, Georgia

Detroit Tigers CF 1905–1926 Philadelphia Athletics OF 1927–28
PERHAPS THE GREATEST PLAYER IN BASEBALL HISTORY
ACHIEVEMENTS AND HONORS
Inducted into the National Baseball hall of Fame in 1936
Holds baseball's highest lifetime batting average at .367*
Batted .400 or better three season:** .420 1911, .409 1912, .401 1922
Ranks second in all - time triples 295, fourth in doubles 724,
fourth in stolen bases 892
Holds major league record for career runs scored at 2,246
Won Chalmers Award AL MVP in 1911 with career high of .420
Led the league in RBI in four of the five years 1907–1911
Captured 1909 Triple Crown pacing both major leagues in batting
average .377, home runs 9 and RBI 107
Was player - manager of Tigers 1921–1926

Sculptors: Julie and Omri R. Amrany   Co - sculptor: Lou Cella
Dedicated: April 5, 2000

*Recent research puts his lifetime average at .366.
**Seasons.

HANK GREENBERG
"HAMMERIN' HANK"

Born: January 1, 1911 New York, N.Y.
Died: September 4, 1986 Beverly Hills, California

Detroit Tigers 1B 1930–46 Pittsburgh Pirates 1B 1947
ONE OF BASEBALL'S GREATEST SLUGGERS
AWARDS AND ACHIEVEMENTS
Inducted into the National Baseball Hall of Fame in 1956
Selected AL MVP in 1935 after leading the league
with 39* homers and 170 RBI
Drove in 183 runs in 1937, one short of Lou Gehrig's 1931
league record
Led the league in 1938 with 58 longballs
Won AL MVP honors in 1940 with a career best of .340
Led the league with 41 homers, 150 RBI and 50 doubles in 1940
Entered the Army in 1941, interrupting his career
Had more than 100 RBI seven times in his career and hit better
than .300 in each of his first eight seasons
Posted a lifetime slugging percentage of .605—fifth in
major league history
Had his uniform number 5 retired on June 12, 1983

Sculptors: Julie and Omri R. Amrany   Co-sculptor: Gary Tillery
Dedicated: April 5, 2000

*Actually 36 homers.

CHARLIE GEHRINGER
"THE MECHANICAL MAN"

Born: May 11, 1903 Fowlerville, Michigan
Died: January 21, 1993 Bloomfield Hills, Michigan

Detroit Tiger 2B 1924–42
A QUIET MAN WHO PLAYED WITH
REMARKABLE GRACE AND EFFICIENCY
ACHIEVEMENTS AND HONORS
Inducted into the National Baseball Hall of Fame in 1949
Batted over .300 in 13 of his 16 full seasons
with a lifetime batting average of .320
Named AL MVP in 1937 after hitting .371 to lead the league
Led the AL in 1929 in hits, runs, doubles, triples, stolen bases,
games, putouts and fielding percentage
Hit 15 or more home runs in a season six times
and had 100 or more RBI seven times
Drilled 60 doubles in 1936 setting a Tiger record for left-handed
hitters
Batted .379* and handled 39 chances without an error in
1935 World Series
Served as the Tigers' general manager from 1951–53
Had his uniform number 2 retired on June 12, 1983

Sculptors: Julie and Omri R. Amrany   Co-sculptor: Gary Tillery
Dedicated: April 5, 2000

*Batted .375.

HAL NEWHOUSER
"PRINCE HAL"

Born: May 20, 1921 Detroit, Michigan
Died: November 10, 1998 Bloomfield Hills, Michigan

Detroit Tigers LHP 1939–53 Cleveland Indians LHP 1954–55
ONE OF THE MOST DOMINANT PITCHERS
OF THE 1940s
ACHIEVEMENTS AND HONORS
Inducted into the National Baseball Hall of Fame in 1992
Captures his first MVP award in 1944 after leading
the majors with a 29-9 record
Named MVP in 1945 leading the entire major leagues in wins 25,
strikeouts 212 and ERA 1.81
Named to the All-Star Team seven times
Won 20 or more games in four of the five years during 1944–48
with 118 wins, 107 games* and 993 strikeouts
Pitched 313.1 innings in 1945 leading the majors
Led the AL in victories four times and twice in strikeouts and ERA
Hurled back-to-back 300 inning seasons in 1944 and 1945
Had his uniform number 16 retired on July 27, 1997

Sculptors: Julie and Omri R. Amrany   Co-sculptor: Lou Cella
Dedicated: April 5, 2000

*Really 126 complete games.

AL KALINE
Born December 19, 1934 Baltimore, Maryland

Detroit Tigers RF 1953–74
A COMPLETE SUPERSTAR WHO COULD HIT, FIELD, THROW AND RUN WITH EQUAL SKILL
ACHIEVEMENTS AND HONORS
Inducted into the National Baseball Hall of Fame in 1980
Won the league's batting crown in 1955 with a .340 batting average
Selected to 18 All-Star Games over his career
Hit .300 or better eight times and drilled 20 or more home
runs nine times
Captured 10 Gold Gloves
Ended career with 3,007 career hits breaking Al Simmons'
30 year old record*
Posted 399 career home runs while maintaining a .297 lifetime average
Elected Player of the Year by The Sporting News in 1955 and 1963
Had his uniform number retired August 17, 1980
Has been in the Tigers' television broadcast booth since 1976

Sculptors: Julie and Omri R. Amrany   Co-sculptor: Lou Cella
Dedicated: April 5, 2000

*The record Kaline broke is for most hits by a right-handed American Leaguer.

Firsts and Lasts

With all of the attention paid to the end of Tiger Stadium as the Tigers' home and the inauguration of Comerica Park as the club's new field, much was made—and rightfully so—of the last time such-and-such happened, or the first time thus-and-such took place. We've committed a lot of that to these pages, but we've also taken care to provide context for events that happened long before Tiger Stadium was a gleam in anyone's eye.

The First Major-League Baseball Game in Detroit

May 2, 1881. The Wolverines lost to Buffalo, 6-4, with 1,265 looking on at the home field, Recreation Park.

First Club to Issue Rain Checks

The Detroit Wolverines—in 1888. They said, "In case rain interrupts the game before three innings are played this check will admit the bearer to grounds for the next league game only."

THE FIRST GAME PLAYED AT MICHIGAN AND TRUMBULL

April 13, 1896. Detroit played a local semipro sandlot team known as the Athletics. It was no contest as Detroit clobbered the Athletics with a six-run first inning en route to a 30-3 win.

THE FIRST WESTERN LEAGUE GAME AT MICHIGAN AND TRUMBULL

April 28, 1896. The Detroits, as they were then known, beat their Western League rivals, the Columbus Senators, 17-2, before an overflow crowd of 8,000 at Bennett Park.

THE TIGERS' FIRST MAJOR-LEAGUE OPENING-DAY BATTING ORDER, APRIL 25, 1901

3B Doc Casey
CF Jimmy Barrett
2B Kid Gleason
RF Ducky Holmes
1B Pop Dillon
SS Kid Elberfeld
LF Doc Nance
C   Fritz Buelow
P   Roscoe Miller

THE LAST TIGER TO PLAY WITHOUT A GLOVE

Joe Yeager. He was Detroit's regular third baseman in 1903, and in 1901 and '02 pitched and played third, second and shortstop. He put in exactly 200 games for the Tigers during his three seasons.

DETROIT'S FIRSTS IN BASEBALL EQUIPMENT

Charles Bennett, the Detroit Wolverines' catcher during the team's 1887 championship year, said his wife made the first chest protector after worrying about his getting hit in the chest from so many fast pitches; remember that, at the time, the few gloves used were much smaller than today's. Mrs. Bennett's test model worked well in a private tryout and Bennett gave it a go in public, where it caught on quickly with other catchers.

Hank Greenberg, who at 6'3-1/2" was huge for a big-leaguer in the 1930s, came up with the idea to enlarge his glove by putting webbing between the sections of his first baseman's mitt, to make it both more comfortable for his hand and easier to pull in a throw. Although some decried the "fisherman's net," his webbing was approved and soon became the norm. Greenberg also initiated the practice of taking his glove with him to the bench. Players ordinarily left their gloves on the field when their team came up to bat. The old ways were still in use, though, until 1954.

THE TIGERS' FIRST SUNDAY GAME AT BENNETT PARK

The Tigers beat the New York Highlanders 13-6 before a crowd of 9,635 on August 18, 1907. Playing Sunday ball in Detroit then was a chancy proposition at best. To compensate, the Tigers took Sundays off or took a train to their opponent's city where Sunday baseball was not a hot issue. On 50 occasions in the 1900s, the Tigers ventured to parks in the suburbs and sometimes as far away as Columbus, Ohio, and Grand Rapids to get in a Sunday game.

Detroit's First Designated Hitter

Gates Brown. He was hitless in four at-bats on Opening Day in Cleveland, April 7, 1973, as the Indians beat the Tigers, 2-1 before 74,420 fans at Municipal Stadium.

Firsts at Comerica Park

Game: Detroit Tigers vs. Seattle Mariners, won 5-2, April 11, 2000
Pitch: Brian Moehler, Det, called Strike to Mark McLemore, Sea, 1st inning, April 11, 2000
Run: Luis Polonia, Det, off Freddie Garcia, Sea, 1st inning, April 11, 2000
Hit: John Olerud, Sea, double off Brian Moehler, Det, 1st inning April 11, 2000
Single: Gregg Jefferies, Det, off Freddie Garcia, Sea, 1st inning, April 11, 2000
Double: John Olerud, Sea, off Brian Moehler, Det, 1st inning, April 11, 2000
Triple: Luis Polonia, Det, off Freddie Garcia, Sea, 1st inning, April 11, 2000
Home Run: Juan Gonzalez, Det, off Ryan Rupe, TB, two men on, 3rd inning, April 14, 2000
Grand Slam: Trot Nixon, Bos, off Jim Poole, Det, 6th inning, April 19, 2000
Inside the Park HR: Juan Gonzalez, Det, off Kenny Rogers, Tex, 1st inning, September 2, 2000
Run Batted In: Gregg Jefferies, Det, off Freddie Garcia, Sea, 1st inning, April 11, 2000
Ground into DP: Mark McLemore, Sea, Jefferies to Cruz to Clark, Det, 2nd inning, April 12, 2000
Line into DP: Mark McLemore, Sea, to Tony Clark, Det, unassisted 6th inning, April 11, 2000
Walk: Brad Ausmus, Det, off Freddie Garcia, Sea, 1st inning, April 11, 2000
Intentional Walk: Mark McLemore, Sea, off Danny Patterson, Det, 7th inning, April 13, 2000
Strikeout: Tony Clark, Det, vs. Freddie Garcia, Sea, 1st inning, April 11, 2000

FIRSTS AND LASTS

Stolen Base: Mark McLemore, Sea, 2B off Dave Mlicki, Det, 5th inning, April 12, 2000

Caught Stealing: Mark McLemore, Sea, 2B, Ausmus to Cruz, Det, 1st inning, April 13, 2000

Pick Off: Mike Cameron, Sea, 1B by Brian Moehler, Det, 1st inning, April 11, 2000

Hit Batter: Dean Palmer, Det, by Jeff Sparks, TB, 5th inning, April 14, 2000

Sacrifice Fly: Dean Palmer, Det, scored Karim Garcia, Det, 8th inning, April 13, 2000

Sacrifice Bunt: Deivi Cruz, Det, moved Juan Encarnacion to 2nd, 2nd inning, April 11, 2000

Putout: Juan Encarnacion, Det, fly to CF from Mark McLemore, Sea, 1st inning, April 11, 2000

Outfield Assist: Bobby Higginson, Det, Mark McLemore, Sea, out at home, 6th inning, April 13, 2000

Error: Deivi Cruz, Det, fielding, GB hit by Mike Cameron, Sea, 1st inning, April 11, 2000

Winning Pitcher: Brian Moehler, Det, beat Freddie Garcia, Sea, April 11, 2000

Save: Todd Jones, Det, pitched a scoreless ninth inning, vs. Seattle, April 11, 2000

Complete Game: Aaron Sele, Sea, allowed three hits vs. Detroit, April 12, 2000

Shutout: Aaron Sele, Sea, final score, 4-0 vs. Detroit, April 12, 2000

Wild Pitch: Dave Mlicki, Det, moved Alex Rodriguez, Sea, to 2B 6th inning, April 12, 2000

Passed Ball: Jorge Posada, NYA, Deivi Cruz, Det, moved to third, 5th inning, May 14, 2000

Balk: Freddie Garcia, Sea, Gregg Jefferies scored, 1st inning, April 11, 2000

Umpires: Home, Rick Reed (Mich. native); 1B, Mark Wegner; 2B, Jim Reynolds; 3B, Charlie Williams, April 11, 2000

Rainout; vs. the Boston Red Sox, made up September 16, 2000, April 20, 2000

Doubleheader: vs. the Kansas City Royals, day-night from May 9 rainout, 8-5 KC, 10-6 Det, July 22, 2000

Tigers Sweep: vs. the New York Yankees 9-7, 6-3, 2-1 May 12–14, 2000

LASTS AT TIGER STADIUM

Game: Detroit Tigers vs. the Kansas City Royals, won 8-2 September
27, 1999

Pitch: Todd Jones, Det, called Strike to Carlos Beltran, KC, 9th inning,
September 27, 1999

Run: Rob Fick, Det, off Jeff Montgomery, KC, 8th inning, September
27, 1999

Hit: Rob Fick, Det, grand slam off Jeff Montgomery, KC, 8th inning,
September 27, 1999

Single: Damion Easley, Det, off Jeff Montgomery, KC, 8th inning,
September 27, 1999

Double: Dean Palmer, Det, off Jeff Montgomery, KC, 8th inning,
September 27, 1999

Triple: Luis Polonia, Det, off Brad Rigby, KC, 8th inning, September 25,
1999

Home Run: Rob Fick, Det, grand slam off Jeff Montgomery, KC,
8th inning, September 27, 1999

Grand Slam: Rob Fick, Det, off Jeff Montgomery, KC, 8th inning,
September 27, 1999

Inside the Park HR: Bobby Higginson, Det, off Alan Mills, Bal,
8th inning, July 6, 1997

Over the Roof HR: Jeromy Burnitz, Mil, off Nelson Cruz, Det,
6th inning, July 9, 1999

Run Batted In: Rob Fick, Det, off Jeff Montgomery, KC, 8th inning,
September 27, 1999

Ground into DP: Joe Randa, KC, Easley to Cruz to Clark, Det,
7th inning, September 27, 1999

Line into DP: Rob Fick, Det, Liner, Dye to Sweeney, KC, 6th inning,
September 27, 1999

Walk: Karim Garcia, Det, off Jeff Montgomery, KC, intentional,
8th inning, September 27, 1999

Intentional Walk: Karim Garcia, Det, off Jeff Montgomery, KC,
8th inning, September 27, 1999

Strikeout: Carlos Beltran, KC vs. Todd Jones, Det, 9th inning,
September 27, 1999

Stolen Base: Gabe Kapler, Det, 2B, off Jeff Suppan, KC, 2nd inning,
September 27, 1999

Caught Stealing: Dean Palmer, Det, 2B, Kreuter to Febles, KC,
1st inning, September 27, 1999

Picked Off: Deivi Cruz, Det, by Dwight Gooden, Cle, 3rd inning, September 20, 1999

Hit Batter: Sal Fasano, KC, by C. J. Nitkowski, Det, 7th inning, September 25, 1999

Sacrifice Fly: Rob Fick, Det, scored Damion Easley, Det, 2nd inning, September 27, 1999

Sacrifice Bunt: Damion Easley, Det, moved Dean Palmer, Det, to second, 6th inning, September 27, 1999

Putout: Brad Ausmus, Det, on Carlos Beltran's strikeout, 9th inning, September 27, 1999

Outfield Assist: Jermaine Dye, KC, Gabe Kapler, Det, out at first, 6th inning, September 27, 1999

Error: Jermaine Dye, KC, throwing error on hit by Easley, Det, 8th inning, September 27, 1999

Winning Pitcher: Brian Moehler, Det, beat Jeff Suppan, KC, vs. Kansas City, September 27, 1999

Save: Todd Jones, Det, pitched the ninth inning vs. Cleveland, September 23, 1999

Complete Game: Brian Moehler, Det, final score 1-0 vs. Texas, August 30, 1999

Shutout: Brian Moehler, Det, allowed three hits vs. Texas, August 30, 1999

Wild Pitch: Chad Durbin, KC, Karim Garcia, Det, to second, 6th inning, September 26, 1999

Passed Ball: Bill Haselman, Det, B. J. Surhoff to second, 1st inning, August 29, 1999

Balk: Freddie Garcia, Sea, Tony Clark to second, 2nd inning, June 17, 1999

Umpires: Home, Rocky Roe; 1B, Rick Reed (Mich. native); 2B, Durwood Merrill; 3B, Jim Reynolds, September 27, 1999

Rainout: vs. the Seattle Mariners, made up August 7, 1998, as DH August 6, 1998

Doubleheader: vs. the TB Devil Rays, from April 9 rainout, 10-6 TB, 8-2 Det, August 29, 1998

Tigers Sweep: vs. the Kansas City Royals, 10-5, 9-8, July 21–22, 1999

TIGER STADIUM FINAL GAME POST-GAME PLAYER PARTICIPANTS, SEPTEMBER 27, 1999

First Five Players, Years with Detroit

Mark Fidrych, 1976–80
Bill Freehan, 1961, 1963–76
Dave Bergman, 1984–92
Dick McAuliffe, 1960–73
Tom Brookens, 1979–88

Last Five Players, Years with Detroit

Kirk Gibson, 1979–87, 1993–95
Cecil Fielder, 1990–96
Al Kaline, 1953–74
Lou Whitaker, 1977–95 with Alan Trammell, 1977–96

Other Players, Years with Detroit (in alphabetical order)

Elden Auker, 1933–38
Brad Ausmus, 1996, 1999–2000
Reno Bertoia, 1953–58, 1961–62
Ray Boone, 1953–58
Red Borom, 1944–45
Doug Brocail, 1997–2000
Gates Brown, 1963–75
Jim Bunning, 1955–63
Damion Easley, 1996–
Harry Eisenstat, 1938–39
Darrell Evans, 1984–88
Joe Ginsberg, 1948, 1950–53
Steve Gromek, 1953–57
Mike Henneman, 1987–95
Ray Herbert, 1950–51, 1953–54
Guillermo Hernandez, 1984–89
Larry Herndon, 1982–88
John Hiller, 1965–70, 1972–80
Billy Hoeft, 1952–59
Willie Horton, 1963–77
Art Houtteman, 1945–50, 1952–53
George Kell, 1946–52
Steve Kemp, 1977–81

179

Dick Kryhoski, 1950–51
Ron LeFlore, 1974–79
Chet Lemon, 1982–90
Mickey Lolich, 1963–75
Don Lund, 1949, 1952–54
Charlie Maxwell, 1955–62
Eddie Mayo, 1944–48
John McHale, 1943–45, 1947–48
Ed Mierkowicz, 1945, 1947–48
Jack Morris, 1977–90
Les Mueller, 1941, 1945
Jim Northrup, 1964–74
Jimmy Outlaw, 1943–49
Lance Parrish, 1977–86
Dan Petry, 1979–87, 1990–91
Billy Pierce, 1945, 1948
Jim Price, 1967–71
Aurelio Rodriguez, 1971–79
Billy Rogell, 1930–39
Dave Rozema, 1977–84
Mickey Stanley, 1964–78
Frank Tanana, 1985–92
Jason Thompson, 1976–80
Dick Tracewski, 1966–69
Virgil Trucks, 1941–43, 1945–52, 1956
Jake Wade, 1936–39
Don Wert, 1963–70
Hal White, 1941–43, 1946–52
Milt Wilcox, 1977–85
Earl Wilson, 1966–70
John Wockenfuss, 1974–83
Jake Wood, 1961–67
Eddie Yost, 1959–60

FINAL GAME UNIFORM NUMBERS*

(starters listed in **bold**)

Catchers	#	Primary Player Honored	Other Players Honored
Brad Ausmus	11^	Bill Freehan**	Dizzy Trout (P)
Bill Haselman	28	Birdie Tebbetts	

Elden Auker, a Tigers submarine-style pitcher during the 1930s, was one of the dozens of Tigers from past eras who got to take a curtain call during the last game at Tiger Stadium in 1999. (Photo courtesy National Baseball Hall of Fame Library, Cooperstown, N.Y.)

FIRSTS AND LASTS

Infielders	#	Primary Player Honored	Other Players Honored
Tony Clark	5	Hank Greenberg**	Jim Northrup (OF)
Damion Easley	2	Charlie Gehringer**	Jake Wood (2B)
Dean Palmer	21	George Kell**	Guillermo Hernandez (P)
Deivi Cruz	3^	Alan Trammell**	Mickey Cochrane (C)
		Eddie Mayo (2B)	
		Dick McAuliffe (SS-2B)	
Gabe Alvarez	4	Aurelio Rodriguez	Goose Goslin (OF)
		Rudy York (C-1B)	
Frank Catalanotto	1	Lou Whitaker	
Robert Fick (DH)	25	Norm Cash	
Gregg Jefferies	45	Cecil Fielder	
Jason Wood	24	Travis Fryman	Mickey Stanley (OF)

Outfielders	#	Primary Player Honored	Other Players Honored
Karim Garcia	6	Al Kaline**	
Gabe Kapler	None	Ty Cobb**	Harry Heilmann (OF)
		Sam Crawford (OF)	
		Heinie Manush (OF)	
Juan Encarnacion	23	Kirk Gibson**	Willie Horton (OF)
Kimera Bartee		Rocky Colavito	Harvey Kuenn (SS)
		Billy Rogell (SS)	
Luis Polonia	8	Ron LeFlore	Ray Boone (3B)
		Ed Brinkman (SS)	
Bobby Higginson	34	Chet Lemon	

Pitchers	#	Primary Player Honored	Other Players Honored
Matt Anderson	39	Mike Henneman	
Willie Blair	26	Frank Tanana	
Dave Borkowski	10^	Tommy Bridges	
Doug Brocail	18	John Hiller	
Francisco Cordero	37	Hank Aguirre	
Nelson Cruz	44	Billy Hoeft	
Seth Greisinger	None	George Mullin	Wild Bill Donovan (P)
		Hooks Dauss (P)	
Erik Hiljus	19	Al Benton	
Todd Jones	59	(Todd Jones wore his own #59)	

182

Pitchers	#	Primary Player Honored	Other Players Honored
Masao Kida	17	Denny McLain	
Dave Mlicki	29	Mickey Lolich**	Aurelio Lopez (P)
Brian Moehler	47	Jack Morris**	
C. J. Nitkowski	16	Hal Newhouser**	
Sean Runyan	None	Ed Killian	Harry Coveleski (P)
Justin Thompson	15	Earl Whitehill	
Jeff Weaver	14	Jim Bunning	Hoot Evers (OF)

Manager/Coaches	#	Primary Person Honored
Larry Parrish	11^	Sparky Anderson
Perry Hill	31	Del Baker
Jeff Jones	32	Steve O'Neill
Lance Parrish	13	(Lance Parrish wore his own #13)
Juan Samuel	10^	Mayo Smith
Alan Trammell	3^	(Alan Trammell wore his own #3)
Dan Warthen	None	Hughie Jennings
Brad Andress	41	Darrell Evans (IF-DH)

Other Available Number: 20—Vic Wertz (OF)

*To honor a century of Tigers greats, the 1999 Tigers for the final game wore jerseys with their numbers on the back. The only exceptions were Parrish and Trammell, coaches who were Tiger greats in their own right as players, and pitcher Jones.
**Tigers All-Time Team Members, voted by fans in 1999.
^Duplicate numbers (3, 10, 11).

FIRST CURTAIN CALL AT COMERICA PARK

Jose Macias, July 22, 2000, after hitting a grand slam as part of the Tigers' 10-6 win over Kansas City. It was also the first grand slam of Macias' career.

Media Savvy

Which came first, the chicken or the egg? Just like in the world of fowl, the relationship between a baseball team and the journalists who report on it is a symbiotic one—although at times one group (guess which one?) thinks of the other as a necessary evil, if that. Each needs the other in both good years and bad. Each uses the other, one to sell tickets and the other to gain market share and advertising revenue. As luck would have it, the communications media is also a wonderful vehicle for spreading one's artistic expressions in song and even poetry. Since not everybody can make it to every ballgame they'd love to see, and since no stadium could be built big enough to accommodate that desire, fans live vicariously through the media the ups and downs of their favorite team in a sort of ritualized soap opera. Every so often, you'll catch a moment of art shining through.

TIGERS RADIO BROADCASTERS THROUGH THE YEARS

Broadcaster	Years
Ty Tyson	1927–42, 1951
Harry Heilmann*	1934–50
**Van Patrick	1949, 1952–59
Paul Williams	1951
Dizzy Trout	1953–55
Mel Ott	1956–58
**George Kell	1959–63
**Ernie Harwell	1960–91, 1993, 1999–
**Bob Scheffing	1964
Gene Osborn	1965–66
Ray Lane	1967–72
Paul Carey	1973–91
Rick Rizzs	1992–94
Bob Rathbun	1992–94
Frank Beckmann	1995–98
Lary Sorenson	1995–98
Jim Price	1998–
Dan Dickerson	2000–

*The first future Hall of Famer to work in the broadcast booth.
**Alternated between radio and TV booths in the middle of the fifth inning, 1959–64.

TIGERS OVER-THE-AIR TV BROADCASTERS THROUGH THE YEARS

Broadcaster	Years
Ty Tyson	1947–52
Harry Heilmann	1947–52
Paul Williams	1947–52
*Van Patrick	1953–59
Dizzy Trout	1953–55
Mel Ott	1956–58
*George Kell	1959–63, 1965–96
*Ernie Harwell	1960–64, 1997–98
*Bob Scheffing	1964
Ray Lane	1965–66
Larry Osterman	1967–77
Don Kremer	1975
Al Kaline	1976– 2001
Joe Pellegrino	1977
Mike Barry	1978
Jim Price	1995–97
Frank Beckmann	1999–
Lance Parrish	2002–

*Alternated between TV and radio booths in the middle of the fifth inning, 1959–64.

TIGERS CABLE TV BROADCASTERS THROUGH THE YEARS

Broadcaster	Years
Larry Adderly	1981–83
Hank Aguirre	1981–83
Norm Cash	1981–83
Larry Osterman	1984–92
Bill Freehan	1984–85
Jim Northrup	1985–94
Jim Price	1993–97
Ernie Harwell	1994–97
Fred McLeod	1995–97
Josh Lewin	1998–2001
Kirk Gibson	1998–

TIGERS RADIO STATIONS THROUGH THE YEARS

WWJ, 950 AM: 1930–32 (home games only; no Sunday games), 1933 (home games only; no Saturday or Sunday games), 1960–63 (day games only)

WXYZ (now WXYT), 1270 AM: 1934–42 (home games only), 1943–51, 2001–

WJBK (now WLQV), 1500 AM: 1950–52, 1953 (simulcast on TV)

WKMH (now WXDX), 1310 AM: 1952, 1953–59 (simulcast on TV), 1960–63

WJR, 760 AM: 1960–63 (night games only), 1964–2000

TIGERS OVER-THE-AIR TV STATIONS THROUGH THE YEARS

WWDT/WWJ/WDIV, Channel 4: 1947–52, 1975–94

WJBK, Channel 2: 1953–74

WKBD, Channel 50: 1995–

TIGERS CABLE AND PAY TV STATIONS THROUGH THE YEARS

On-TV*: 1981–83

Pro-Am Sports System (PASS): 1984–97

Fox Sports Net Detroit: 1998–

*On-TV was a pay-TV service that used the signal of WXON, Channel 20 in Detroit (now WDWB), during prime time, and a decoder was needed to watch the signal unscrambled.

SONGS ABOUT THE TIGERS

Go Get 'Em, Tigers

Written by Artie Fields. Commissioned by the National Bank of Detroit. Introduced during the 1967 season when NBD was a Tigers radio sponsor and played during the Tigers' World Series championship year of 1968.

(woman's voice, spoken)
Go GET 'em, Tigers. Rrowr!

(vocal group)
We're all behind our baseball team
Go get 'em, Tigers
World Series bound and pickin' up steam
Go get 'em, Tigers

Bridge:
    There'll be joy in Tigertown
    We'll sing you songs
    When the Bengals bring the pennant home
    Where it belongs

We're all behind our baseball team
Go get 'em

(female solo voice)
Detroit Tigers

(group)
Go get 'em, Tigers!
(bridge instrumental)

(group)
We're all behind our baseball team
Go get 'em
(female solo voice)
Detroit Tigers

(group)
Go get 'em, Tigers!

Thanks for the Memories

Authorship unknown. To the tune of Bob Hope's theme song.
Sung by Mel Torme at Tiger Stadium August 2, 1970, Al Kaline
Day.

Thanks for the memories
Of sunny afternoons, beaming August moons
Good field, good hit are words you fit
You left St. Louis in ruins
We thank you, so much

Thanks for the memories
Of records you have set, the list is growing yet
Your golden mitts and booming hits
And throws we can't forget
We thank you, so much

You came here when you were eighteen
And the years have quickly passed
But you've earned our highest rating
And countless friends amassed

So thanks for the memories
Of a batting title won, a Series job well done
All Star Games and Halls of Fame
That wait to add your name
We thank you, so much

Tigers On Parade

Authorship unknown. A fight song for the 1935 World Series season. The words and melody were remembered by Jeannine Pattison, co-author Mark's mother, 65 years after the fact, when she had been not that long an immigrant from French Canada.

> See the flags a-wavin'
> O'er the field of Navin
> Oh, you Tigers on parade
> Mickey's aces have sure gone places
> Around those bases on parade
>
> Cochrane, Cochrane, what a man you are
> What a team! And every man a star
> All the world is telling
> Every fan is yelling
> Oh, you Tigers on parade

Away Down South

A parody of "Dixie" penned by Eddie Ainsmith after the Tigers got off to a horrible start in 1920. The team blamed it on a pre-season barnstorming tour through the deep South with the Boston Braves where they encountered rain, hail, floods, and lousy diamonds.

> Away down South in the land of cotton
> Where the sky is high and the grounds are rotten
> Stay away! Stay away! Stay away! Stay away!

TIGER POETRY!

Speaking of Greenberg

Edgar A. Guest, 1934

The Irish didn't like it when they heard of Greenberg's
fame
For they thought a good first baseman should possess an
Irish name;
And the Murphys and Mulrooneys said they never
dreamed they'd see
A Jewish boy from Bronxville out where Casey used to be.
In the early days of April not a Dugan tipped his hat
Or prayed to see a "double" when Hank Greenberg came
to bat.

In July the Irish wondered where he'd ever learned to
play.
"He makes me think of Casey!" Old Man Murphy dared
to say;
And with fifty‑seven doubles and a score of homers
made
The respect they had for Greenberg was being openly
displayed.
But on the Jewish New Year when Hank Greenberg
came to bat
And made two home runs off pitcher Rhodes—they
cheered like mad for that.

Came Yom Kippur—holy feast day world wide over to
the Jew
And Hank Greenberg to his teaching and the old tradi-
tion true
Spent the day among his people and he didn't come to
play.
Said Murphy to Mulrooney, "We shall lose the game
today!"

We shall miss him on the infield and shall miss him at the bat,
But he's true to his religion—and I honor him for that!"

TRADEMARK SAYINGS BY TIGERS BROADCASTERS

"Good afternoon, boys and girls, this is Ty Tyson speaking to you from Navin Field."—Ty Tyson
"Bugaboo! Another fly is dead!"—Harry Heilmann
"Trouble! Trouble!"—Harry Heilmann
"Listen to the voice of baseball."—Harry Heilmann
"Up high."—George Kell
"Down low."—George Kell
"Have a confab out on the mound."—George Kell
"He didn't like that one too much."—George Kell
"Hello, everybody, I'm George Kell"—George Kell
"HE struck him out!"—George Kell
"HE hit it a mile!"—George Kell
"It's long gone!"—Ernie Harwell
"Strike, Mr. (umpire's name here) said so."—Ernie Harwell
"He stood there like the house at the side of the road and watched that one go by."—Ernie Harwell
"Two for the price of one."—Ernie Harwell
"The Tigers need some instant runs."—Ernie Harwell
"The umpires who paid to get in didn't agree with that call."—Ernie Harwell
"Goodbye, baseball!"—Rick Rizzs

MOVIES INVOLVING THE TIGERS

Somewhere in Georgia, 1916, starring Ty Cobb as a bank clerk who winds up playing for the Tigers. In the process, he thwarts the villains and wins the heart of the heroine, played in this six-reeler by Elsie MacLeod. Grantland Rice wrote the script, and Cobb became the first pro athlete to star in a movie.

Sparky Anderson, shown here in the dugout in Cooperstown, N.Y., managing the Tigers in the 1995 Hall of Fame game, has written or co-written three books, had a book written about him, and has been featured in a movie. (Photo courtesy National Baseball Hall of Fame Library, Cooperstown, N.Y.)

College, 1927, about a high school valedictorian who tries out for every sport in college to win the girl. Starring Buster Keaton, Anne Cornwall, Harold Goodwin, Snitz Edwards, Florence Turner, Flora Bramley, Tigers Hall-of-Famer Sam Crawford, Grant Withers, Charlie Hall and the University of Southern California baseball team.

Alibi Ike, 1935, a comedy about an idiosyncratic new baseball recruit, Francis X. "Ike" Farrell, who tries to help the Chicago Cubs to the pennant with his pitching and hitting. Starring Joe E. Brown, Olivia de Havilland, Ruth Donnelly, Roscoe Karns, William Frawley, Eddie Shubert, G. Pat Collins, and featuring Jim Thorpe and former Tigers pitchers Guy Cantrell and Ed Wells, third baseman Babe Pinelli and catchers Johnny Bassler and Gene Desautels.

The Kid From Cleveland, 1949, about a ballclub helping a troubled teen fan. Starring George Brent, Lynn Bari, Russ Tamblyn, Tommy Cook, Ann Doran, Louis Jean Heydt, K. Elmo Lowe, John Beradino, retired Tigers great Hank Greenberg, future Tigers players Gene Bearden, Ray Boone, Larry Doby, Steve Gromek and Bob Kennedy and future Tigers manager Joe Gordon.

The Stratton Story, 1949, an autobiographical account of pitcher Monty Stratton, who made it to the big leagues even after losing a leg in a hunting accident. Starring Jimmy Stewart, June Allyson, Frank Morgan, Agnes Moorehead, Bill Williams, Bruce Cowling, Cliff Clark, Mary Lawrence, Dean White, Robert Gist, Tigers infielder George Vico plus actors Louie Novikoff and Dwight Adams in uncredited roles as Tigers players, future Tigers pitcher Gene Bearden and future Tigers manager Jimmy Dykes.

Angels in the Outfield, 1951, about celestial help for the woeful Pittsburgh Pirates. It spurred a 1994 sequel about the California Angels. Starring Paul Douglas, Janet Leigh, Donna Corcoran, Keenan Wynn, Lewis Stone, Spring Byington, Bruce Bennett, Ellen Corby, Joe DiMaggio, Bing Crosby, Harry Ruby, Tigers Hall-of-Famer Ty Cobb and Jeff Richards.

The Winning Team, 1952, a glossy biography of pitching great Grover Cleveland Alexander starring Doris Day, Ronald Reagan, Frank Lovejoy, Eve Miller, Bob Lemon, then-Tigers second baseman Jerry Priddy, Peanuts Lowery, George (Catfish) Metkovich, Irv Noren, Hank Sauer, Al Zarilla and Gene Mauch.

One in a Million: The Ron LeFlore Story, 1978, a CBS made-for-TV movie starring LeVar Burton as LeFlore, based on LeFlore's autobiography, *Breakout,* chronicling his route from the ghetto to prison to All-Star status as a ballplayer. Also starring Madge Sinclair, Paul Benjamin, James Luisi, former Tigers manager Billy Martin, Larry B. Scott, and Tigers greats Al Kaline, Norm Cash, Jim Northrup and Bill Freehan.

Tiger Town, 1983, a Disney Channel made-for-TV movie starring Roy Scheider as a famed Detroit Tiger on the verge of seeing his career end without ever playing in the World Series until he gets inspiration from a young fan (Justin Henry). Also starring Ron McLarty, then-Tigers manager Sparky Anderson, Tigers broadcaster Ernie Harwell, Bethany Carpenter and Noah Moazezi.

The Natural, 1984, starring Robert Redford as Roy Hobbs, an old rookie with a sweet swing. Also starring Robert Duvall, Glenn Close, Barbara Hershey, Robert Prosky, Richard Farnsworth, Darren McGavin, Joe Don Baker, Michael Madsen and Sibbi Sisti. Because active pro ballplayers could not be used, retired and college players were used in filming. Retired Tigers third baseman Phil Mankowski played the unfortunate third sacker for the sad-sack New York Knights, victimized early in the film by a batted ball to his crotch.

The Slugger's Wife, 1985, starring Michael O'Keefe as an Atlanta Braves outfielder and Rebecca De Mornay as his rock-star wife who try to juggle the two-career household. Also starring Martin Ritt, Randy Quaid, Cleavant Derrick, retired Tigers pitcher Mark Fidrych, Al Hrabosky, Ted Turner, Pete Van Wieren, Ernie Johnson, Skip Caray and Nick Charles.

Cooperstown, 1993, a TNT made-for-TV movie starring Alan Arkin as a pitcher who feels he's been snubbed by the Hall of Fame because he served up a home-run pitch that kept his team out of the World Series. Also starring Graham Greene, Hope Lange, Josh Charles, Ed Begley Jr., Maria Pitillo, Ann Wedgeworth, Paul Dooley, Charles Haid (who also directed) and Tigers broadcaster Ernie Harwell.

Little Big League, 1994, starring Luke Edwards as a 12-year-old who inherits the Minnesota Twins from his grandfather and names himself to manage the team. Also starring Timothy Busfield, John Ashton, Ashley Crow, Kevin Dunn, Jason Robards, Jonathan Silverman, Dennis Farina, Leon Durham, Kevin Elster, Ken Griffey Jr., Lou Piniella, then-Tigers catcher-outfielder Mickey Tettleton, Ivan Rodriguez, Sandy Alomar Jr., Eric Anthony, Carlos Baerga, Alex Fernandez, Randy Johnson, Wally Joyner, Dave Magadan, Lenny Webster, Paul O'Neill, Rafael Palmeiro, future Tigers third baseman Dean Palmer, Tim Raines and Chris Berman.

Cobb, 1994, based on author Al Stump's efforts to write Ty Cobb's autobiography on Cobb's terms but finding a hateful, spiteful, bigoted—yet compelling—man, even shortly before death. Starring Tommy Lee Jones, Robert Wuhl, Lolita Davidovich, Lou Myers, Tyler Logan Cobb, Roger Clemens, Jay Tibbs and Tigers broadcaster Ernie Harwell.

For Love of the Game, 1999, starring Kevin Costner as a near-certain Hall-of-Fame Tigers starter near the end of the line, wondering whether he should accept a trade with the team being sold or quitting the sport to be with his lady love—all while he's in the process of pitching a perfect game. Also starring Kelly Preston, Jena Malone and John C. Reilly.

The Life and Times of Hank Greenberg, 2000, a documentary about the slugger's life inside and outside of baseball, bringing his feats for Detroit and his Jewish ethnic and religious heritage into sharp relief. Greenberg and several of his contemporaries on the diamond, most of them fellow Tigers, are featured in interviews, and archival newsreel and film footage is on the mark when advancing the narrative. Among the Tigers interviewed are Elden Auker, Flea Clifton, Harry Eisenstat, Charlie Gehringer, George Kell, Barney McCosky, Hal Newhouser, Billy Rogell,

Birdie Tebbetts, Virgil Trucks, Tigers clubhouse manager Rip Collins, and Tigers broadcaster Ernie Harwell.

TIGERS APPEARING ON TV

Denny McLain: A whiz on the Hammond organ, McLain appeared on "The Ed Sullivan Show," CBS' prime-time variety staple, after the Tigers won the World Series in 1968. McLain in the 1990s also hosted a morning-drive talk radio program on WXYT (1270 AM) in Detroit in the 1990s before quitting at the peak of his popularity to enter private business.

Mickey Lolich: Because he won three World Series games in 1968, somebody thought Lolich could make a go of it in the off-season a singer. He appeared on the ABC late-night entry, "The Joey Bishop Show," in the 1968 offseason.

Lou Whitaker and Alan Trammell: As themselves, they gave "Magnum, P.I." (Tom Selleck) tickets to a sold-out Tigers game. The episode was filmed after the Tigers' 1984 World Series win. The Magnum character usually wore a Tigers cap and was a huge Tigers fan (as was Selleck). When he asked them where they'd be sitting at the park, Whitaker replied, "Behind second base." It took Magnum a while to realize who he had been talking to, but by then they were gone.

BOOKS ON THE TIGERS

Alexander, Charles. *Ty Cobb*. New York: Oxford University Press. 1984.

Allen, Maury. *Damn Yankee: The Billy Martin Story*. New York: New York Times Books. 1980.

Anderson, William. *The Detroit Tigers: A Pictorial Celebration of the Greatest Players and Moments in Tigers History*. South Bend, Ind.: Diamond Communications. 1991; updated edition, Detroit: Wayne State University Press. 1999.

Anderson, Sparky. *Bless You Boys: Diary of the Detroit Tigers' 1984 Season*. Chicago: Contemporary Books. 1984. First edition (paperback) ends at the division clincher; second edition (hardcover) ends after the World Series.

Anderson, Sparky, and Dan Ewald. *Sparky!* New York: Prentice-Hall. 1990.

———. *They Call Me Sparky.* Chelsea, Mich.: Sleeping Bear Press. 1998.

Auker, Elden, with Tom Keegan. *Sleeper Cars and Flannel Uniforms: A Lifetime of Memories from Striking Out the Babe to Teeing It Up With the President.* Chicago: Triumph Books. 2001.

Bak, Richard. *Cobb Would Have Caught It: The Golden Age of Baseball in Detroit.* Detroit: Wayne State University Press. 1991.

———. *Ty Cobb: His Tumultuous Life and Times.* Dallas: Taylor. 1994.

———. *A Place for Summer: A Narrative History of Tiger Stadium.* Detroit: Wayne State University Press. 1998.

Bak, Richard, Charlie Vincent, and the Free Press staff. *The Corner.* Chicago: Triumph. 1999.

Barrow, Ed. *My 50 Years in Baseball.* New York: Coward-McCann. 1951.

Bartell, Dick, with Norman Macht. *Rowdy Richard.* Berkeley, Calif.: North Atlantic Books. 1987.

Benagh, Jim, and Jim Hawkins. *Go Bird Go.* New York: Dell. 1976.

Berkow, Ira, and Mick Ellison. *Hank Greenberg: Hall of Fame Slugger.* Philadelphia: Jewish Publication Society. 1991.

Betzold, Michael. *Tiger Stadium: Where Baseball Belongs.* Detroit: Tiger Stadium Fan Club. 1988.

———. *Casey and the Bat.* Philadelphia: buybooksontheweb.com. 1999. (F)

Betzold, Michael, and Ethan Casey. *Queen of Diamonds.* West Bloomfield, Mich.: Altwerger and Mandel. 1992; updated edition, West Bloomfield, Mich.: Northmont Publishing. 1997.

Bevis, Charlie. *Mickey Cochrane: The Life of a Baseball Hall of Fame Catcher.* Jefferson, N.C.: McFarland. 2001.

Bunning, Jim, as told to Ralph Bernstein. *The Story of Jim Bunning.* Philadelphia: Lippincott. 1965.

Bunning, Jim, Whitey Ford, Mickey Mantle, and Willie Mays. *Grand Slam.* New York: Viking Press. 1965.

Burchard, Marshall. *Sports Hero Ron LeFlore.* New York: Putnam. 1979. (C)

Burchard, S. H. *Sports Star Mark "The Bird" Fidrych.* New York: Harcourt Brace Jovanovich. 1977. (C)

Butler, Hal. S*tormin' Norman Cash.* New York: Julian Messner. 1968.

————. *The Willie Horton Story.* New York: Julian Messner. 1970.

————. *Al Kaline and the Detroit Tigers.* Chicago: Henry Regnery Co. 1973.

Cantor, George. *The Tigers of '68: Baseball's Last Real Champions.* Dallas: Taylor. 1997.

Cobb, Ty. *Bustin' Em, And Other Big League Stories.* New York: E. J. Clode. 1914.

Cobb, Ty, and Al Stump. *My Life in Baseball: The True Record.* New York: Doubleday. 1961. Reprint, Lincoln, Neb.: University of Nebraska Press. 1993.

Cobbledick, Gordon. *"Don't Knock the Rock": The Rocky Colavito Story.* Cleveland: World Publishing Co. 1966.

Cochrane, Mickey. *Baseball: The Fan's Game.* New York: Funk and Wagnalls Co. 1939. Reprint, Cleveland: Society for American Baseball Research. 1992.

Craig, Roger, and Vern Plagenhoef. *Inside Pitch: Roger Craig's '84 Tiger Journal.* Grand Rapids, Mich.: Eerdmans Publishing Co. 1984.

Davis, Eric, and Ralph Wiley. *Born To Play: The Eric Davis Story.* New York: Viking. 1999.

Detroit Free Press. *From Corner to Copa.* Chicago: Triumph. 2000.

Detroit News. *The 1984 Detroit Tigers: The Magic Season.* Indianapolis: News Books International. 1984.

————. *Home, Sweet Home: Memories of Tiger Stadium, From the Archives of the Detroit News.* Champaign, Ill.: Sports Publishing. 1999.

————. *They Earned Their Stripes: The Detroit Tigers All-Time Team.* Champaign, Ill.: Sports Publishing, Inc. 2000.

Detroit Tigers. Roster Books, 1932–1947. Detroit: Detroit Tigers.

————. Press-TV-Radio/Media/Information Guides, 1948–present. Detroit: Detroit Tigers.

————. Team Yearbooks, 1955, 1957–1992. Detroit: Detroit Tigers.

Dolson, Frank. *Jim Bunning, Baseball and Beyond.* Philadelphia: Temple University Press. 1998.

Driscoll, David, and the Mayo Smith Society. *Tiger Tracks: 1988.* London, Ontario: self-published. 1988.

Eldridge, Grant, and Karen Elizabeth Bush. *Willie Horton: Detroit's Own "Willie the Wonder."* Detroit: Wayne State University Press. 2001. (C)

Evers, Crabbe. *Tigers Burning: A Duffy House Mystery.* New York: William Morrow & Co. 1994. (F)

Ewald, Dan. *John Fetzer: On a Handshake—The Times and Triumphs of a Tiger Owner.* Champaign, Ill.: Sagamore Press. 1997.

Falkner, David. *The Last Yankee: The Turbulent Life of Billy Martin.* New York: Simon and Schuster. 1992.

Falls, Joe. *Baseball's Great Teams: Detroit Tigers.* New York: MacMillan. 1975.

———. *So You Think You're a Die-Hard Tiger Fan.* Chicago: Contemporary Press. 1986.

———. *Detroit Tigers: An Illustrated History.* New York: Walker. 1989.

Falls, Joe, and Irwin Cohen. *So You Love Tiger Stadium Too . . . Give It a Hug.* Grand Ledge, Mich.: Connection Graphics. 1999.

Fidrych, Mark, with Tom Clark. *No Big Deal.* Philadelphia: Lipincott. 1977.

Freehan, Bill, edited by Steve Gelman and Dick Schaap. *Behind the Mask: An Inside Diary.* New York: The World Publishing Co. 1970.

Gibson, Kirk, with Lynn Henning. *Bottom of the Ninth.* Chelsea, Mich.: Sleeping Bear Press. 1997.

Golenbock, Peter. *Wild High and Tight: The Life and Death of Billy Martin.* New York: St. Martin's Press. 1994.

Grabowski, John. *Detroit Tigers Trivia.* Boston: Quinlan Press. 1988.

Green, Jerry. *The Year of the Tiger: The Diary of Detroit's World Champions.* New York: Coward-McCann. 1969.

Greenberg, Hank, with Ira Berkow. *The Story of My Life.* New York: Times Books. 1989.

Groch, Dick, and Bill Lajoie. *Baseball, the Major League Way: Featuring the Detroit Tigers.* Dubuque, Iowa: Kendall/Hunt Publishing Co. 1976.

Harrigan, Patrick. *The Detroit Tigers: Club and Community, 1945–1995.* Toronto: University of Toronto Press. 1997.

Harwell, Ernie. *Tuned to Baseball.* South Bend, Ind.: Diamond Communications. 1985.

———. *Diamond Gems.* Ann Arbor, Mich.: Momentum Books Ltd. 1991.

———. *The Babe Signed My Shoe.* South Bend, Ind.: Diamond Communications. 1994.

———. *Stories From My Life in Baseball.* Detroit: Detroit Free Press. 2001.

Hawkins, John. *This Date in Detroit Tigers History: A Day-By-Day*

Listing of the Events in the History of the Detroit Tigers Baseball Team. New York: Scarborough/Stein and Day. 1981.

Henrich, Tommy. *Five O'Clock Lightning.* New York: Carol Publishing Group. 1992.

Herzog, Whitey, and Kevin Horrigan. *White Rat: My Life in Baseball.* New York: Harper & Row. 1987.

Hill, Art. *"I Don't Care If I Never Get Back": A Baseball Fan and His Game.* New York: Simon and Schuster. 1980.

Hirschberg, Al. *The Al Kaline Story.* New York: Julian Messner. 1964.

Italia, Bob. *Detroit Tigers.* Edina, Minn.: Abdo & Daughters. 1997. (C)

Jackson, Robert. *Thirty-One and Six: The Story of Denny McLain.* New York: Walsh. 1969.

Janoff, Barry. *Alan Trammell—Tiger on the Prowl.* Chicago: Children's Press. 1985. (C)

Jordan, David. *A Tiger in His Time: Hal Newhowser and the Burden of Wartime Ball.* South Bend, Ind.: Diamond Communications. 1990.

Kell, George, and Dan Ewald. *Hello Everybody, I'm George Kell.* Chicago: Sports Publishing. 1998.

Knapp, Ron. *From Prison to the Big Leagues: The Picture Story of Ron LeFlore.* New York: Messner. 1980. (C)

Kuenn, Harvey, and Jim Smilgoff (introduction by Al Kaline). *Big League Batting Secrets.* New York: Prentice-Hall. 1978.

LeFlore, Ron, and Jim Hawkins. *Breakout: From Prison to the Big Leagues.* New York: Harper & Row. 1978. (It was translated into French and published in 1980 by Domino after LeFlore was traded to the Montreal Expos.)

Lieb, Fred. *The Detroit Tigers.* New York: G. P. Putnam's Sons. 1946.

Macht, Norman. *Ty Cobb.* New York: Chelsea House Publishers. 1993. (C)

Martin, Billy, and Peter Golenbock. *Number 1.* New York: Delacorte Press. 1980.

Martin, Billy, and Phil Pepe. *Billyball.* New York: Doubleday. 1987.

Martin, Mollie. *Detroit Tigers.* Mankato, Minn.: Creative Paperbacks. 1982. (C)

Mathews, Eddie, and Bob Buege. *Eddie Mathews and the National Pastime.* Milwaukee: Douglas American Sports Publications. 1994.

Mayo Smith Society. *Tiger Tracks: 1989.* London, Ontario: self-published. 1989.

McCallum, John. *The Tiger Wore Spikes: An Informal Biography of Ty Cobb.* New York: Barnes. 1956.

———. *Ty Cobb.* New York: Praeger. 1975.

McCollister, John. *The Tigers and Their Den: The Official Story of the Detroit Tigers.* Lenexa, Kan.: Addax Publishing Group. 1999.

McLain, Denny, and Dave Diles. *Nobody's Perfect.* New York: Dial Press. 1975.

McLain, Denny, with Mike Nahrstedt. *Strikeout: The Story of Denny McLain.* St. Louis: The Sporting News. 1988.

Monaghan, Tom, and Robert Anderson. *Pizza Tiger.* New York: Random House. 1986.

Newhouser, Hal. *Pitching to Win.* Chicago: Ziff-Davis. 1948.

Okkonen, Marc. *The Ty Cobb Scrapbook: An Illustrated Chronology of Significant Dates in the 24-Year Career of the Fabled Georgia Peach—Over 800 Games From 1905 to 1928.* New York: Sterling. 2001.

Owen, Vi. *The Adventures of a Quiet Soul.* San Jose, Calif.: Rosicrucian Press. 1996.

Phillips, John. *The Tigers vs. the Cubs: The 4-F World Series of 1945.* Perry, Ga.: Capital Publishing Co. 1997.

Poremba, David Lee. *Baseball in Detroit, 1886–1968.* Charleston, S.C.: Arcadia Press. 1998.

Rambeck, Richard. *Detroit Tigers: AL East.* Mankato, Minn.: Creative Education. 1992. (C)

Rambeck, Richard. *The History of the Detroit Tigers.* Mankato, Minn.: Creative Education. 1999. (C)

Regan, Phil, as told to Jim Hefley. *Phil Regan.* Grand Rapids, Mich.: Zondervan Publishing House. 1968.

Rothaus, James. *Detroit Tigers.* Mankato, Minn.: Creative Education. 1987. (C)

Rubin, Robert. *Ty Cobb: The Greatest.* New York: Putman. 1978.

Sandman, Peter R. *"Doc" The Story of Roger Cramer, The Best Baseball Player of the Twentieth Century Not In Cooperstown.* Frankfort, Mich.: Review and Forecast Publications. 2001

Schoor, Gene, and Henry Gilfond. *The Story of Ty Cobb: Baseball's Greatest Player.* New York: Julian Messner. 1952.

Shine, Neal, and Bill McGraw. *The Roar of '84.* Detroit: Detroit Free Press. 1984.

Smith, Fred. *The 995 Tigers.* Lathrup Village, Mich.: self-published. 1981.

————. *Fifty Years With the Tigers.* Lathrup Village, Mich.: self-published. 1983.

————. *Tiger Facts.* Lathrup Village, Mich.: self-published. 1986.

————. *Tiger Tales and Trivia.* Lathrup Village, Mich.: self-published. 1988.

————. *Tiger S.T.A.T.S.* Lathrup Village, Mich.: self-published. 1993.

Smith, Fred, and Ernie Harwell. *Son of Tiger Trivia.* Lathrup Village, Mich.: self-published. 1980.

Soos, Troy. *Hunting a Detroit Tiger.* New York: Kensington Books. 1997. (F)

Stanton, Tom. *The Final Season: Fathers, Sons, And One Last Season in a Classic American Ballpark.* New York: Thomas Dunne Books/St. Martin's Press. 2001.

Stewart, Mark. *Cecil Fielder.* New York: Children's Press. 1996. (C)

Stump, Al. *Cobb: The Life and Times of the Meanest Man Who Ever Played Baseball.* Chapel Hill, N.C.: Algonquin Books. 1994.

Sullivan, George, and David Cataneo. *Detroit Tigers: The Complete Record of Detroit Tigers Baseball.* New York: Macmillan. 1985.

Topps Chewing Gum Inc. *Topps Baseball Cards of the Detroit Tigers.* New York: Topps. 1987.

————. *Topps Baseball Cards of the Detroit Tigers.* Los Angeles: Price Stern Sloan. 1989.

Weber, Bruce, edited by Michael Goodman. *Sparky Anderson.* Mankato, Minn.: Crestwood House. 1988. (C)

Wills, Maury, as told to Steve Gardner. *It Pays to Steal.* Beverly Hills, Calif.: Book Company of America. 1963.

Word, A. H. *Word's Base Ball Album and Sketch Book, Detroit Tigers.* Detroit: publisher unknown. 1912.

(C)=Children's book.
(F)=Fiction book.

Note: These are all of the books we know of that have been written on the Detroit Tigers and their players. Books on Tigers such as Billy Martin and Sparky Anderson that pre-date their Tiger days are not included. Also not included are items such as pamphlets and magazine articles. For a bibliography of such items, see B*aseball Bibliography* by Myron Smith, published by McFarland (original edition in 1986, supplements in 1993 and 1998).

EAR-CATCHING PERFORMERS OF THE NATIONAL ANTHEM AT TIGER STADIUM

Before Game Four of the 1968 World Series, Jose Feliciano sang "The Star-Spangled Banner" with his characteristic jazz-pop acoustic guitar accompaniment. It was so novel at the time the performance stirred outrage, coming as it did at the height of America's involvement in the divisive war in Vietnam.

Before Game Five, Motown vocalist Marvin Gaye sang the anthem in the manner in which most people expected it to be sung. After the game, Gaye said there was a time and a place for everything, and before a World Series game was not the time for such a rendition of the National Anthem. He challenged Feliciano to a "soul-off," which Feliciano declined.

Robert Taylor, otherwise known as "Fat Bob the Singing Plumber" often took to the microphone before Tigers games in the 1970s and '80s with his operatic baritone voice.

In the 1990s, taking the field once a year would be the Eugene V. Debs Memorial Kazoo Band, named after the labor leader and Socialist Party presidential candidate of the early twentieth century. While ostensibly for fun, the sound of dozens of kazoos made for an anthem rendition not often heard in Detroit or elsewhere.

What's in a Name?

With more than 1,300 men who have played for the Tigers, it's
inevitable that certain similarities—or oddities—will crop up
over time. Goodness knows how many Tigers there are whose
last names are also the first names of other big leaguers.
(Actually, WE know, but we'll save that for the next edition!)
Not to mention all the nicknames bestowed upon players—
although this book mentions a good many of them. This chapter
is meant to be fun and to amuse, and maybe even amaze you.

Tigers Known by Their Initials

C. J. Nitkowski (Christopher John)
J. W. Porter (he was born with initials only)
A. J. Sager (Anthony Joseph)

Type Consecutive Letters on a Keyboard to Spell His Name

TY Cobb
Don WERT

WHAT'S IN A NAME?

TIGERS WHO BECAME NAMESAKES FOR FUTURE MAJOR LEAGUERS

Mickey Cochrane for Mickey Mantle
Frank Lary for Lary Sorenson
Joe P. Coleman for Joe H. Coleman
Billy Sullivan Sr. for Billy Sullivan Jr.
George C. Susce for George D. Susce

YOUR NAME SOUNDS FAMILIAR

Bill Bailey—not that he won't come home
Jim Brady—not President Reagan's press secretary
George Burns—not the cigar-chomping vaudevillian
Davey Crockett—not the king of the wild frontier
Roberto Duran—not the boxing champion
Bill Graham—not the Fillmore East concert promoter
Willie Horton—not the negative-campaigning poster boy of 1988
Bill James—not the dean of baseball statistical research
Howard Johnson—not the hotel and restaurant chain
Bob Jones—not the controversial South Carolina preacher
Davy Jones—not the sailor with the undersea "locker"
Deacon Jones—not the football All-Pro defensive end
Tom Jones—not the swivel-hipped singer
Bob Kennedy—not the slain New York senator
John Knox—not the 16th century religious reformer
Jim Morrison—not the Doors lead singer
Mike Myers—not the comic actor or the "Halloween" movie killer
Bob Reynolds—not the longtime Detroit sportscaster
Al Unser—not the race-car driver
John Warner—not the U.S. senator from Virginia
Jo-Jo White—not the Boston Celtics basketball player

TIGERS ODD COUPLES

Jose Lima-Billy Bean
Elroy Face-Dave Beard
Don Buddin-Ben Flowers
Fred Hatfield-Benny McCoy
Billy Martin-Mark Lewis
Richie Lewis-Tony Clark
Mickey Stanley-Scott Livingstone
Mark Parent-Stan Papi
Raul Casanova-Sandy Amoros
Dean Chance-John Gamble
Ike Blessitt-Bob Christian
Ralph Young-Heinie Elder
Matt Batts-Charlie Spikes
Donie Bush-Greg Gohr
Gene Michael-Cliff Bolton
Joe Sargent-Steve Bilko
Lu Blue-Pat Meany
Buddy Groom-Jim Brideweser
Brian Harper-Schoolboy Rowe
Hugh High-Bobby Lowe
Chuck Cary-Billy Hoeft
John Knox-Jake Wood
Herman Long-Chick Shorten
Bob Nieman-Marcus Jensen
Charlie Carr-Virgil Trucks
Curtis Pride-Bill Faul
Slicker Parks-Bruce Fields
Larry Sherry-Billy Lush
Shawn Hare-Jimmy Wiggs
Ted Power-Lew Drill
Jim Stump-Franklin Stubbs
Dwayne Henry-Rube Kisinger
Jim Small-Johnny Groth
Charlie Lau-Walter Justis
Slim Love-Owen Friend
Rick Schu-Boots Poffenberger

THE MOST COMMON TIGERS SURNAMES

Surname	No.	First Names
Johnson	9	Alex, Brian, Dave, Earl, Howard, Ken, Mark, Roy, Syl
Jones	13	Alex, Bob, Dalton, Davy, Deacon, Elijah, Ken, Lynn, Ruppert, Sam, Todd, Tom, Tracy
Miller	8	Bob G., Bob L., Ed, Hack, Matt, Orlando, Roscoe, Trever
Smith	8	Bob, Clay, George C., George S., Heinie, Jack, Rufus, Willie
Sullivan	8	Billy Sr.*, Billy Jr.*, Charlie, Jack, Joe, John E., John P., Russ
Walker	7	Dixie, Frank, Gee*, Hub*, Luke, Mike, Tom
Wilson	8	Earl, Glenn, Icehouse, Jack, Mutt, Red, Squanto, Walter

*Related.

Through 2001, 358 Tigers, more than 25 percent of all Tigers who have played in the club's first 101 years, share a surname with another Tiger; a total of 125 surnames are involved.

SHORTEST NAMES: 6 LETTERS TOTAL

Al Aber
Lu Blue
Ty Cobb
Red Cox
Ed High
Al Koch
Don Lee
Jim Ray
Al Shaw
Bob Uhl

What's in a Name?

Longest Surnames

12 letters:	Steve Partenheimer
	Boots Poffenberger
	Vito Valentinetti
13 letters:	Lou Schiappacasse

Terms the Tigers Added to the Baseball Lexicon

"April Cobb"—not used much now, it refers to a spring phenom who looks, at least for a while, to be the next Ty Cobb.

"Bengals"—a synonym for the Tigers, its usage slipped after the Cincinnati Bengals joined the then-American Football League. Other synonyms that had pretty much faded from use by the end of World War II included "Felines" and "Jungleers."

"Bubble-gum ball"—a spitball pitch pioneered by onetime Tigers hurler Orlando Peña. He would chew tobacco and bubble-gum at the same time and, occasionally, put a bit of the concoction on a ball he was about to pitch.

"Cobb's Lake"—an area in front of dirt in front of home plate at Navin Field. When Cobb played for the Tigers, the groundskeepers kept the area wet in order to slow down Cobb's bunts and cause infielders to slip as they tried to field them.

"Curtain call"—a clamor from fans for a player to return to the field to acknowledge a heroic feat. The modern era had its curtain-call genesis June 28, 1976, when the Yankees played the Tigers in a night game televised nationally by ABC. Mark Fidrych, the Tigers' rookie sensation, upped his record to 8-1 with a 5-1 win over the Yankees in just 1:51. With 47,855 fans packing Tiger Stadium to see "The Bird" vanquish the foe, they started a postgame chant, "We want the Bird! We want the Bird!" and kept it up for minutes on end until Fidrych, unaware that it had been his nickname they were chanting, finally stepped out of the dugout to the fans' delirious delight.

"Eleven Immortals"—Ty Cobb was one of these, a group of living inductees present for the dedication in 1939 of the

National Baseball Hall of Fame in Cooperstown, N.Y. The others were, in alphabetical order, Grover Cleveland Alexander, Eddie Collins, Walter Johnson, Nap Lajoie, Connie Mack, Babe Ruth, George Sisler, Tris Speaker, Honus Wagner and Cy Young.

"Fast Food Fall Classic"—a nickname given to the 1984 World Series between the Tigers, owned by Domino's Pizza founder Tom Monaghan, and the San Diego Padres, controlled by the heirs to the McDonald's Hamburgers fortune.

"Kaline's Corner"—a section in the lower-deck box seats in right field fair territory at Tiger Stadium removed in 1955.

"Sleeper rabbit play"—invented by Tigers third baseman George Moriarty, it involves runners at second and third. The runner at second tries to get the catcher's attention by going lazily back to the base after each pitch. If he lures the catcher to throw to second to try and get him out, he breaks for third while the runner at third dashes for home.

"The Corner"—an appellation given by broadcaster Ernie Harwell for the intersection of Michigan and Trumbull, the site of Tiger Stadium.

"Tygers"—a nickname for the Tigers when Ty Cobb was playing with the team (1905–26).

"Wave"—while practiced on occasion at a handful of college football games, the Tigers' 35-5 start in 1984 prompted wave action in the stands. Fans would—seat by seat and section by section of the fully enclosed Tiger Stadium, which enjoyed a record-setting 2.7 million attendance that year—stand up, bring their hands way above their head and cheer. Some variations of the basic wave, now common in most stadiums, included: a slow-motion wave; the upper and lower decks going in opposite directions; and waves going in opposite directions on the same deck, making for exhilarating crescendos.

"You can't steal first"—except that Tigers second baseman and resident comic Germany Schaefer did during a September 4, 1908, game. He said he went from second base to first to disrupt the pitcher's concentration, allowing the runner at third to score when Schaefer tried to go back to second on a steal. (The maneuver was first tried July 13, 1902, by Philadelphia against the Tigers.) After the 1908 season, the major leagues created a rule meant to prevent stealing first.

TIGERS GROUP NICKNAMES

"G-Men"—For the pennant-winning stars of 1934–35: first baseman Hank Greenberg, second baseman Charlie Gehringer, and outfielder Goose Goslin.

"James Boys"—Given to the Tigers' two 1955 bonus babies, Jim Brady and Jim Small.

"K-K Kids"— Given to Al Kaline and Harvey Kuenn, the young Tigers stars of the 1950s.

"Nine Old Men"—For the 1945 Tigers, whose starters' average age was 33. Led by 40-year-old Doc Cramer in left, every starter was at least age 30, including rookie third baseman Bob Maier, who turned 30 during the season.

"T-N-T"— For the pitching trio of Dizzy Trout, Hal Newhouser and Virgil Trucks in their glory years of the 1940s.

"The Twelve Apostles"—For the Tigers' late-1950s ownership syndicate. The moniker was given by 1958–59 manager Bill Norman. Told that the syndicate had only 11 members, Norman shot back, "Yeah, but one of them always bring his wife to the meetings."

"The Battalion of Death"— Given to the 1934 Tigers infield of Hank Greenberg (first base), Charlie Gehringer (second base), Billy Rogell (shortstop) and Marv Owen (third base) for their combined offensive and defensive prowess. Other nicknames included "First Line of Defense," "Punch and Protection of Bounding Bengals," "Tigers Million Dollar Infield," "Detroit's Big Guns" and "The Infield of Dreams."

"Pine Brothers"— The 1980-era Tigers bench, most notably Lynn Jones and John Wockenfuss.

NICKNAMES BASED ON PHYSICAL ATTRIBUTES

Elden "Big Six" Auker (he was 6 feet tall, tall in his day)
Jack "The Blade" Billingham (he stood 6'4" and weighed 195)
"Big John" Bogart (he was 6'2" and 195, big in 1920)
Edward "Red" Borom
George "Curly" Bullard
"Sleepy Bill" Burns
Allen "Red" Conkwright
John "Red" Corriden
Plateau "Red" Cox
Harry "Stinky" Davis (he smoked smelly cigars)
Gene "Red" Desautels
Francis "Red" Donahue
Jerome "Red" Downs
Mal "Kid" Eason (he was 21 when he played his first major league
    game in 1900)
Zeb "Red" Eaton
Norman "Kid" Elberfeld
Ferris "Burrhead" Fain (because of a bad haircut)
Ferris "Cocky" Fain (a trainer thought his eyes were cockeyed)
Al "Whitey" Federoff
Cecil "Big Daddy" Fielder (he was listed at 6'3" and 230 pounds but
    was even heavier)
Bob "Fats" Fothergill (he was 5'10" but weighed 230 pounds)
"Rotund Robert" Fothergill (ditto)
John "Tito" Francona (it's Italian for "small")
Owen "Red" Friend
"Fat Freddie" Gladding (for his portly physique)
William "Kid" Gleason
Leon "Goose" Goslin (for his big nose)
Kyle "Skinny" Graham (plausible at 6'2" and 172 pounds)
Fred "Pudge" Haney (he was 5'6" and 170 pounds)
Charlie "Slim" Harding (he was 6'2-1/2" and weighed 172 pounds)
Don "Jeep" Heffner
Art "Sandy" Herring (short for "Sandblower"; Bob Fothergill said
    Herring was so short—5'7"—that if he passed gas he'd blow
    sand in his shoes)

What's in a Name?

Dorrel "Whitey" Herzog (for his light blond hair)
Charles "Piano Legs" Hickman (for his stocky legs)
Michael "Pinky" Higgins (for his complexion)
Frank "Pig" House (he had manicured nails and fastidious grooming)
William "Baby Doll" Jacobson
"Big Bill" James (he stood 6'4" and weighed 195 pounds)
Wade "Red" Killefer
Ralph "Red" Kress
Ron "Twinkle Toes Bosco" LeFlore (given by his fellow prisoners for
    his blazing speed and for putting Bosco syrup in his milk)
Don "Footsie" Lenhardt (for his hard-to-fit narrow feet)
William "Baldy" Louden
Elmer "Slim" Love (indeed, at 6'7" and only 195 pounds)
Grover "Slim" Lowdermilk (he was 6'4" and 190 pounds)
"Wee Willie" Ludolph (at 6'1-1/2", he wasn't wee at all)
Japhet "Red" Lynn
Jose "Chooch" Macias (teammates say he runs like a choo-choo
    train)
Fred "Firpo" Marberry (he resembled boxer Louis Firpo)
Billy "Barrymore" Martin (he had a nose job)
Frank "Red" McDermott
Jim "Reds" McGarr
Raymond "Red" McKee
Carl "Skinny" McNabb (he was 5'9" and weighed 155 pounds)
Dan "Whitey" Meyer (for his blond hair)
Gene "Stick" Michael (for his dimensions, 6'2", 183 pounds)
Tom "Plowboy" Morgan (his gait reminded broadcaster Mel Allen of
    a farmer walking behind his plow)
Don "Ears" Mossi (he may have had the biggest ears in baseball)
Don "The Sphinx" Mossi (his hangdog look and big ears helped)
William "Kid" Nance
Jim "Sweet Lips" Northrup
John "Red" Oldham
Frank "Stubby" Overmire (fitting at 5'7", 170 pounds)
Marv "Freck" Owen (his face was covered with freckles)
Clarence "Red" Phillips
Henry "Cotton" Pippen (for his extremely light-colored hair)
Johnny "The Point" Podres (for his thinning hair and somewhat
    pointy hairline)
"Baby Joe" Presko

Shown from left are "Hammerin' Hank" Greenberg, Joyner "Jo-Jo" White, and Leon "Goose" Goslin, who got his sobriquet from the size of his protruding proboscis. (Photo courtesy Ray Billbrough and the National Baseball Hall of Fame Library, Cooperstown, N.Y.)

"Little Joe" Presko
Dick "The Monster" Radatz (he hulked at 6'5", 235 pounds)
Joe "The Joker" Randa (his upturned mouth makes it seem as if he's
    always smiling)
Frank "Tubby" Reiber (he stood 5'8-1/2" and weighed 169 pounds)
Saul "Sleepy" Rogovin (he could sleep anywhere)
Robert "Red" Rolfe (for his hair)
Lynwood "Schoolboy" Rowe
Roman "Baby" Semproch

What's in a Name?

George "Kid" Speer
Edward "Tubby" Spencer
Joe "Slim" Staton (he stood 6'3" and weighed 175 pounds)
Daniel "Rusty" Staub (for his red hair)
Rusty Staub "Le Grand Orange" (Montreal's French-speaking fans
    gave him this moniker)
Mike "Skinny" Strahler (indeed, at 6'4" and 180 pounds)
"Big Sam" Thompson (he stood 6'2" and weighed 207)
Mark "Peanut" Wagner (he was 6 feet tall and weighed 165 pounds)
Dick "Legs" Weik (at 6'3-1/2" and only 184 pounds, all you could see
    were his legs)
"Big Jim" Wiggs (he was 6'4", tall for 1903)
Robert "Red" Wilson
Al "Red" Wingo
Joe "Little General" Wood (he was 5'9-1/2" and 160 pounds)
"Little Joe" Wood
"Little Joe" Yeager (he stood 5'10", 160 pounds)

Nicknames Based on Baseball Ability, Either Real or Hoped-For

Al "Lefty" Aber
Ernie "Lefty" Alten
George "Glider" Alusik
Elden "Submarine" Auker (he threw the ball submarine style)
Frank "Lefty" Barnes
Walter "Boom-Boom" Beck (when he was taken out of one game, he
    fired the ball at the right-field fence and it made a boom sound)
Werner "Babe" Birrer
Ray "Ike" Boone (after top-hitting minor leaguer Ike Boone)
"Steady Eddie" Brinkman (he set an AL record for errorless games
    at shortstop)
Chris "Tin Man" Brown (he got hurt easily)
Jack "Slug" Burns
"Stormin' Norman" Cash (for his slugging output)
Al "Lefty" Clauss
Rocky Colavito "The Rock" (for his homer-hitting prowess)
Rocky "Lucky Strike" Colavito (for his batting practice pitching ability)
"Wild Bill" Connelly

What's in a Name?

Harry Coveleski "The Giant Killer" (he quelled the Giants' NL pennant
   hopes in 1908 while pitching for the Phillies)
George "Hooks" Dauss (for his curve ball)
Woody "Babe" Davis
"Wild Bill" Donovan
Norman "The Tabasco Kid" Elberfeld (a tribute by sportswriter Sam
   Crane to his spicy play)
Herbert "Babe" Ellison
Alfred "Cy" Ferry (the thought was he could be another Cy Young)
Ervin "Pete" Fox (shortened from "Peter Rabbit" for his speed)
Arthur "Cy" Fried (yet another Cy Young wannabe)
Phil "Scrap Iron" Garner (for his toughness)
Charlie "Champ" Gehringer ("because he was the best," said Marv Owen)
Charlie Gehringer, "The Mechanical Man" (his fielding at second
   base was automatic)
Kirk "Hall of Famer" Gibson (for his talent as a prospect)
"Hammerin' Hank" Greenberg (for his homer-hitting prowess)
Hank "Five-Strike" Greenberg (for getting close calls from umps)
Bob "The Hammer" Hamelin (when he hit, he hit 'em far)
Luke "Hot Potato" Hamlin (he'd bounce the ball from hand to hand
   between pitches)
Richie "Hacker" Hebner
Harry "Slug" Heilmann
Floyd "Babe" Herman
Hugh "Lefty" High
"Willie the Wonder" Horton (for his promise as a young player)
Art "Hard Luck" Houtteman (pitching with little run support)
Frank "The Capital Punisher" Howard (given during the slugger's
   time with Washington)
Augie "Lefty" Johns
Earl "Lefty" Johnson
Ken "Hooks" Johnson (for his curveballs)
Todd "Rollercoaster" Jones (for hair-raising save situations)
Walter "Smoke" Justis (a pitcher, he was presumed to have some on
   the ball; he walked 6 and struck out none in a 3.1-inning career)
Charlie "King Kong" Keller (he was his era's strongest player)
Harvey "Radar" Kuenn (for how his hits seemed to drop in)
Harvey "Slug" Kuenn
Frank Lary, "The Yankee Killer" (he was 28-13 against the Yanks)
Ralph "Razor" Ledbetter (he pitched one inning for Detroit)

WHAT'S IN A NAME?

"Hot Rod" Lindsey (he was almost exclusively a pinch-runner)
"Lightning Rod" Lindsey (ditto)
"Rocket Rod Lindsey" ("He's got more nicknames than all the other
    Tigers," Ernie Harwell said in 2000)
Bob "Lefty" Logan
Aurelio "Señor Smoke" Lopez (for his fastballs)
Adolph "Lefty" Lorenzen
Jeff "Mickey" Manto (a Mantle pun for the light-hitting Manto)
Charlie "Sunday Punch" Maxwell (35 of his 133 Tigers home runs
    were hit on a Sunday)
Eddie "Hotshot" Mayo
"Rifle Jim" Middleton (good nickname for a pitcher)
James "Hack" Miller
Julio "Whiplash" Navarro (on account of his breaking balls)
Lynn "Line Drive" Nelson
Frank "Lefty" Okrie
Lance "Big Wheel" Parrish (given by Mel Allen on "This Week in
    Baseball")
Ralph "Cy" Perkins
John "Big Pete" Peters (he was 6'1" and 192 pounds, big for 1915)
Jack "Stretch" Phillips
Lynwood "Schoolboy" Rowe (once shut out a team of older church-
    men in a sandlot game)
Art "Speedy" Ruble
Johnny "Man of 1,000 Curves" Sain
Kevin "Hot Sauce" Saucier (for his brief skill at saving games)
"Bucketfoot Al" Simmons (from the style of his swing)
Walter "Lefty" Stewart
Jason "Rooftop" Thompson (given by broadcaster Ernie Harwell
    after Thompson hit two stadium-clearing blasts)
Bob "Lefty" Uhl
Earl "King of Doublin'" Webb (he hit 67 doubles in 1931)
Bill "Lefty" Wight
Claude "Lefty" Williams
Eddie Yost "The Walking Man" (he led the AL six times in walks)

TIGERS WITH PERSONALITY-BASED NICKNAMES

George "Sparky" Anderson
Dick "Rowdy Richard" Bartell
"Tyrus the Untamed" Cobb
"Rowdy Bill" Coughlin
Charlie "Jolly Cholly" Dressen
"Honest John" Eubank
"Eatin' Ed" Farmer (a good metabolism for 6'5" and 200 pounds)
Joe "Happy" Finneran
Charlie "Silent Night" Gehringer (for his quiet demeanor)
Wedsel "Buddy" Groom
"Cheerful Charlie" Hickman
Ralph "Major" Houk (he attained that rank in the Army)
Fred "The Great Stoneface" Hutchinson
Hughie "Ee-Yah" Jennings (for his call as he raised his right leg in joy)
"Sad Sam" Jones
"Toothpick Sam" Jones (he chewed a toothpick on the mound)
Al "Mr. Tiger" Kaline
Eddie "Sparky" Lake
Archie "Happy" McKain
George "Win" Mercer
Dave "Grumpy" Philley
Bob "Grump" Scheffing (after he chewed out Charlie Root for missing a game-winning golf putt)
Mayo "America's Guest" Smith (he was a renowned moocher)
"Gentleman George" Stallings
Paul "Dizzy" Trout (for his eccentricities)
"Whistlin' Jake" Wade (he whistled whenever he got nervous)
"Sweet Lou" Whitaker

TIGERS WITH NICKNAMES BASED ON ETHNIC OR GEOGRAPHIC ORIGIN

George "Turk" Alusik

Bob "The Hammond Hammer" Anderson (after the Indiana town)

Charles "Paddy" Baumann

Gene "Arkansas Traveler" Bearden (he was born in Lexa, Ark.)

Ervin "Dutch" Beck

Henry "Heinie" Beckendorf (for his German ancestry)

Juan "The Panamanian Express" Berenguer (he was born in Panama)

Tommy "Little T from Tennessee" Bridges (born in Gordonsville, Tenn.)

Tom Brookens "The Pennsylvania Poker" (born in Chambersburg, Pa.)

"Tioga George" Burns (from the Philadelphia street he grew up on)

Frank "Tex" Carswell (born in Palestine, Texas)

Ty Cobb "The Georgia Peach" (so named by Detroit Free Press sportswriter Joe S. Jackson)

Ty Cobb "The Georgia Phantom"

Mickey "Black Mike" Cochrane (dark-haired Irish have been called the "Black Irish")

Kevin "Casey" Collins (for his Irish ancestry)

"Scranton Bill" Coughlin (from his Pennsylvania home town)

Bill "Tex" Covington (he lived in Texas)

"Wahoo Sam" Crawford (after his Nebraska home town)

George "Clancy" Cutshaw

Clyde "Tony" DeFate (after his Italian ancestry)

Walt "Moose" Dropo (his home town was Moosup, Conn.)

Henry "Heinie" Elder (after his German heritage)

Eric "Swatting Swede" Erickson (for his Swedish roots)

Ross "Tex" Erwin (he was born in Forney, Texas)

Lorenzo "Chico" Fernandez (after his Latino ancestry)

Alex "Golden Greek" Grammas

Hank "Hankus Pankus" Greenberg (after his Jewish origin, popularized by broadcaster Ty Tyson)

Earl "Irish" Harrist (after his Irish ancestry)

Elon "Chief" Hogsett (he roomed with a full-blooded Kiowa Indian, but he's 1/32 Cherokee on his mother's side)

Al "Dutch" Klawitter

What's in a Name?

Hubert "Dutch" Leonard
Herman "Flying Dutchman" Long
Herman "Germany" Long
Aurelio "El Lanzallama" Lopez (after his Mexican home town)
Harry "Swede" Malmberg (after his Swedish heritage)
Henry "Heinie" Manush (after his German ancestry)
Charlie "Paw Paw" Maxwell (he grew up in Paw Paw, Mich.)
Lambert "Dutch" Meyer
"Wabash George" Mullin (for his Indiana hometown)
Henry "Prince" Oana (born in Waipahu, Hawaii, which still had royalty before American annexation)
Arthur "Ole" Olsen (after his Swedish heritage)
Karl "Ole" Olson (ditto)
Frank "Blackie" O'Rourke (like Mickey Cochrane, a "black Irish")
Frank "Yip" Owen (he hailed from Ypsilanti, Mich.)
Edward "Dixie" Parsons (he was born in Talladega, Ala.)
Charles Poffenberger, "The Baron von Sauerkraut" (he was German)
Herman "Germany" Schaefer (as was he)
Charley "Dutch" Schmidt
Henry "Heinie" Schuble (after his German ancestry)
Johnnie Seale, "The Durango Kid"
Al "Duke of Milwaukee" Simmons (after his home town)
Lou Skizas "The Nervous Greek" (for his pre-at-bat mannerisms)
George "Heinie" Smith
Earl Torgeson "The Earl of Snohomish" (after his Washington home)
Fred "Dixie" Walker (born in Georgia, his dad, pitcher Ewart Walker, was also nicknamed Dixie)
Joyner "Jo-Jo" White (that's how his home state, Georgia, sounded when he said it)
"Honolulu Johnnie" Williams (his birthplace)

TIGERS WITH ANIMAL NICKNAMES

Dale "Moose" Alexander
Ralph "Hawk" Branca
Gates "The Gator" Brown
Jim "The Lizard" Bunning
Frank "Cat Man" Catalanotto
Herman "Flea" Clifton (manager Del Baker thought he has the tenac-
　ity and bite of a sand flea)
Jim "Catfish" Crawford
Walt "Moose" Dropo
Mark "The Bird" Fidrych (he resembled "Sesame Street's" Big Bird)
Tito "Parakeet" Fuentes (for his constant on-field chatter)
Frank "Rabbit" Fuller
Harold "Chick" Gagnon
Clarence "Chick" Galloway
Fred "Bear" Gladding
Leon "Goose" Goslin
Charlie "Bugs" Grover
Charley "Sea Lion" Hall (he often would bark like a sea lion)
"Harry the Horse" Heilmann
Dorrel "The White Rat" Herzog
Hugh "Bunny" High
James "Ducky" Holmes
Frank "Pig" House
Frank "Horse" Howard (a Dodgers teammate hung this one on him)
Fred "The Big Bear" Hutchinson (he paced in the dugout like a bear
　on the prowl, according to Joe Garagiola)
Bob "Ducky" Jones
Davy "Kangaroo" Jones
Charlie "Chick" King
George "Moose" Korince
Wayne "Chick" Krenchicki
Al "Moose" Lakeman
Frank "Mule" Lary
Charles "Chick" Lathers
Don "Moose" Lee
Ron "Bosco Bear" LeFlore (because of his favorite beverage)
Chris "The Crab" Lindsay
Bill "Mad Dog" Madlock (a play on words of his surname)

WHAT'S IN A NAME?

Cliff "Tiger" Mapes
Ed "Mouse" Mierkowicz
Chet "Chick" Morgan
Jim Northrup, "The Gray Fox" (he had prematurely graying hair)
Ray "Rabbit" Powell
Arthur "Bugs" Raymond
Phil "The Vulture" Regan (for blowing saves of starters' wins, then
    getting the win himself when teammates rallied)
Clyde "Rabbit" Robinson
Joe "Horse Belly" Sargent
Joe "Dode" Schultz (short for "dodo")
Ivey "Chick" Shiver
Charles "Chick" Shorten
Tom "Snake" Sturdivant (for his outstanding curveball)
Jackie "Rabbit" Tavener
George "Birdie" Tebbetts (for his high, squeaky voice)
George "The Bull" Uhle
Jon "Warbler" Warden (he always seemed to whistle)
Earl "Moose" Wilson
William "Mutt" Wilson

NICKNAMES BASED ON POPULAR CULTURE

George "Captain Hook" Anderson (for pulling starting pitchers, after the character in J. M. Barrie's "Peter Pan")

"Diamond Jim" Brady (after the Roaring Twenties personality)

Bert "King" Cole (after the nursery rhyme)

Daniel "Davey" Crockett (after the frontier hero)

Alvin "General" Crowder (the head of the federal draft board during World War I was a general named Crowder)

Talbot "Jack" Dalton (after a Wild West bad guy)

Walter "Hoot" Evers (after Western movie actor Hoot Gibson)

Elroy "Sam Spade" Face (after the fictional detective)

Phil "Yosemite Sam" Garner (after the cartoon character)

"Fred Flintstone" Gladding (after the TV cartoon character)

Joe "Flash" Gordon (after the movie serial hero)

Jack "Hairbreadth Harry" Hamilton (after movie serial villains)

Clyde "Mad" Hatter (after the "Alice in Wonderland" character)

John "Ratso" Hiller (after the "Midnight Cowboy" character)

Howard "Hojo" Johnson (after the same-named restaurant chain)

Dave "Tarzan" Lemanczyk (from the Edgar Rice Burroughs character)

Johnny "Skids" Lipon (from the Skid Row gang)

Alfred "Billy the Kid" Martin (after the Wild West outlaw)

Denny "Mighty Mouth" McLain (a pun on the cartoon superhero)

Denny "Sky King" McLain (after the 1950s radio and TV show)

"Prince Hal" Newhouser (after the Shakespearean character)

Ben "Spiderman" Oglivie (his build seemed like a spider's)

"Gentle Ben" Oglivie (after the TV bear)

Ben "Benji" Oglivie (after the movie dog)

Gus "Ozark Ike" Zernial (after a comics character of the era)

PUN NICKNAMES GIVEN TIGERS

Bob "Sugar" Cain (almost every Cain/Kane has this nickname)
Bill "Soup" Campbell (almost every Campbell gets this nickname)
Bruce "Soupy" Campbell (or a variant)
Dave "Soupy" Campbell (see what we mean?)
"Colby Jack" Coombs (after the cheese)
Bob "Hurricane" Hazle
Art "Red" Herring
Johnny "Hippity" Hopp
Don "Cab" Kolloway (after nightclub performer Cab Calloway)
Fred "Whip" Lasher
John "Holy" Moses
William "Pol" Perritt (there was a shoe brand named Pol Parrot)
Jim "Sting" Ray
George Washington "Hack" Simmons (who cut down the cherry tree?)
John "Rocky" Stone
Virgil "Fire" Trucks

FUN NICKNAMES GIVEN TIGERS

William "Gates" Brown (at age 5, he'd hang out at the front gate)
James "Doc" Casey (he was a dentist in the offseason)
Al "Bozo" Cicotte (he ate Bozo brand ice cream as a boy)
Herman "Mohammed" Clifton ("I had to be something. Nobody ever
    thought anything about it," Clifton once said)
Roger "Doc" Cramer (as a boy, he hung out at the house of his
    physician neighbor)
Stanley "The Boy Wonder" Harris (he managed a World Series win-
    ner at 27)
Richie "Digger" Hebner (he dug graves in the offseason)
Frank "Taters" Lary (he wrote "taters" on a blank railroad dining car
    menu)
Charlie "Chinese" Lau (teammates thought his surname sounded
    Chinese)
Denny "Maestro" McLain (for his prowess at the Hammond organ)
Roscoe "Rubberlegs" Miller (for jumping from the Tigers to the
    Giants in 1902, before the AL and the NL made peace)
Norman "Bobo" Newsom (he called everyone that, including him-
    self)

224

What's in a Name?

Larry "Bobo" Osborne (thought to be the manager's pet, or "bobo")
Marv "Merv" Owen (given by Schoolboy Rowe, a case of loose
     vowels)
Harold "Muddy" Ruel (after he fell in a puddle as a kid)
"Kickapoo Ed" Summers (after the Kickapoo Indian tribe)
Jim "Abba Dabba" Tobin (he'd say it when he did his magic act)

Still Other Tigers Nicknames

A: Eddie "Dorf" Ainsmith, Bill "Bump" Akers, Luis "Pimba"
Alvarado, Edmundo "Sandy" Amoros, Earl "Rock" Averill, Yancy
"Doc" Ayers.

B: Robert "Billy" Baldwin, William "Skeeter" Barnes, "Cousin" Ed
Barrow, Wayne "Footsie" Belardi, Roy "Beau" Bell, William
"Bud" Black, Everett "Rocky" Bridges, Edward "Ike" Brookens,
Bob "Bluecheese" Bruce, Les "Buck" Burke, Owen "Donie"
Bush.

C: Guy "Gunner" Cantrell, Owen "Ownie" Carroll, Frank "Wheels"
Carswell, Tiller "Pug" Cavet, Eddie "Knuckles" Cicotte, George
"Slick" Coffman, Harry "Rip" Collins, Duff "Sir Richard" Cooley,
Duff "Dick" Cooley, Roger "Flit" Cramer, Frank "Dingle"
Croucher.

D: Harold "Doc" Daugherty, George "Storm" Davis, Woodrow
"Babe" Davis, Frank "Pop" Dillon, "Tricky Dick" Donovan, "Long
Tom" Doran, Raymond "Snooks" Dowd, Jean "Chauncey"
Dubuc, "Jumping Joe" Dugan, Don "Duffy" Dyer.

E: Howard "Bob" Ehmke.

F: Elroy "The Baron" Face, "Smokey Joe" Finneran, Ira "Pete"
Flagstead, Les "Moe" Fleming, Leslie "Bubba" Floyd, George
"Bud" Freese, Rigoberto "Tito" Fuentes, Elias "Liz" Funk.

G: Del "Sheriff" Gainer, Harry "Doc" Gessler, Harry "Brownie"
Gessler, Bob "Bunch" Gillespie, Myron "Joe" Ginsberg, John
"Bert" Glaiser, Juan "Igor" Gonzalez, Patrick "Willie" Greene,
Ed "Battleship" Gremminger, Charlie "Bert" Grover, Cesar
"Coca" Gutierrez.

H: Sam "Bad News" Hale, Herb "Iron Duke" Hall, William "Pinky"
Hargrave, Stanley "Bucky" Harris, Jim "Pie" Hegan, Clarence
"Buddy" Hicks, Vern "Woody" Holtgrave, Gene "Slick" Host,

Gene "Twinkies" Host, Frank "Hondo" Howard, Waite "Schoolboy" Hoyt, Clarence "Gilly" Huber.

J: Carroll "Deacon" Jones, Elijah "Bumpus" Jones, Ken "Broadway" Jones.

K: Harry "Klondike" Kane, Wade "Lollypop" Killefer, "Twilight Ed" Killian, Clyde "Chad" Kimsey, Judson "Jay" Kirke, Charles "Rube" Kisinger, Don "Butch" Kolloway, Lou "Lena" Kretlow, Russell "Rusty" Kuntz.

L: Ed "Doc" Lafitte, Alfred "Roxie" Lawson, Rick "Bone" Leach, Hubert "Pete" LePine, Christian "Pinky" Lindsay, Henry "Jack" Lively, Bobby "Link" Lowe.

M: Duane "Duke" Maas, Miles "Alex" Main, Herm "Tug" Malloy, Clyde "Pete" Manion, Charles "Buck" Marrow, Alfred "Billy" Martin, "Captain" Eddie Mathews, Charlie "Smokey" Maxwell, Lewis "Sport" McAllister, Maurice "Mickey" McDermott, James "Deacon" McGuire, Wayne "Nubbin" McLeland, Eric "Boob" McNair, Bill "Rebel" McTigue, Russell "Rusty" Meacham, Frank "Scat" Metha, Ed "Butch" Mierkowicz, Roscoe "Roxy" Miller, Bill "Monbo" Monbouquette, Manny "Pete" Montejo, Julio "Jerry" Morales, Wycliffe "Bubba" Morton, Lloyd "Shaker" Moseby, John "Soldier Boy" Murphy.

N: William "Doc" Nance, Francis "Bots" Nekola, Norman "Buck" Newsom, Fred "Shoemaker" Nicholson.

O: Forrest "Joe" Orell.

P: Francis "Salty" Parker, Vernon "Slicker" Parks, Harold "Steve" Partenheimer, Joseph "Pepper" Peploski, Wally "Hub" Pernoll, William "Hank" Perry, William "Socks" Perry, John "Shotgun" Peters, John "Bubba" Phillips, Herman "Old Folks" Pillette, Ralph "Babe" Pinelli, Cletus "Boots" Poffenberger, John "Augie" Prudhomme.

R: Raymond "Rip" Radcliff, Ed "Rock" Rakow, Tony "Pug" Rensa, "Bullet" Bob Reynolds, Ross "Doc" Reynolds, Emory "Topper" Rigney, Leon "Bip" Roberts, Aurelio "Radio" Rodriguez.

S: Joe "Skabotch" Samuels, Walter "Biff" Schaller, Lou "Skippy" Schiappacasse, Charles "Boss" Schmidt, Heinie "Kid Boots" Schuble, Bob "Bill" Schultz, George "Barney" Schultz, Wayne "Chuck" Scrivener, Roman "Ray" Semproch, Truett "Rip" Sewell, Duane "Duke" Sims, John "Buckshot" Skopec, Rufus "Shirt" Smith, "Wonderful Willie" Smith, Steve "Bud" Souchock, George "Tuck" Stainback, Ulysses Simpson Grant "Lil" Stoner,

Jesse "Scout" Stovall, Ralph "Sailor" Stroud, Carl "Jack" Sullivan, Ed "Chief" Summers, John "Champ" Summers, George C. "Good Kid" Susce, Gary "Suds" Sutherland, Harvey "Suds" Sutherland .

T: Bill "Cash" Taylor, Forrest "Frosty" Thomas, Luther "Bud" Thomas, Charles "Tim" Thompson, Alan "Tram" Trammell, Thomas "Bubba" Trammell, Robert "Bun" Troy, John "Jerry" Turner, Guy "King Tut" Tutwiler.

V: Orville "Coot" Veal, George "Sam" Vico.

W: Harvey "Hub" Walker, Joseph "Hap" Ward, James "Skeeter" Webb, David "Boomer" Wells, Ed "Satchelfoot" Wells, Carl "Big Train" Willis, George "Icehouse" Wilson, George "Squanto" Wilson, Walter "Lank" Wilson, George "Sassafras" Winter, Kendall "Casey" Wise, Ralph "Judge" Works, George "Yats" Wuesling, John "Whit" Wyatt.

Y: Tom "Kibby" Yewcic, Ralph "Pep" Young.

CHRIS BERMAN-STYLE TIGERS NICKNAMES

Bill "Green" Akers
Doyle "Brandy" Alexander
Jimmy "Mayor" Archer
Paul Bako "Bits"
Kimera Bartee "Like It's 1999"
Frank Bolling "For Dollars"
Arlo "Guthrie" Brunsberg
Chuck "Cash and" Cary
Al "Santa" Clauss
Deivi Cruz "Control"
Hoot Evers "and the Blowfish"
Ferris "Wheel" Fain
Shane Halter "Top"
Mike "O my God! They" Kilkenny
Ed Killian "Me Softly With His Song"
Frank "Fidel" Kostro
Mark Leiter "Than Air"
Scott "The Caped" Lusader
Wendell "Fibber" Magee
Walt "Bat" Masterson
Tom "Don't Play With" Matchick
Billy "Don't Be a Hero" McMillon
Cotton "Scottie" Pippen
Jack Russell "Terrier"
Rick "Really Big" Schu
Ruben "High" Sierra
Frank "Chiquita" Tanana
Tom "Take Out the" Tresh
Carl "What Choo Talkin' 'Bout" Willis
Ron "Tiger" Woods
Bill "Led" Zepp

TIGERS BORN UNDER ANOTHER NAME

As a Pro	Born As
Harry Frank Coveleski	Harry Frank Kowalewski
George August "Hooks" Dauss	George August Daus
Jean Joseph Octave Dubuc	Jean Baptiste Arthur Dubuc
John Joseph Perry Gorsica	John Joseph Perry Gorczyca
Willie Greene	Pat Foley*
Charles Bert Grover	Charles Byrd Grover
Charles Louis Hall	Carlos Clolo
Kenneth Eugene Holloway	Kenneth Eugene Hollaway
Sylvester W. Johnson	Sylvester Johnson
Harry Kane	Harry Cohen
Arthur Loudell	Arthur Laudel
Dwight Lowry	Dwight Lowery
Eddie Mayo	Eddie Mayoski
Charlie Metro	Charles Moreskonich
Robert L. Miller	Robert Lane Gemeinweiser
William G. Nance	Willie G. Cooper
Ronald Peter Perranoski	Ronald Peter Perzanowski
Johnny Pesky	John Michael Paveskovich
Tony Piet	Anthony Francis Pietruszka
Ralph Arthur (Babe) Pinelli	Rinaldo Angelo Paolinelli
Ray Wilson Scarborough	Rae Wilson Scarborough
Aloysius Harry Simmons**	Alois Szymanski
Jack Smith	John Joseph Coffey
Robert Earl Wilson	Earl Lawrence Wilson

*Used this name breaking in to the major leagues.
**Simmons took his new surname from a Milwaukee hardware store.

HISPANIC TIGERS' NAMES

Many—but not all—Hispanics follow a custom in which their mother's maiden name, the last name, is part of their full name, and their father's name—the name under which they play pro ball—is the second-to-last name. What follows are the full names of Hispanic Tigers over the years who followed this custom:

Luis Cesar Alvarado Martinez
Fausto Cruz Santiago
Rigoberto Fuentes Peat
Pedro Modesto Garcia Delfi
Juan Alberto Gonzalez Vazquez
Julio Cesar Gonzalez Hernandez
Guillermo Hernandez Villanueva
Jose Desiderio Rodriguez Lima*
Aurelio Alejandro Lopez Rios
Orlando Dejesus McFarlane Quesada
Orlando Mercado Rodriguez
Manuel Montejo Bofill
Julio Navarro Ventura
Benjamin Ambrosio Oglivie Palmer
Omar Olivares Palqu
Johnny Alfonso Paredes Isambert
Rudy Hector Pemberton Perez
Orlando Gregorio Peña Quevara
Ramon Peña Padilla
Luis Andrew Polonia Almonte
Aurelio Rodriguez Ituarte
Edgardo Ralph Romero Rivera
Luis Ernesto Salazar Garcia
Alejandro Sanchez Pimentel
Elias Sosa Martinez
Antonio Nemesio Taylor Sanchez
Osvaldo Jose Virgil Pichardo

---

*Uses his mother's maiden name professionally.

BY THE NUMBERS

Baseball statistics are far from the only way one can have fun with numbers. Take into account players' uniform numbers, stadium dimensions and starting times, ticket prices, plus heights and weights, and you can come to a clearer view of the long and short of Tigers baseball.

THE ONLY FOUR TIGERS PITCHERS WITH SINGLE-DIGIT UNIFORM NUMBERS

2 Chief Hogsett, 1944
2 Al Aber, 1953
5 Billy Pierce, 1945
8 Bots Nekola, 1933

BEST TIGERS BY UNIFORM NUMBER
(INCLUDES YEARS WORN ONLY)
(CLOSE SECONDS IN PARENTHESES)

1 Lou Whitaker, 1978–95
2 Charlie Gehringer, 1932–42
3 Alan Trammell, 1978–96 (Mickey Cochrane, 1934–38)

4   Rudy York, 1938–45
5   Hank Greenberg, 1934–41
6   Al Kaline, 1954–74
7   Rocky Colavito, 1960–63
8   Ron LeFlore, 1975–79
9   Pete Fox, 1935–39 (Damion Easley, 1996–)
10   Tommy Bridges, 1934–43, 1945–46
11   Bill Freehan, 1962–76
12   Bobo Newsom, 1939–41
13   Lance Parrish, 1977–86
14   Jim Bunning, 1956–63
15   Joe H. Coleman, 1971–76
16   Hal Newhouser, 1939–52
17   Denny McLain, 1965–70 (Frank Lary, 1955–64)
18   John Hiller, 1967–70, 1972–79
19   Al Benton, 1940–42, 1945–48
20   Mickey Tettleton, 1991–94 (Vic Wertz, 1947–50, 1952)
21   George Kell, 1946–52 (Guillermo Hernandez, 1984–89)
22   Virgil Trucks, 1942–43, 1946–52
23   Willie Horton, 1964–77 (Kirk Gibson, 1979–87, 1993–95)
24   Travis Fryman, 1990–97 (Mickey Stanley, 1966–78)
25   Norm Cash, 1960–74
26   Frank Tanana, 1985–92
27   Gee Walker, 1932–33
28   Tom Timmerman, 1969–73
29   Mickey Lolich, 1963–75
30   Jason Thompson, 1976–80
31   Larry Herndon, 1982–99
32   Ruppert Jones, 1984
33   Steve Kemp, 1977–81
34   Chet Lemon, 1982–90
35   Walt Terrell, 1985–88, 1990–92
36   Bill Gullickson, 1991–94
37   Hank Aguirre, 1960–67
38   Bill Bruton, 1961–64 (Brian Moehler, 1996–)
39   Milt Wilcox, 1977–85 (Mike Henneman, 1987–95)
40   Felipe Lira, 1995–97, 1999
41   Darrell Evans, 1984–88
42   Buddy Groom, 1992–95
43   Darryl Patterson, 1968–71

44   Billy Hoeft, 1952–59
45   Cecil Fielder, 1990–96
46   Dan Petry, 1979–87, 1991
47   Jack Morris, 1977–90
48   Paul Gibson, 1988–91
49   A. J. Sager, 1996–98
50+ Todd Jones, 1997–2001 (wore #59)

During the first three decades of the Tigers, players didn't wear numbers on their jerseys. Here, pitcher Earl Whitehill tunes up in a 1927-era Tigers uniform. (Photo courtesy Ray Billbrough and the National Baseball Hall of Fame Library, Cooperstown, N.Y.)

TIGERS WEARING NUMBERS OTHER THAN THEIR BEST-KNOWN ONE

Name	Famous #	Original #	Years
Charlie Gehringer	2	3	1931
Hank Greenberg	5	7	1933
John Hiller	18	39	1965–66
Al Kaline	6	25	1953–54
Harvey Kuenn	7	26	1953–54
Denny McLain	17	34	1964
Jim Northrup	5	30	1965–66
Schoolboy Rowe	14	24	1933
Mickey Stanley	24	49	1965
Dick Tracewski	53	44	1966–69
Alan Trammell	3	42	1977
Dizzy Trout	11	15	1939–40
Don Wert	8	36	1962
Lou Whitaker	1	43	1977

RETIRED TIGERS UNIFORM NUMBERS

#	Retired For	Last Worn By*	Retired
2	Charlie Gehringer	Richie Hebner, 1982	June 12, 1983
5	Hank Greenberg	Howard Johnson, 1983	June 12, 1983
6	Al Kaline	Pat Mullin, 1953	August 17, 1980
16	Hal Newhowser	David Wells, 1995	July 27, 1997
23	Willie Horton	Hideo Nomo, 2000	July 15, 2000
42	Jackie Robinson	Jose Lima, 2001–**	April 15, 1997

*The only exception to this column is the final game at Tiger Stadium, September 27, 1999, when players wore these numbers to honor the Tigers greats who wore them earlier.

** Although Robinson was never a Tiger, the commissioner's office decreed that, to commemorate the 50th anniversary of Robinson breaking baseball's "color line" in 1947, no other player would be allowed to wear #42. Players who wore the number before could continue to wear it, though. Lima wore 42 as a Tiger during his first stint with the team, which ended when he was traded to Houston after the 1996 season. He continued to wear 42 while with the Astros, and again with the Tigers following a 2001 midseason trade.

The History of #29
Since Mickey Lolich Wore It

Player	Years
Mickey Lolich	1963–75
Steve Foucault	1977–78
Aurelio Lopez	1979–85
Dave Collins	1986
Billy Beane	1988
Pete Incaviglia	1991
Danny Bautista	1993–96
Frank Catalanotto	1997–98
Geronimo Berroa	1998
Karim Garcia	1999
Luis Polonia	1999
Wendell Magee	2000–

Note that #29 was the "fat pitcher" number until Collins came to the Tigers. Given that Collins wore #29 in Cincinnati and New York, he may have requested it. Since then, it's been a hitter's number—often a guy with some speed (generally smaller players).

Highest Uniform Numbers
Worn by a Tigers Player

Number	Player
60	Howard Bailey, 1981–83
59	Todd Jones, 1997–2001
58	Glenn Dishman, 1997; Will Brunson, 1998–99
57	Greg Keagle, 1996–98; Matt Miller, 2001; Adam Pettyjohn, 2001
56	Dean Crow, 1998; Brandon Villafuerte, 2000

All were pitchers.

The Lightest Tigers

Player	Weight
Alex Jones	135
Jackie Tavener	138
Win Mercer	140
Bill Coughlin	140
Donie Bush	140
Frank Scheibeck	145
Frank Browning	145
Steve Partenheimer	145
Rabbit Robinson	148
14 tied at	150

The Tallest Tigers

Player	Height
Tony Clark	6'8"
Slim Love	6'7"
Frank Howard	6'7"
Roger Mason	6'6"
Jeff Robinson	6'6"
Alex Main	6'5"
Walt Dropo	6'5"
Hal Erickson	6'5"
Purnal Goldy	6'5"
Dick Radatz	6'5"
Lerrin LaGrow	6'5"
Ed Farmer	6'5"
Enos Cabell	6'5"
Phil Meeler	6'5"
Sheldon Burnside	6'5"

The Shortest Tigers

Player	Height
Billy Maharg	5'4"
Frank Browning	5'5"
Ralph Young	5'5"
Jackie Tavener	5'5"
Alex Jones	5'6"
Ducky Holmes	5'6"
Doc Casey	5'6"
Lew Drill	5'6"
Rabbit Robinson	5'6"
Donie Bush	5'6"
Red McDermott	5'6"
Fred Haney	5'6"

Dimensions of Tigers' Ballparks

Navin Field, 1912: 340 to left, 400 to center, 365 to right

Navin Field, 1936: 340 to left, 400 to center, 325 to right Navin Field, 1937: 340 to left, 400 to center, 325 to right (upper-deck overhang, 315)

Briggs Stadium, 1946: 340 to left, 440 to center, 325 to right (upper-deck overhang, 315)

Tiger Stadium, 1972: 340 to left, 365 to left-center, 440 to center, 370 to right center, 325 to right (upper-deck overhang, 315)

Comerica Park, 2000: 345 to left, 395 to left-center, 420 to center, 365 to right-center, 330 to right

Ticket Prices Since the Advent of Divisional Play in 1969

Years	Box	Reserved	Grandstand	Bleacher	Other
1969	$3.50	$2.75	$1.50	$1	
1970	$3.75	$3	$2	$1	
1971–73	$4	$3	$2	$1	Ladies/Retirees Day: $0.50
					Family Day: $3 HOH*,
					$0.50 others
1974	$4.25	$3.25	$2	$1	Family Day: $3.25 & $0.50
1975–76	$4.50	$3.50	$2	$1	Family Day: $3.50 & $0.50
1977	$5	$4	$2.50	$1.50	Tiger Day: $0.75 women, boys,
					girls, retirees, youth groups
					Family Day: $4 and $0.75
1978–79	$6	$5	$3.50	$2	Tiger Day: $1.50
					Family Day: $5 and $1.50
1980	$6	$5	$3.50	$2	Family Day: $5.50 and $1.50
1981	$7.50	$6.50	$4.25	$2.75	Tiger Day: $2
					Family Day: $6.50 and $2
1982	$8	$7	$4.50	$3	Tiger Day: $2.25
					Family Day: $7 and $2.25
1983–85	$9	$7.50	$5	$3	Tiger Day: $2.75
					Family Day: $7.50 and $2.75
1986–90	$10.50	$8.50	$6	$4	Bargain Day: $4.50 for all
1991–92	$12.50	$10	$7	$4	Bargain Day: $5
1993	$14	$11	$7	$4	Tiger Den $20
					Bargain Day: $7 and $5
1994	$15	$12	$8	$5	Bargain Day: $10 and $5
1995	$15	$12	$8	$2.50	Bleachers for 14-unders $1

1997–98: Tiger Den $20; upper and lower deck box $15; lower deck reserved $12; upper deck box (outfield) $10; upper deck reserved $8; grandstand $8; bleacher $4 (14-under $1)

1999: Tiger Den $25; upper and lower deck box $20; upper deck box (outfield) and lower deck reserved $15; upper deck reserved $12; left field grandstand (Coca-Cola Fan Stands) $10**; upper deck reserved (outfield) and right field grandstand $8; bleacher $5

2000 (Comerica Park): Tiger Den $75 and $60***; On-Deck Circle $60***; club level, $50***; infield box $30; outfield box $25; upper box $20; mezzanine $15; pavilion $14; upper reserved $12; Pepsi Family Stands $8

2001: Tiger Den $75 and $60***; On-Deck Circle $60; club level $35***; Terrace $35; infield box $30; outfield box $25 and $15;

upper box $20; mezzanine $15; pavilion $14; upper reserved $12; bleachers $8

*Head of household.
**Included soft drink and choice of pizza slice or hot dog.
***Available only through season-ticket packages.
By contrast, the top ticket price at Bennett Park in the 1900s was $1.25.

STARTING TIMES SINCE THE ADVENT OF DIVISIONAL PLAY IN 1969 (ALL TIMES P.M.)

Years	Day	Night	Doubleheader	Twi-Night/Other
1969–71	1:30	8:00	1:30	Twi-Night 5:30
				Saturdays 1:15
1972	1:30	8:00	1:30	Twi-Night 5:30
				Saturdays 1:15 and 2:15
				Monday nights 7:15
1973	1:30	8:00	1:30	Twi-Night 5:30
				Saturdays 2:15
				Monday nights 8:15
1974–81	1:30	8:00	1:30	Twi-Night 5:30
				Saturdays 2:15
1982–84	1:30	7:35	1:30	Twi-Night 5:30
				Saturdays 2:15
1985	1:30	7:35	1:30	Twi-Night 5:30
				Saturdays 1:15
1986–87	1:30	7:35	7:35	Twi-Night 5:30
				Saturdays 1:15
				Sundays 1:35
1988–91	1:35	7:35	1:35	Twi-Night 5:35
				Saturdays 1:15
1992	1:35	7:35	1:35	Twi-Night 5:35
				Saturday days 1:15
				Saturday nights 7:05
1993	1:35	7:05	1:35	Twi-Night 5:35
1994–96	1:15	7:05	1:15	Twi-Night 5:35
1997–98	1:05	7:05	—	—
1999	1:05	7:05	—	Some Saturdays 4:05, 5:05
2000–01	1:05	7:05	—	Some Saturdays 5:05

RUNNING THE SHOW

Sometimes when a manager gets fired after the team is playing poorly, his defenders will say things along the lines of, "Well, I didn't see the manager blow that six-run lead against Cleveland, or hit .212 batting cleanup." This may be true, but it's also true that games can be won or lost long before the 25-man roster is finalized. Not only are the executives responsible for fielding a competitive team, they're also responsible for the fan's enjoyment, balancing whether a fan would prefer an unobstructed seat to see a .441 ballclub or an obstructed-view seat to see a .586 club. No Tigers executive has ever dismissed an entire team for shoddy play, although some of the moves they've made qualify as unique. Here's a look at the folks who put the players on the field in hopes of putting fans in the stands.

DETROIT OWNERSHIP THROUGH THE YEARS

1881: (Detroit Wolverines, National League) Mayor William G. Thompson and his backers paid $20,000 for a National League franchise.

1883: Thompson sold the club to businessman Joseph H. Marsh.

1885: Pharmaceutical heir Frederick K. Stearns, who played college baseball, bought a majority interest in the club.

1889: Merrill B. Mills, prominent in Detroit's stove and tobacco trades, bought an International Association franchise after the Wolverines dissolved following the 1888 season.

1894: George Arthur Vanderbeck started up the Detroit franchise in the Western League.

1900: On the cusp of the Western League becoming the American League and a bona fide competitor to the National League, Vanderbeck sold his stake for $12,000.

1901: Wayne County Sheriff James D. Burns, a hotelier, became owner-president of the Tigers as the American League declared itself a major league. Manager George Stallings had a minority stake. AL President Ban Johnson, though, controlled 51 percent of the team's stock.

1901: Railroad tycoon and insurance man Samuel F. Angus bought the franchise November 14 after Johnson forced Burns and Stallings to stop their squabbling by selling their interest. Johnson still retained his 51 percent control, however.

1904: William Hoover Yawkey, son and heir of Michigan lumber and ore titan William Clymer Yawkey and uncle of future Boston Red Sox owner Tom Yawkey, bought the franchise January 22 for $50,000. For arranging the sale, manager Ed Barrow got $2,500 in stock. Bookkeeper Frank J. Navin, retained after Angus had hired him in 1902, got $5,000 in stock.

1905: Barrow, no longer manager, sold his interest to Yawkey for $1,400.

1907: Navin bought a half-interest in the team September 24 for $20,000 and became president. Yawkey remained a silent partner and headed east, where his fortune grew from $10 million to $40 million.

1920: Auto industrialists Walter O. Briggs Sr. and John Kelsey bought 25 percent shares from the estate of Yawkey, who died March 5, 1919, for $250,000 each.

1927: Briggs bought Kelsey's stock from Kelsey's estate for $250,000.

1935: Navin died November 13 after suffering a heart attack while riding his horse, Masquerader, at the Detroit Riding and Hunt Club. His estate sold Navin's stock to Briggs, who then had complete ownership and became team president.

1952: Briggs died January 17 with his stock going into estate. Briggs' son Walter Jr. ("Spike") became president.

1956: A court order sold Briggs' Tigers stock for a then-record $5.5 million October 1 to a radio-TV syndicate headed by John E. Fetzer, Fred A. Knorr and Kenyon Brown. Fetzer, Carl Lee, a long-time executive in Fetzer's broadcast holdings, and Paul O'Bryan, senior partner of a Washington law firm made up one group in the syndicate. Knorr, owner of Detroit radio station WKMH, headed the second group, which also included Harvey Hansen, who owned various lumber firms, and William McCoy, general agent for a Detroit insurance agency and secretary-treasurer of Knorr Broadcasting. Brown, based in Wichita Falls, Texas, and owner of several radio stations in the Southwest, headed the third group. Other members were George Coleman, an Oklahoma banker and truck manufacturer; New York securities firm partner Joseph Thomas; New York securities firm expert R. F. Woolworth, an heir to the F. W. Woolworth dime store fortune; and film and recording star Bing Crosby, who once had a minority interest in the Pittsburgh Pirates.

1960: Fetzer announced October 11 he was acquiring majority stock control through the purchase of Kenyon Brown's shares. Fetzer became team president nine days later after Bill DeWitt resigned.

1961: Fetzer became sole owner of the Tigers November 14, purchasing the remaining interest that was held by the estate of Knorr, who had died December 27, 1960, two weeks after being on the critical list for serious injuries suffered when he slipped in a bathtub in Fort Lauderdale, Florida.

1983: Fetzer sold the Tigers October 10 to Domino's Pizza co-founder and chairman Tom Monaghan on October 10. The price was $53 million.

1992: Monaghan, after running into financial difficulties, sold the team August 26 to his rival Michigan pizza baron, Michael Ilitch, founder of Little Caesars, for $85 million.

Mayo Smith, pointing in dugout, in the penultimate game of his Tigers tenure, September 30, 1970. He would be replaced by Billy Martin. (Photo courtesy Ernie Harwell Collection/Burton Historical Collection, Detroit Public Library)

TIGERS PRESIDENTS

1901	James D. Burns
1902–03	Samuel F. Angus
1904–07	William H. Yawkey
1908–35	Frank J. Navin
1936–52	Walter O. Briggs Sr.
1952–56	Walter O. Briggs Jr.
1957	Frederick A. Knorr
1957–59	Harvey R. Hansen
1959–60	William O. DeWitt
1961–78	John E. Fetzer
1978–90	James A. Campbell
1990–92	Glenn E. "Bo" Schembechler
1992–95	Michael Ilitch
1995–2001	John McHale Jr.
2001	Michael Ilitch
2001–	David Dombrowski

TIGERS GENERAL MANAGERS SINCE WORLD WAR II

1946–48	George Trautman
1949–51	Billy Evans
1951–53	Charlie Gehringer (vice president)
1954–56	Muddy Ruel
1957	Walter Briggs Jr.
1958	John McHale Sr.
1959–62	Rick Ferrell (vice president, director of major league personnel)
1962–83	James A. Campbell
1984–90	William Lajoie
1991–92	Joe McDonald (senior VP, player procurement and development)
1993–94	Jerry Walker
1995	Joe Klein
1996–	Randy Smith

BEST SIX WINNING PERCENTAGES AMONG TIGERS MANAGERS

.582	Mickey Cochrane (1934–38, 413-297)
.560	Mayo Smith (1967–70, 363-285)
.551	Steve O'Neill (1943–48, 509-414)
.549	Billy Martin (1971–73, 253-208)
.5483	Bob Scheffing (1961–63, 210-173)
.5481	George Stallings (1901, 74-61)

WORST SIX WINNING PERCENTAGES AMONG TIGERS MANAGERS

.385	Frank Dwyer (1902, 52-83)
.397	Fred Hutchinson (1952–54, 155-235)
.399	Buddy Bell (1996–98, 184-277)
.441	Larry Parrish (1998–99, 82-104)
.450	Ralph Houk (1974–78, 363-443)
.453	Ed Barrow (1903–04, 97-117)

LEADERS IN GAMES MANAGED

2,579	Sparky Anderson	1979–95 (1,331-1,248, .516)
2,103	Hughie Jennings	1907–20 (1,131-972, .538)
1,073	Bucky Harris	1929–33, 1955–56 (516-557, .481)
923	Steve O'Neill	1943–48 (509-414, .551)
923	Ty Cobb	1921–26 (479-444, .519)
806	Ralph Houk	1974–78 (363-443, .450)

MANAGERS OF FEWEST TIGERS GAMES (EXCLUDING INTERIM-ONLY)

Les Moss	53	1979
Joe Gordon	57	1960
Bill Norman	122	1958–59
George Stallings	135	1901
Frank Dwyer	135	1902

THE ONLY MANAGERS' TRADE IN MAJOR LEAGUE HISTORY

Tigers skipper Jimmie Dykes was "traded" for Cleveland's Joe Gordon Aug. 3, 1960. Gordon had a 26-31 record with Detroit, which never climbed past sixth place, and was not brought back for 1961. It was not a trade in the strict sense of the word; both managers were given their releases, but in the knowledge that the other team would sign them to a new contract.

DETROIT MANAGERS WHO MANAGED TWO MAJOR-LEAGUE CLUBS IN ONE SEASON

Bill Watkins, 1888 (Wolverines of the National League, then Kansas City of the American Association)
Jimmie Dykes, 1960 (Tigers, then Cleveland)
Joe Gordon, 1960 (Cleveland, then Tigers)
Billy Martin, 1973 (Tigers, then Texas)

TWO WOULD-HAVE-BEEN TIGERS MANAGERS

Frank Navin wanted to interview fading Yankees great Babe Ruth to manage the Tigers for 1934. Ruth was interested but had already scheduled a vacation to Hawaii and left by boat for Honolulu without giving an answer. Navin then acquired Mickey Cochrane to be player-manager. Cochrane responded with pennants his first two years at the helm and the Tigers' first World Series championship in 1935. Ruth played part of the 1934 season for the Boston Braves before retiring as an active player, later joining the Brooklyn Dodgers as a coach.

Schoolboy Rowe, long a favorite Tigers pitcher, was considered to manage the team for the remainder of the 1952 season after Walter Briggs Jr. had decided to fire Red Rolfe. But, Rowe was, literally, gone fishin'—and, in an age before cell phones, couldn't be reached. Briggs instead tapped pitcher Fred Hutchinson to manage the club.

TIGERS PLAYER-MANAGERS

Bobby Lowe (1904) finished out the last 74 games of the 1904 season after Ed Barrow got fired, going 30-44 for a .405 mark. He was the team's regular second baseman that year, but a substitute infielder-outfielder for the Tigers afterward in a career than ran until 1907.

Hughie Jennings (1907–20) suited up rarely for games in 1907, 1909, 1912 (the game where Detroit dressed a squad of Philadelphia semipros to play the Athletics) and 1918, playing five games total. But he hit .333 (3-for-9) in his short stints, his last hit coming when he was 49 years old.

Ty Cobb (1921–26) retained his starting spot in center field during his six years managing the club and continued to hit for average—and occasional power in the live-ball era. But his managerial efforts never got the Tigers to the World Series, the reason the club sacked Jennings after 11 seasons without a pennant.

Bucky Harris (1929–31), a second baseman with his playing days past him, inserted himself into the lineup for seven games in 1929 and four more in 1931, going a combined 2-for-19. His managing was no great shakes, either, as the Tigers got no closer to the flag as they had in the 1910s and '20s.

Mickey Cochrane (1934–38) may have been the prototypical player-manager—a man who could inspire his charges both on the field and in the clubhouse. He led the Tigers to pennants his first two seasons and a World Series win in 1935. The 1934 series with St. Louis marked the last time two player-managers faced each other (second baseman Frankie Frisch was Cochrane's Cardinals counterpart). Cochrane and the Tigers suffered from 1936 on, with Mickey undergoing nervous exhaustion in '36 and being beaned in '37; he never played again after the beaning. But his .582 winning percentage still ranks as the Tigers' all-time best.

Fred Hutchinson (1952–53) was the Tigers' last player-manager, and its only pitcher-manager. (Win Mercer would have been the first, but he committed suicide in a San Francisco hotel room after he was signed to manage the 1903 season.) An All-Star in 1951, Hutch faded quickly, pitching only 15 games combined 1952–53 (including those pitched before he was given the managerial reins), going 2-1 to close out a 10-year playing career.

FANTASY TEAMS

The co-authors of this book go to many ballgames together. Some of them turn out to be yawners, games where Yogi Berra was wrong—it WAS over before it's over. We started passing the time by making teams. Some of our favorite teams were our All Tigers-(insert other team here) teams. We'd pick a team and try to find the best players who played for both teams. Generally, we based it on the stats for both teams, using Tigers stats or career stats (with all teams) as a tiebreaker. When we started writing this book, we quickly agreed that our little ballpark game deserved a spot in this chapter.

Note how much better the American League teams are than the National League. Trades between leagues were seldom accomplished before the 1950s, and the Tigers were no exception. (For details, see the "Trades and Drafts" chapter.) That's why the Tigers-Cardinals team stinks; Steve Bilko at first? (Hey, it could have been Mike Laga.) To contrast, some of the American League teams would win any pennant in a cakewalk, especially the Tigers-Indians and Tigers-White Sox teams. Which is the best? You decide.

We've included other fantasy teams. Several all-time Tigers teams have been chosen, some by sportswriters, some by fans. We list them all and then pick our own, justifying our choices. You can see if you agree or if you think we're just crazy.

ALL-TIGERS-ANAHEIM/CALIFORNIA/ LOS ANGELES ANGELS TEAM

1B	Jason Thompson
2B	Damion Easley
SS	Mick Kelleher
3B	Aurelio Rodriguez
LF	Alex Johnson
CF	Fred Lynn
RF	Al Cowens
C	Lance Parrish
DH	Phil Nevin
SP	Frank Tanana
SP	Dean Chance
SP	Paul Foytack
SP	Dan Petry
RP	Ron Perranoski

ALL-TIGERS-BALTIMORE ORIOLES/ ST. LOUIS BROWNS TEAM

1B	Lu Blue
2B	Del Pratt
SS	Tom Matchick
3B	George Kell
LF	Vic Wertz
CF	Jim Northrup
RF	Heinie Manush
C	Mickey Tettleton
DH	Eric Davis
SP	Doyle Alexander
SP	Bobo Newsom
SP	David Wells
SP	Elden Auker
RP	Gregg Olson

ALL-TIGERS-BOSTON RED SOX TEAM

1B	Dale Alexander
2B	Dick McAuliffe
SS	Billy Rogell
3B	George Kell
LF	Fred Lynn
CF	Doc Cramer
RF	Ben Oglivie
C	Rudy York
DH	Vic Wertz
SP	Earl Wilson
SP	Howard Ehmke
SP	Dan Petry
SP	Dutch Leonard
RP	Bill Campbell

ALL-TIGERS-CLEVELAND INDIANS/NAPS/SPIDERS TEAM

1B	Cecil Fielder
2B	Tony Bernazard
SS	Travis Fryman
3B	Ray Boone
LF	Larry Doby
CF	Harvey Kuenn
RF	Rocky Colavito
C	Johnny Bassler
DH	Willie Horton
SP	Hal Newhouser
SP	George Uhle
SP	Hank Aguirre
SP	Art Houtteman
RP	Steve Gromek

ALL-TIGERS-CHICAGO WHITE SOX TEAM

1B	Norm Cash
2B	Tony Bernazard
SS	Skeeter Webb
3B	George Kell
LF	Steve Kemp
CF	Chet Lemon
RF	Ron LeFlore
C	Milt May
DH	Rocky Colavito
SP	Ed Cicotte
SP	Don Mossi
SP	Billy Pierce
SP	Virgil Trucks
RP	Don McMahon

ALL-TIGERS-KANSAS CITY ROYALS TEAM

1B	Bob Hamelin
2B	Juan Samuel
SS	Tom Matchick
3B	Joe Randa
LF	Al Cowens
CF	Pat Sheridan
RF	Kirk Gibson
C	Chad Krueter
DH	Dean Palmer
SP	Tim Belcher
SP	Storm Davis
SP	Jim Rooker
SP	Juan Berenguer
RP	Aurelio Lopez

ALL-TIGERS-MINNESOTA TWINS/PRE-1961 WASHINGTON SENATORS TEAM

1B	Rich Reese
2B	Jim Delahanty
SS	Donie Bush
3B	Eddie Yost
LF	Heinie Manush
CF	Gee Walker
RF	Goose Goslin
C	Dave Engle
DH	Gary Ward
SP	Bobo Newsom
SP	Earl Whitehill
SP	Jim Perry
SP	Jack Morris
RP	Ron Perranoski

ALL-TIGERS-NEW YORK YANKEES/HIGHLANDERS TEAM

1B	Cecil Fielder
2B	Billy Martin
SS	Ed Brinkman
3B	George Moriarty
LF	Charlie Keller
CF	Steve Kemp
RF	Rocky Colavito
C	Wally Schang
DH	Tom Tresh
SP	Doyle Alexander
SP	Waite Hoyt
SP	David Wells
SP	Bill Gullickson
RP	Lance McCullers

ALL-TIGERS-OAKLAND/KANSAS CITY/PHILADELPHIA ATHLETICS TEAM

1B	Ferris Fain
2B	Jerry Lumpe
SS	Tony Phillips
3B	George Kell
LF	Al Simmons
CF	Ty Cobb
RF	Rocky Colavito
C	Mickey Cochrane
DH	Willie Horton
SP	Denny McLain
SP	Joe H. Coleman
SP	Howard Ehmke
SP	Jack Coombs
RP	Doug Bair

ALL-TIGERS-SEATTLE MARINERS TEAM

1B	Dan Meyer
2B	Torey Lovullo
SS	Tony Bernazard
3B	Darnell Coles
LF	Ruppert Jones
CF	Leon Roberts
RF	Al Cowens
C	Lance Parrish
DH	Willie Horton
SP	Omar Olivares
SP	Milt Wilcox
SP	Glenn Abbott
SP	Mike Moore
RP	Dean Crow

ALL-TIGERS-TEXAS RANGERS/POST-1960 WASHINGTON SENATORS TEAM

1B	Frank Howard
2B	Frank Catalanotto
SS	Ed Brinkman
3B	Aurelio Rodriguez
LF	Willie Horton
CF	Ruben Sierra
RF	Juan Gonzalez
C	Mickey Tettleton
DH	Rusty Staub
SP	Denny McLain
SP	Joe H. Coleman
SP	Frank Tanana
SP	Jim Perry
RP	Mike Henneman

ALL-TIGERS-TORONTO BLUE JAYS TEAM

1B	Cecil Fielder
2B	Pedro Garcia
SS	Tony Phillips
3B	Darnell Coles
LF	Willie Horton
CF	Lloyd Moseby
RF	Junior Felix
C	Lance Parrish
DH	Rick Leach
SP	Jack Morris
SP	Doyle Alexander
SP	David Wells
SP	Joe H. Coleman
RP	Dave Lemanczyk

ALL-TIGERS-ATLANTA/MILWAUKEE/ BOSTON BRAVES TEAM

1B	Darrell Evans
2B	Frank Bolling
SS	Chico Fernandez
3B	Eddie Mathews
LF	Al Simmons
CF	Bill Bruton
RF	Danny Bautista
C	Bubbles Hargrave
SP	Denny McLain
SP	Doyle Alexander
SP	Joe Niekro
SP	Frank Lary
RP	Don McMahon

ALL-TIGERS-CHICAGO CUBS TEAM

1B	Richie Hebner
2B	Tony Taylor
SS	Billy Rogell
3B	Howard Johnson
LF	Luis Gonzalez
CF	Harvey Kuenn
RF	Davy Jones
C	Jimmy Archer
SP	Joe H. Coleman
SP	Hank Aguirre
SP	Hank Borowy
SP	Woodie Fryman
RP	Guillermo Hernandez

ALL-TIGERS-CINCINNATI REDS TEAM

1B	Walt Dropo
2B	Billy Martin
SS	Mark Lewis
3B	Ray Knight
LF	Harry Heilmann
CF	Eric Davis
RF	Sam Crawford
C	Joe Oliver
SP	David Wells
SP	Jack Billingham
SP	Woodie Fryman
SP	Milt Wilcox
RP	C. J. Nitkowski

ALL-TIGERS-HOUSTON ASTROS/ COLT .45s TEAM

1B	Dave Bergman
2B	Gary Sutherland
SS	Andujar Cedeño
3B	Eddie Mathews
LF	Luis Gonzalez
CF	Brian Hunter
RF	Rusty Staub
C	Brad Ausmus
SP	Jose Lima
SP	Jack Billingham
SP	Bill Gullickson
SP	Joe Niekro
RP	Todd Jones

ALL-TIGERS-LOS ANGELES/ BROOKLYN DODGERS TEAM

1B	Frank Howard
2B	Dick Tracewski
SS	Gene Michael
3B	Bill Madlock
LF	Eric Davis
CF	Heinie Manush
RF	Kirk Gibson
C	Tom Haller
SP	Schoolboy Rowe
SP	Hank Aguirre
SP	Jim Bunning
SP	Wild Bill Donovan
RP	Phil Regan

ALL-TIGERS-MILWAUKEE BREWERS/ SEATTLE PILOTS TEAM

1B	Bob Hamelin
2B	Gary Sutherland
SS	Ray Oyler
3B	Tom Matchick
LF	Rob Deer
CF	Wayne Comer
RF	Ben Oglivie
C	Joe Oliver
SP	Jim Slaton
SP	Hideo Nomo
SP	Bryce Florie
SP	Bill Krueger
RP	Mike Marshall

ALL-TIGERS-MONTREAL EXPOS TEAM

1B	Jason Thompson
2B	Gary Sutherland
SS	Doug Flynn
3B	Wayne Krenchicki
LF	Jim Northrup
CF	Ron LeFlore
RF	Rusty Staub
C	Dave Engle
SP	Joe Sparma
SP	Dan Schatzeder
SP	Woodie Fryman
SP	Bill Gullickson
RP	Elroy Face

ALL-TIGERS-NEW YORK METS TEAM

1B	Richie Hebner
2B	Doug Flynn
SS	Tony Phillips
3B	Howard Johnson
LF	Gregg Jefferies
CF	Juan Samuel
RF	Rusty Staub
C	Duffy Dyer
SP	Mickey Lolich
SP	Willie Blair
SP	Frank Lary
SP	Walt Terrell
RP	Dennis Ribant

FANTASY TEAMS

ALL-TIGERS-PHILADELPHIA PHILLIES TEAM

1B	Rico Brogna
2B	Tony Taylor
SS	Dick Bartell
3B	Richie Hebner
LF	Alex Johnson
CF	Harvey Kuenn
RF	Sam Thompson
C	Lance Parrish
SP	Woodie Fryman
SP	Jim Bunning
SP	Schoolboy Rowe
SP	Mark Leiter
RP	Guillermo Hernandez

ALL-TIGERS-PITTSBURGH PIRATES TEAM

1B	Jason Thompson
2B	Bill Madlock
SS	Dick Bartell
3B	Richie Hebner
LF	Hank Greenberg
CF	Heinie Manush
RF	Kirk Gibson
C	Lance Parrish
SP	Joe H. Coleman
SP	Jim Bunning
SP	Woodie Fryman
SP	Walt Terrell
RP	Elroy Face

All-Tigers-St. Louis Cardinals Team

1B	Steve Bilko
2B	Jerry Morales
SS	Ed Brinkman
3B	Skeeter Barnes
LF	Alex Johnson
CF	Larry Herndon
RF	Eric Davis
C	Eddie Ainsmith
SP	Dave LaPoint
SP	Syl Johnson
SP	Randy O'Neal
SP	Bob Sykes
RP	Aurelio Lopez

All-Tigers-San Diego Padres Team

1B	Nate Colbert
2B	Tito Fuentes
SS	Chris Gomez
3B	Phil Nevin
LF	Melvin Nieves
CF	Fred Lynn
RF	John Grubb
C	Brad Ausmus
SP	Pat Dobson
SP	Mickey Lolich
SP	Joe Niekro
SP	Earl Wilson
RP	Doug Brocail

ALL-TIGERS-SAN FRANCISCO/ NEW YORK GIANTS TEAM

1B	Dave Bergman
2B	Tito Fuentes
SS	Dick Bartell
3B	Darrell Evans
LF	Pat Sheridan
CF	Larry Herndon
RF	Harvey Kuenn
C	Matt Nokes
SP	Doyle Alexander
SP	Joe H. Coleman
SP	Dan Schatzeder
SP	Billy Pierce
RP	Don McMahon

ALL .300 LIFETIME TIGERS TEAM

1B	Hank Greenberg, .313
2B	Charlie Gehringer, .320
SS	Harvey Kuenn, .303
3B	George Kell, .306
LF	Sam Crawford, .309
CF	Ty Cobb, .366
RF	Harry Heilmann, .342
C	Mickey Cochrane, .324
P	Don't make us laugh!

ALL-MICHIGAN TIGERS TEAM

C	Bill Freehan, Detroit/Royal Oak
1B	Rick Leach, Ann Arbor
2B	Charlie Gehringer, Fowlerville
SS	Johnny Lipon, Detroit
3B	Steve Boros, Flint
OF	Jim Northrup, Breckenridge
OF	Ron LeFlore, Detroit
OF	Kirk Gibson, Pontiac/Waterford
DH	Willie Horton, Detroit
SP	Hal Newhouser, Detroit
SP	Frank Tanana, Detroit
SP	Billy Pierce, Detroit
SP	Dave Rozema, Grand Rapids
RP	Phil Regan, Evart

ALL-TIGERS MANAGERS/COACHES TEAM

1B	Hughie Jennings	manager, 1907–20
2B	Charlie Gehringer	coach, 1942
SS	Alan Trammell	coach, 1999
3B	Buddy Bell	manager, 1996–98
LF	Vada Pinson	coach, 1985–91
CF	Ty Cobb	manager, 1921–26
RF	Larry Parrish	manager, 1999
C	Mickey Cochrane	manager, 1934–38
DH	Gates Brown	coach, 1978–84
SP	Schoolboy Rowe	coach, 1954–55
SP	Roger Craig	coach, 1980–84
SP	Jon Matlack	coach, 1996
SP	Fred Hutchinson	manager, 1952–54
RP	Fred Gladding	coach, 1976–78

Tommy Bridges, one of the Tigers' underrated pitchers in the team's history, had a career spanning seventeen years with the club, missing one season due to World War II service. (Photo courtesy Ernie Harwell Collection/Burton Historical Collection, Detroit Public Library)

GREATEST TIGERS TEAM FROM ITS FIRST 50 YEARS IN THE AMERICAN LEAGUE

C	Mickey Cochrane
1B	Hank Greenberg
2B	Charlie Gehringer
SS	Donie Bush
3B	George Kell
OF	Ty Cobb
OF	Harry Heilmann
OF	Sam Crawford
P	Schoolboy Rowe
P	Tommy Bridges
P	George Mullin
P	Wild Bill Donovan
P	Hal Newhouser
Mgr.	Hughie Jennings

Note that while Billy Rogell was much fresher in the minds of the voters, they chose Donie Bush at shortstop. Also, while Tigers fans today have heard of George Mullin, if only because of his domination of the Tigers all-time pitching leaders, Wild Bill Donovan was also a fine pitcher, although largely forgotten today.

GREATEST TIGERS TEAM, AS VOTED BY THE FANS IN 1969 TO CELEBRATE PRO BASEBALL'S CENTENNIAL

C	Mickey Cochrane
1B	Hank Greenberg
2B	Charlie Gehringer
SS	Billy Rogell
3B	George Kell
OF	Harry Heilmann
OF	Ty Cobb
OF	Al Kaline
LHP	Hal Newhouser
RHP	Denny McLain

It's interesting that Denny McLain was the all-time right-handed pitcher. That probably would not have been true if the poll had been taken any year but 1969, after the 31-win season and during another Cy Young season.

ALL-FETZER TEAM
(chosen by former Tigers PR director Dan Ewald from among Tigers playing during John Fetzer's ownership)

C	Bill Freehan
1B	Norm Cash
2B	Lou Whitaker
SS	Alan Trammell
3B	Aurelio Rodriguez
LF	Willie Horton
CF	Mickey Stanley
RF	Al Kaline
LHP	Mickey Lolich
RHP	Jack Morris
RP	John Hiller

ALL-TIME TIGERS TEAM, AS VOTED BY THE FANS IN 1999 TO COMMEMORATE THE END OF THE 20TH CENTURY AND THE CLOSING OF TIGER STADIUM

C	Bill Freehan
1B	Hank Greenberg
2B	Charlie Gehringer
SS	Alan Trammell
3B	George Kell
OF	Kirk Gibson
OF	Ty Cobb
OF	Al Kaline
LHP	Hal Newhouser and Mickey Lolich (tie)
RHP	Jack Morris
RP	John Hiller
Mgr.	Sparky Anderson

A tie for left-handed starter? Lucky that baseball doesn't use arcane tie-breakers like the NFL or NHL. Probably the name most out-of-place on this list is Kirk Gibson. While Gibby was a leader of the 1984 World Championship team, Harry Heilmann was much the better player, as was Sam Crawford.

THE AUTHORS' ALL-TIME TIGERS TEAM

Pos.	1st Team	2nd Team
C	Bill Freehan	Lance Parrish
1B	Hank Greenberg	Norm Cash
2B	Charlie Gehringer	Lou Whitaker
SS	Alan Trammell	Donie Bush
3B	George Kell	Travis Fryman
OF	Harry Heilmann	Bobby Veach
OF	Ty Cobb	Willie Horton
OF	Al Kaline	Sam Crawford
LHP	Hal Newhouser	Mickey Lolich
RHP	Jack Morris	Tommy Bridges
RP	John Hiller	Guillermo Hernandez
Mgr.	Sparky Anderson	Hughie Jennings

We went out on a limb and picked a first and second team.

Catcher was tough in that we left off Mickey Cochrane. However, we could not ignore the fact that Black Mike only played two full seasons for the Tigers; his best days were spent with the Athletics. Freehan over Parrish was in many ways a case of longevity. They had similar offensive stats in Detroit (200 HR, 758 RBI, .262 BA for Freehan; 212 HR, 700 RBI, and .263 BA for Parrish). Parrish accomplished his feats in about two-thirds of the games and seasons, but Freehan played during the worst hitting era since the advent of the lively ball. Freehan made 11 All-Star teams as a Tiger, starting seven times, Parrish "only" five times, two as a starter.

First base was easy. Greenberg was the obvious first choice. Cash was a shoo-in for the second team. People do not realize what a great player Cash was because he played in the 1960s pitchers' era; much of his offensive value was in drawing walks; and he was not the biggest hitting star on the team (which also hurt Harry Heilmann). What's compelling is that Cash had 6.5 runs created per game lifetime in a league where 4.0 was the average. (For a definition of runs created per game, see "More Hitting and Offense.")

Second base was even easier. "The Mechanical Man" is one of the greatest ever, and Lou Whitaker deserved more consideration for the Hall of Fame. Honorable mention goes to Dick McAuliffe, a teammate of Cash's whose offensive skills were similar to Cash's (given that he was a second baseman) in a tough era for hitters, and therefore not given enough credit.

Shortstop has a clear #1 in Trammell and a battle for second that is not as close as one might think. We chose Donie Bush over Billy Rogell. Rogell is better known, in part for a successful political career on the Detroit Common Council, but Bush was a star. He played 14 years in Detroit (Rogell played 10), led the league in walks five times, and had the most runs created per game of any American League shortstop three times.

Third base is probably the weakest position in the Tigers' history. George Kell was a fine player but spent only seven seasons in Detroit. In those seven seasons, though, he led the league in hits twice, doubles twice (56 in 1950!), and batting average once. The race for the second spot came down to three players most current fans remember: Don Wert, Aurelio Rodriguez and Travis Fryman. Rodriguez played the most games for the Tigers, but his poor bat (.235 average with 85 homers in nine years of mostly regular play) eliminate him. Wert's bat was a little stronger (.244 and 77 home runs in eight years in a tougher hitters' era), but still not impressive. Fryman, even given a better period for hitters, was much the superior hitter (.274 with 149 homers plus 80–100 RBI a year over eight years), with a fine glove too.

We tried to pick a LF-CF-RF combo for each team. We failed in that we couldn't leave either Heilmann or Kaline, both right fielders, off the team. If we had to choose between them, it would be truly difficult. This is not to slight Kaline, a genuine all-time great player, but that's how good Heilmann was. Heilmann, as we said earlier, was overshadowed playing with Cobb, but for seven consecutive years and eight out of nine, he had one of the top three runs created per game marks of any American League outfielder (1921–27, 1929). In other words, he was one of the three best offensive outfielders in the league eight times. Kaline, to contrast, was among the top three four times (1955, 1959, 1966, and 1967). Defensively, there is no contest: Kaline was a great defensive outfielder while Heilmann was considered poor in the outfield. It's a close call; a more detailed look at the statistics might prompt a choice of Kaline by a hair—if one had to make that choice.

On the second team in the outfield, Sam Crawford is the definite star, Veach and Horton a step down. The last cut was Kirk Gibson, and it was tough. We could have taken him over Horton. Veach and Horton aren't that far apart, either, but Veach was a little better; for example, Veach led the league in several offensive categories—once in hits, twice in doubles, once in triples when it meant something, and RBI three times. Horton never led the league in a major category. Then again, Horton was a four-time All-Star while a Tiger; Gibson, despite being one of the greatest Tigers clutch hitters in recent memory, never made an All-Star squad with Detroit—or with anybody else.

Left-handed pitchers were easy: the Hall-of-Famer first, the one-step-from-the-Hall guy second.

We had a tough choice for right-handed starter, because of one of the three men on this list, Tommy Bridges (along with Bush and Heilmann), who we see as seriously underrated. The names Dizzy Trout and Schoolboy Rowe from that era are much more famous (good nicknames?). We consider Morris a marginal Hall of Famer, and Bridges is not far behind him. Morris and Bridges are close in games (as a Tiger), wins, and innings pitched. Both pitched during hitters' times. Bridges pitched for the Tigers for 16 years, more than any other Tigers pitcher (Hooks Dauss had 15). Both Morris and Bridges were far ahead of any other right-handed Tigers pitchers. McLain was a great pitcher, but for a short time in a brief career.

The choice for relief pitcher may have been toughest of all. At first we picked Hernandez over Hiller on the basis of his MVP year on a World Series team; Hiller's best years came when the Tigers were nowhere near contenders. But Hiller pitched for the Tigers for 15 seasons to Hernandez' six, and

Hiller was a top relief pitcher for six seasons and helped define the role of relief pitching throughout baseball. Hernandez never topped Hiller's 125 Tigers saves, and Hiller's 38 saves in a season in 1973 wasn't bettered until Todd Jones in 2000. And need we mention Hiller's stirring comeback from a 1971 heart attack?

Another tough choice for the #1 and #2 spots with no competition beyond that was for the manager. Sparky won out because he won more games. Jennings finished first three times to Anderson's twice, but Anderson's job in leading the 1987 team to the division and the best record in baseball was superb. Sparky also did not have a Ty Cobb to manage, either. So did that make him lucky or unlucky?

TRADES AND DRAFTS

Tigers fans who followed the 1968 World Championship team had the luxury of seeing most of their players homegrown. Pitcher Earl Wilson may have been the most prominent Tiger from that year to have been acquired in a trade; Denny McLain was claimed on waivers from the White Sox before he ever pitched a big-league game. But as players come, so do they go: McLain and Don Wert to the Washington Senators, Jim Northrup and Joe Sparma to the Montreal Expos, Dick McAuliffe to the Boston Red Sox, Ray Oyler to the Seattle Pilots, Mickey Lolich to the New York Mets, Willie Horton to the Texas Rangers. Trades and other forms of player movement can be a sobering reminder that baseball is not just a game but also a business. Yet for every player traded away, a new player from another club brings with him the hope—even if only in his own mind—that he'll make a more significant contribution to his new team than he did for the team that let him go. By looking at the names listed in this chapter, you'll get a trip down memory lane, but also insights at what could have been.

THE FIVE BEST TRADES IN TIGERS HISTORY

1. October 1970: Tigers got: P Joe Coleman, SS Ed Brinkman, 3B Aurelio Rodriguez, P Jim Hannan
Washington Senators got: P Denny McLain, 3B Don Wert, OF Elliot Maddox, P Norm McRae

The Tigers made one of the best deals in baseball history here, with help from Commissioner Bowie Kuhn, who wanted McLain to move on after three suspensions in 1970. In fact, Kuhn had to lift McLain's suspension for the trade to happen since suspended players could not be traded. Senators owner Bob Short salivated at the chance to get a "star." Short, one of the worst owners ever in baseball, got what he deserved. The trade was made on the eve of the World Series, and the baseball minds gathered in Cincinnati all agreed the Tigers had taken the Senators. Even Senators manager Ted Williams disavowed the deal.

The key in the deal for the Tigers was Rodriguez, a 22-year-old third baseman who had hit 19 home runs and driven in 83 for the Nats under the tutelage of Hall of Fame manager Williams. While Rodriguez eventually ended up playing more games at third than any other Tiger, 1970 turned out to be his high-water mark as a hitter. The same was true for Brinkman, who hit .266 and .262 under Williams but between .203 and .237 as a Tiger. Coleman turned in a solid five-plus seasons with Detroit, with two 20-win years and one All-Star nod. Hannan lasted seven games with Detroit moving on to the Milwaukee Brewers.

The Tigers got a top starting pitcher and the left side of an infield for a pitcher who was through and three other players. McLain only pitched for the Senators in 1971, who played and were run so poorly they abandoned Washington for Texas. McLain pitched briefly for the Rangers, A's, and Braves before disappearing from the majors in 1972. Wert was on an even greater downside, appearing in 20 games for the Nats, batting .050 on 2-for-40 hitting. Maddox, a 21-year-old outfielder, never made it, nor did the hard-throwing but wild McRae. The Tigers had finished below .500 in 1970, but won 91 games in

1971 and the American League East in 1972. Without that deal, it is likely both the 1971 and '72 teams would have been below .500, too.

2. April 1960: Tigers got: 1B Norm Cash
   Cleveland Indians got: 3B Steve Demeter
Norm Cash was a 24-year-old rookie in 1959 who was on his second organization. Steve Demeter was a 24-year-old rookie in 1959 with the Tigers. The Tigers wanted a first baseman, the Indians needed a third baseman. Neither player was that highly regarded, but the Tigers did not need a third baseman with Eddie Yost manning the hot corner while the Indians wanted some protection at the position. Steve Demeter played just four games with Cleveland. Norm Cash hit 373 home runs for the Tigers.

3. December 1933: Tigers got: C Mickey Cochrane
   Philadelphia Athletics got: C Johnny Pasek and $100,000
This was not really a trade; it was a sale with Pasek (who never played for Philadelphia) thrown in. Athletics owner Connie Mack needed money, and the Tigers wanted to win the pennant. Longtime Tigers owner Frank Navin did not have the money himself, but co-owner Walter Briggs offered to put it up. The Tigers won the pennant in 1934 and the World Series in 1935 under catcher-manager Mickey Cochrane. Cochrane's goals were to get outfielder Goose Goslin from the Senators, third baseman Pinky Higgins from the A's, and outfielder Al Simmons from the White Sox. He got Goslin before 1933 was out (for outfielder John "Rocky" Stone, a decent player), but not the others. (As it happened, each wound up with the Tigers, Simmons in 1936 and Higgins in 1938.)

4. March 1984: Tigers got: RP Willie Hernandez, 1B Dave Bergman
   Philadelphia Phillies got: OF Glenn Wilson, C John Wockenfuss
This deal may have put the "Bless You Boys" Tigers team over the top in 1984. This deal, made the last week of spring training, got the Tigers the eventual 1984 American League Most

Valuable Player and Cy Young Award winner, plus a solid back-up infielder and clubhouse presence for nine years. Wilson was an OK outfielder with one All-Star year (in 1985 with the Phils, when he was fifth in the NL with 102 RBI) but had low on-base and slugging averages throughout his career. Wockenfuss had been a longtime fan favorite and led the Tigers in seniority (joining the team in 1974), but he had complained about his limited role. He had asked to be traded but never thought it would actually happen. He ended up with 217 at-bats—a big drop from his Detroit numbers—over the next two years, his last in the bigs.

5. May 1946: Tigers got: 3B George Kell
Philadelphia Athletics got: OF Barney McCosky
Athletics owner-general manger-manager Connie Mack was down on the 23-year-old Kell, believing he was too slow and would not hit enough, so he traded him to the Tigers for McCosky, who was off to a slow start after returning from World War II. McCosky played three seasons as a regular for Philadelphia with little power—three home runs in an A's uniform. He was out of the majors by 1953. Kell starred for the Tigers until 1952, winning the 1949 batting title and leading the league in hits and doubles in 1949 and 1950.

THE FIVE WORST TRADES IN TIGERS HISTORY

1. November 1948: Tigers got: C Aaron Robinson
Chicago White Sox got: P Billy Pierce
The Tigers were coming off a disappointing fifth-place finish in 1948 after four years near the top of the league, and they were looking to move back into the hunt in 1949. Detroit wanted more punch behind the plate; the incumbent catcher, Bob Swift, had hit .223 with four home runs. Robinson was 32, but the Tigers weren't concerned because they had phenom Frank House on the way. They knew the 21-year-old Pierce, a native

Detroiter, was a top prospect, but they were willing to pay the price. Baseball rules required the Tigers to keep Pierce on the roster in 1948 and he did not pitch well, striking out 36 and walking 51 in 55.1 innings.

Robinson had decent seasons in 1949 and 1950 for Detroit, hitting .269 with 13 home runs in 1949, but he was traded to the Red Sox during the 1951 season, his last in the majors. Pierce pitched 13 seasons for the White Sox and three for the Giants, winning 211 games in his big-league career, leading the league in strikeouts, wins, and ERA one time each.

2. November 1927: Tigers got: P Emil Vangilder, OF Harry Rice, SS Chick Galloway, St. Louis Browns got: OF Heinie Manush, 1B Lu Blue

The Tigers were trying to improve their pitching staff and felt the 31-year-old Vangilder was the man (even though his ERA was above the league average the last four seasons). The 26-year-old Manush had won the batting title with a .378 mark in 1926 but had fallen to .298 in 1927. Vangilder was almost through; he pitched in 1928 and a bit in '29 before his career ended. Galloway had only one more season in him. Rice and Blue were veterans whose stats roughly canceled each other out. Manush went on to complete a Hall of Fame career and, although is probably a weak Hall of Fame selection, he played in the majors until 1939 for the Browns, Senators, Red Sox, Dodgers, and Pirates, amassing 2,524 hits in a 17-year career.

3. December 1963: Tigers got: OF Don Demeter, P Jack Hamilton Philadelphia Phillies got: P Jim Bunning, C Gus Triandos

Several factors went into the making of this deal. The Tigers had traded Rocky Colavito to the Athletics the month before for pitching and a second baseman and needed a replacement. Manager Charlie Dressen and Bunning did not get along and Dressen coveted Demeter, who had been with the Dodgers when he was a coach there. Dressen felt Demeter was better than Colavito because of his outfield range and his speed; he ignored the fact that Demeter did not walk much while Colavito walked a lot, and that statistics indicated Demeter had poor range.

Demeter played creditably with the Tigers, amassing a 232-game errorless streak in the outfield, and hitting 22 and 16 home runs in 1964 and '65, respectively. Perhaps his best contribution is what he himself brought in trade: pitcher Earl Wilson, a starter on the 1968 World Championship team. But Demeter's contributions in Detroit paled next to Bunning's in Philly. He won 19 games each 1964–66, pitched a perfect game in 1964, and lasted in the majors with the Phillies, Pirates and Dodgers until 1971. Bunning was later elected to the Hall of Fame, although like Manush he is a marginal Hall of Famer.

4. July 1995: Tigers got: IF Mark Lewis, P C. J. Nitkowski, P Dave Tuttle Cincinnati Reds got: P David Wells

The Tigers had an old team in 1995, and the age was starting to show. Detroit had been doing well—as of July 7, they were 37-33 and in second place, three games out of first in the AL East. Then things started falling apart, and as the deadline to make a deal without requiring waivers approached at the end of July, the Tigers sank to 40-47, 8-1/2 games out of first, although they were only four games out of the wild-card race.

General manager Joe Klein decided it was time to trade some veterans for kids. The 32-year-old Wells had been a fair pitcher since coming to the majors in 1987 with Toronto—and since 1993 when the Tigers signed him after the Jays released him. He had come into his own in 1995, though, going 10-3 with a 3.04 ERA, and Klein felt it was time to cash in on him. Nitkowski had been the 12th overall pick in the 1994 amateur draft and was thought a top prospect. The Tigers' choice of a "player to be named later" after the 1995 season was Lewis, another top prospect who had been the second overall pick in the draft in 1988 and was coming off a fine 1995 season with Cincinnati.

Nitkowski never developed as a starting pitcher, although he might have been hurt by both the Reds and the Tigers having him face major league competition too soon. Nitkowski was traded to the Astros and later back to Detroit, finding a niche as a lefty relief specialist. Lewis' power never developed as expected and after one year as Detroit's starting second baseman spent a career as a utility infielder. Wells struggled early with the Reds, and had a 5.14 ERA for the Orioles in 1996 but blossomed after signing with the Yankees in 1997, hurling a perfect game in 1998. He has remained a star, even after subsequent trades to Toronto (1999–2000) and the White Sox (2001). While he became one of the top left-handers of his era, the Tigers tried without success in the succeeding years to find a legitimate number-one starter.

5. November 1997: Tigers got: 3B Joe Randa, 3B Gabe Alvarez, one player picked and returned in the expansion draft (P Matt Drews) Arizona Diamondbacks got: 3B Travis Fryman

The Tigers rebounded from a terrible 53-109 1996 season with a credible 79-83 campaign in 1997 and were looking to add players to continue the upward movement. They thought they had a big deal done to get OF Bernie Williams from the Yankees but it fell through (see "Two Done Deals That Weren't Done"). General Manager Randy Smith felt the team needed more depth but lacked money to acquire the talent. Fryman was asking for a contract in the $6 million-a-year range after his current pact expired following the 1998 season, more than the Tigers felt he was worth. Randa had been a decent, if not spectacular, third baseman throughout his career with the Royals and Pirates, known for a decent average and low-to-medium power. Alvarez was considered a good prospect in the Padres system and had been drafted during Smith's time there. The Tigers felt their farm system had improved, too, and were reluctant to lose three players in the expansion draft.

What gets this trade on the list is not as much the deal but the aftermath. Alvarez caught a case of the throwing "yips," registering an .875 fielding average with the Tigers in 1998. He never fully rid himself of them before being dealt to San Diego in a minor league deal in July 2000. Drews rang up ERAs of 6.57 and 8.27 as a starter in the minors once the Tigers got him back; even the pitching-poor Tampa Bay Devil Rays cut him loose soon after picking him up early in 2000. The Tigers used the $5 million saved on Fryman's contract to sign free agents: pitchers Frank Castillo and Scott Sanders, designated hitter Bip Roberts and outfielder Luis Gonzalez. With the exception of Gonzalez, the signings were huge mistakes; in fact, the dissension caused by Roberts helped get manager Buddy Bell fired before the 1998 season ended. Tigers went 65-97 to finish behind every American League team but the expansion Devil Rays. After the season, the Tigers signed a third baseman quite comparable to Fryman, Dean Palmer, to a five-year deal averaging $7 million a year, over a million bucks more per year than Fryman cost the Cleveland Indians (to whom Arizona dealt Fryman).

TWO DONE DEALS THAT WEREN'T DONE

These are two trades the Tigers made with other teams that the other teams shook hands on and reneged on at the last moment.

December 1974: Tigers would have gotten: C Bob Boone, OF Mike
    Anderson
Philadelphia Phillies would have gotten: C Bill Freehan, OF Mickey
    Stanley, P Jim Ray, P Luke Walker, P Bill Slayback
The teams agreed to the deal, even getting Bill Freehan to waive his 10-and-5 no-trade clause (ten years in the majors, five with the same team). The Phils pulled back a short time before the deal was to have been announced.

Freehan said, "I had it in my mind that I was a member of the Philadelphia Phillies. I had already said my good-byes to (Tiger GM) Jim (Campbell) and (manager) Ralph Houk. I wasn't hurt. . . . It was a very maturing, emotional experience, but . . . it is a lot harder on the family."

Campbell was incensed. "In my 25 years in baseball I've never seen anything like this happen. I've seen deals fall through but not after they've agreed upon it and the other club even talks to your players."

The 27-year-old Boone, the son of former Tiger Ray Boone, was coming off his second season as a regular and was considered to be one of the best young catchers in the game. Leaving the Phils after the 1981 season, he played 16 seasons after the non-deal for Philadelphia, California, and Kansas City. The Phils backed out in part because they decided to deal away another young catcher instead, John Stearns, to the Mets for relief pitcher Tug McGraw, who became a mainstay on their 1980 World Championship team. Freehan and Stanley each retired a Tiger, Freehan in 1976, Stanley in 1978. None of the other players ever did anything consequential after the aborted deal.

November 1997: Tigers would have gotten: OF Bernie Williams
New York Yankees would have gotten: P Mike Drumright, P Roberto Duran
This deal was agreed to as the expansion draft for Arizona and Tampa Bay took place. Williams was set to be a free agent after the 1998 season and the Yankees were afraid of losing him. The Tigers were coming off a surprisingly strong 79-83 season and had visions of using Williams to take the next step. However, after the first round of the draft, Yankees general manager Bob Watson told Tigers GM Randy Smith the deal was off. Reportedly, New York owner George Steinbrenner nixed the deal. Smith was disappointed and believed the Yanks should have lived up to their commitment.

Had this trade gone through, it would have changed base-ball history. The 1998 Yankees, with Williams as their biggest star, became one of the best teams in baseball history, going 114-48, and taking the postseason at a 12-1 clip to win the World Series. The Tigers had a disappointing 1998, dropping to 65-97. Drumright never made the majors and eventually was dealt to Florida. Duran made it up but his wildness kept him from a long stay.

PLAYERS WHO WERE TIGERS PROPERTY BUT NEVER TIGERS

Carl Hubbell, a Tigers property for three years before he was cut loose—because Ty Cobb did not like Hubbell using a screw-ball—and became a Hall of Famer for the New York Giants.

TRADES AND DRAFTS

Johnny Sain, one of 91 Tigers, 87 of them farmhands, who were made free agents early in 1940. Pitcher Sain was arguably the best of the 23 farmhands who made it to the majors.

John Smoltz, a Lansing native in AA ball who was traded July 1987 to Atlanta for Doyle Alexander.

John Wetteland, a Rule 5 draft pick from Los Angeles in 1988. Under Rule 5, a player must stay with the new club for a full year or be offered back to the team that lost him. That the Tigers did before spring training ended. Wetteland returned to Los Angeles and became a top closer for the Expos, Yankees and Rangers, with more than 300 saves to his credit.

Maury Wills, the first man to break Ty Cobb's single-season base-stealing record, languished in the Tigers' farm system through spring training of 1959. He was passed over for the starting shortstop job in favor of Coot Veal, and was claimed on waivers by the Los Angeles Dodgers.

TIGERS NOTABLES WHO FINISHED THEIR CAREERS WITH OTHER TEAMS

Player	Team	Last Year
George Mullin	Newark (Federal League)	1915
Donie Bush	Washington Senators	1923
Ty Cobb	Philadelphia Athletics	1928
Harry Heilmann	Cincinnati Reds	1932
Billy Rogell	Chicago Cubs	1940
Hank Greenberg	Pittsburgh Pirates	1947
Schoolboy Rowe	Philadelphia Phillies	1949
Dizzy Trout	Baltimore Orioles	1957
Frank Lary	Chicago White Sox	1965
Hank Aguirre	Chicago Cubs	1970
Jim Northrup	Baltimore Orioles	1975
Dick McAuliffe	Boston Red Sox	1975
Ed Brinkman	New York Yankees	1975
Mickey Lolich	San Diego Padres	1979
Willie Horton	Seattle Mariners	1980
Aurelio Rodriguez*	Chicago White Sox	1983

Player	Team	Last Year
Darrell Evans	Atlanta Braves	1989
Frank Tanana	New York Yankees	1993
Jack Morris	Cleveland Indians	1994

*The Original "A-Rod"!

NOTABLE PLAYERS WHO ENDED THEIR CAREERS AS TIGERS

Jack Coombs, 1930
Eddie Mathews, 1967–68
Frank Howard, 1973
Bill Madlock, 1987

TIGERS DEALS BY THE DECADE

Decade	w/AL	w/NL	Total
1900s	6	0	6
1910s	3	0	3
1920s	7	0	7
1930s	12	1	13
1940s	13	0	13
1950s	25	5	30
1960s	21	19	40
1970s	17	23	40
1980s	24	30	54
1990s/2000s	29	36	65

The first trade with an NL team was in 1939: The Cubs dealt Detroit shortstop Dick Bartell for shortstop Billy Rogell. The lack of deals with the NL was due to the fact that a team needed waivers on a player to deal him to the other league. To see the effects of this policy, go to "Fantasy Teams."

TIGERS FIRST-ROUND DRAFT PICKS WHO PLAYED FOR THE TIGERS

Gene Lamont, C (13th overall)	June 1965
Jim Foor, P (17th)	June 1967
Tom Veryzer, IF (11th)	June 1971
Jerry Manuel, IF (20th)	June 1972
Lance Parrish, C (16th)	June 1974
Tom Brookens, IF (4th)	January 1975
Steve Kemp, OF (1st)	January 1976
Pat Underwood, P (2nd)	June 1976
*Chris Codiroli, P (11th)	January 1979
Kirk Gibson, OF (12th)	June 1979
Rick Leach, OF (13th)	June 1979
Mike Laga, 1B (17th)	January 1980
Glenn Wilson, IF (18th)	June 1980
Rich Monteleone, P (20th)	June 1982
Randy Nosek, P (26th)	June 1985
Phil Clark, C (18th)	June 1986
*Steve Pegues, OF (21st)	June 1987
Rico Brogna, 1B (26th)	June 1988
Greg Gohr, P (21st)	June 1989
Tony Clark, 1B (2nd)	June 1990
Justin Thompson, P (32nd)	June 1991
Seth Greisinger, P (6th)	June 1996
Matt Anderson, P (1st)	June 1997
Jeff Weaver, P (14th)	June 1998
Eric Munson, C (3rd)	June 1999

*Played elsewhere in the majors.
Note: The January draft was discontinued after 1987.

TIGERS BONUS BABIES

Player	Year	Bonus
Dick Wakefield	1941	$52,000 and a new car
Lou Kretlow	1946	$30,000
Frank House	1949	$75,000 and two new cars
Harvey Kuenn	1952	$65,000
Reno Bertoia	1953	$13,000 plus $10,000 salary for 1953−55*
Al Kaline	1953	$15,000 plus $20,000 salary for 1953−55
Bob Miller	1953	$60,000
Jim Brady	1955	$37,500
Jim Small	1955	$30,000
Steve Boros	1957	$26,000
George Thomas	1957	$25,000

*Bertoia also got $1,000 to send his mother to her native Italy.

Other Teams, Other Leagues

Despite your obvious affection—and ours—for the Tigers, it would be incorrect to think that they existed in a vacuum, that somehow in 1901 they suddenly materialized out of seemingly nowhere to play major-league baseball. The truth, then as now, is that cities have looked to attract and keep sports teams as evidence of their high self-regard as a city. Detroit's quest began twenty years before the Tigers with a National League entry called the Detroit Wolverines. And due to the restrictive color line the majors drew until 1947, there were parallel developments in Negro League baseball, in which Detroit also was a participant. This book could not possibly do justice to the Negro National League Detroit Stars or the NL's Detroit Wolverines; for a more comprehensive perspective on the former, read Richard Bak's *Turkey Stearnes and the Detroit Stars: The Negro Leagues in Detroit, 1919–1933*, published by Wayne State University Press. But it would be at least as wrong, if not more so, to neglect them entirely. This chapter also looks at the Tigers' spring training locales, its farm system, the team's exhibitions in Cuba and Japan, and its players' involvement in still other leagues.

WOLVERINES NATIONAL LEAGUE LEADERS

Dan Brouthers	1886	Doubles: 40
Dan Brouthers	1886	Home runs: 11*
Dan Brouthers	1887	Doubles: 36
Dan Brouthers	1887	Runs scored: 153
Dan Brouthers	1888	Runs scored: 118
Dan Brouthers	1888	Doubles: 33
Charlie Getzien	1887	Winning percentage: .690 (29-13)
Hardy Richardson	1886	Hits: 189
Hardy Richardson	1886	Home runs: 11*
Sam Thompson	1887	Triples: 23
Sam Thompson	1887	RBI: 166**
George Wiedman	1881	ERA: 1.80**
George Wood	1882	Home runs: 7

*Tie.
**Statistics for RBI and ERA were not kept at the time, but twentieth-century baseball research ascertained the numbers retroactively from extant records.

THE LONGEST 1-0 GAME DECIDED BY A HOME RUN

August 17, 1882, Providence 1, Wolverines 0. Pitcher Hoss Radbourn, playing right field that day, hit a home run over the left-field fence in the 18th inning. It could have ended sooner, in the 15th inning, when Providence's George Wright hit the ball through a carriage gate in the outfield, but Detroit's Lon Knight in right field chased the ball under the horses' hooves and started a relay which cut down Wright at the plate. Despite Providence's contention that the ball should have been an automatic home run, the umpire ruled that the ball was playable.

THE DETROIT WOLVERINES' BIGGEST PURCHASE

Owner Frederick Stearns, after the 1885 season, bought the "Big Four" infield—Dan Brouthers, first base; Hardy Richardson, second base; Jack Rowe, shortstop; Jim "Deacon" White, third base—from Buffalo for $8,000. They helped get the Tigers from the second division in 1885 to second place in 1886, and become a championship club in 1887.

WOLVERINES-BROWNS GAMES OF THE 1887 "WORLD SERIES"

Game 1, October 10 at St. Louis: St. Louis 6, Detroit 1

To begin with, the American Association champions played the National League champs for a "world championship" each year from 1884 to 1890. For this 15-game barnstorming series, Detroit and St. Louis alternated batting last through the first 12 games. The AA champ Browns had little home-field advantage, with three of the 15 scheduled games played on their home turf, while the Wolverines had only two. It worked to St. Louis' advantage in the series opener as pitcher Bob Caruthers held Detroit scoreless until the last inning, and the Browns played errorless ball—rare for its day.

Game 2, October 11 in St. Louis: Detroit 5, St. Louis 3

A pair of two-run innings in the second and third paced Detroit to a 5-3 victory, holding off a late Browns charge in the seventh and eighth frames.

Game 3, October 12 in Detroit: Detroit 2, St. Louis 1 (13 innings)

Here the series' closest game was played. Charles "Pretzels" Getzien, who lost the first game on the mound for Detroit, helped his own cause in the bottom of the 13th inning by leading off with a single, advancing to third on two ground outs, and then scoring on an infield error—the Browns' seventh miscue of the game—to provide the winning margin.

Game 4, October 13 in Pittsburgh: Detroit 8, St. Louis 0

The Wolverines began to assert their dominance in the series with a four-run first inning and pitcher Lady Baldwin shutting down the Browns on two hits.

Game 5, October 14 in Brooklyn: St. Louis 5, Detroit 2
The Browns crept to within one game of the Wolverines, as Caruthers pitched a seven-hitter to lead St. Louis to victory.

Game 6, October 15 in New York: Detroit 9, St. Louis 0
Getzien starred again, twirling a two-hit gem as the Wolverines pounded the Browns, scoring three runs each in the first, second and ninth innings.

Game 7, October 17 in Philadelphia: Detroit 3, St. Louis 1
Tip O'Neill's ninth-inning solo home run for St. Louis wasn't enough to overcome a three-run Detroit second as the Wolverines won their second straight.

Game 8, October 18 in Boston: Detroit 9, St. Louis 2
The Wolverines' Sam Thompson crashed two home runs as Detroit, behind the eight-hit pitching of Getzien, crushed the Browns.

Game 9, October 19 in Philadelphia: Detroit 4, St. Louis 2
Detroit extended its winning streak to four as pitcher Pete Conway held the Browns to two runs while the Wolverines erased a 2-1 deficit with two runs in the seventh and an insurance marker in the eighth.

Game 10, October 21 (morning) in Washington: St. Louis 11, Detroit 4
St. Louis, one loss away from losing the series, came back with a thrashing of the Wolverines. Third baseman Arlie Latham and outfielder Curt Welch smashed homers for the Browns, while second baseman Hardy Richardson led off the game with a circuit clout for Detroit.

Game 11, October 21 (afternoon) in Baltimore: Detroit 13, St. Louis 3
Detroit won the series in style, cruising in the nightcap of a morning-afternoon doubleheader with Game 10 in Washington, Game 11 in Baltimore 40 miles to the north. Outfielder Larry Twitchell hit a home run for the Wolverines, who put the game away with 11 runs in the middle three innings.

Game 12, October 22 in Brooklyn: St. Louis 5, Detroit 1 (6-1/2 innings, darkness)

Even with Detroit assured of a series win, the two teams played the remaining four games on their schedule, this time returning to Brooklyn, where Silver King won his only game of the series against three losses, besting the Wolverines' Pete Conway, 5-1 in a contest shortened by darkness.

Game 13, October 23 in Detroit: Detroit 6, St. Louis 3

Back in Detroit, the champion Wolverines, curiously, had fewer folks turn out to greet their conquering heroes than in Game 2 (3,389 vs. 4,509). The result was the same, though, as Lady Baldwin won his fourth game against the Browns.

Game 14, October 24 in Chicago: Detroit 4, St. Louis 3

Only 378 bothered to see the game. The Wolverines built a 3-0 lead after one inning and extended it to 4-0 in the fifth, a margin big enough to hold on to a 4-3 win behind Charlie Getzien, who won his fourth game of the series.

Game 15, October 26 in St. Louis: St. Louis 9, Detroit 2 (6 innings, cold)

Back where they started in St. Louis, Caruthers evened his series record at 4-4 with a 9-2 win over the Wolverines. Only 659 came to see the meaningless contest.

TIGERS WHO PLAYED FOR BOTH THE AL AND NL DETROIT CLUBS

Player	Wolverines	Tigers
Deacon McGuire	1885, 1888	1902–3, 1912
Frank Scheibeck	1888	1906
Sam Thompson	1885–88	1906

DETROIT IN THE INTERNATIONAL ASSOCIATION

Five American and three Canadian cities surrounding Lake Erie formed the league: Detroit, Buffalo, Toledo, Syracuse, and Rochester in the States, and Toronto, London, and Hamilton in the Ontario province of Canada. Detroit won the league championship in 1889 and 1890, its first two years in the league—and its first two years after the city's National League team bit the dust.

DETROIT IN THE NORTHWESTERN LEAGUE

A short-lived entry, it lasted only into June 1891, 28 games into its first and only season. It had moved from Recreation Park, close to the site of present-day Harper Hospital in Detroit, to Riverside Park, across from Belle Isle on land now occupied by Owens Park. Officials in Hamtramck Township, which had jurisdiction over the field, frustrated the club's attempts to play games on Sunday.

MEMBERS OF THE 1894 WESTERN LEAGUE*

Detroit (first called the "Creams," later the Tigers)
Milwaukee (later the Baltimore Orioles via St. Louis Browns)
Sioux City (later the Chicago White Sox via St. Paul)
Grand Rapids
Indianapolis
Kansas City
Minneapolis
Toledo

*The Western League became the American League in 1900, and declared itself a major league in 1901.

DETROIT'S FIRST
WESTERN LEAGUE GAME

April 25, 1894, at Toledo. Detroit 8, Toledo 7. Detroit lost its first home game, May 2, 1894, 4-3 to Toledo, before an estimated 4,000 paying customers, plus a few hundred watching the game for free from trees and rooftops.

WHEN DETROIT ALMOST REJOINED
THE NATIONAL LEAGUE

After the 1920 season, a movement was afoot within the major leagues to have one commissioner oversee both the American and National League. This was opposed by AL president Ban Johnson, who suspected it would curb his power; he supported the existing three-man National Commission to preside over the sport. The owners of three AL clubs—Boston, Chicago and New York—none of whom liked Johnson much, joined the unanimous National League and voted to form a 12-team "New National League" that would include all of them plus the Tigers while conveniently making Johnson's job superfluous. While putting Detroit owner Frank Navin in a tight spot, it also gave him negotiating leverage. Soon, all 16 major-league clubs were invited to a conference at which—with neither league president on hand—Judge Kenesaw Mountain Landis was appointed as the first commissioner. The New National League plan was quickly scrapped.

THE SEASONS WE HAD THE STARS

The Detroit Stars played in the Negro National League, 1919–33, including 1932 as the Detroit Wolves, replacing the Indianapolis ABCs in May 1933 in a season that ended after only the first half was played. They played in only one championship series, losing that one, which unfortunately made them less of a team in the eyes of many high-profile writers, whose East Coast bias carried over from whites-only baseball to Negro League ball as well. Until his induction into the Hall of Fame in 2000, Norman (Turkey) Stearnes could be considered a tragic hero along the lines of an Al Kaline, but at least Kaline finally grabbed the brass ring of a championship club as well as a first-ballot Hall of Fame induction. Stearnes was an obvious star among Stars but could never claim a championship. The larger truth, though, is that all of the Detroit Stars were tragic heroes, confined to playing in a league where virtually everything was substandard except the quality of play. That the major leagues' color line didn't dissolve until it was too late for the Stars only compounded the tragedy.

STARS TEAM HITTING LEADERS

Name	Year/Career	Record
Jimmy Lyons	Year	Stolen bases: 22 (1920)
Orville (Mule) Riggins	Year	Games played: 84 (1925)
Ed Rile	Year	Doubles: 27 (1928)
Clarence Smith	Year	At-bats: 341 (1925)
Norman (Turkey) Stearnes	Career	Games played: 585 (1923–31)
Norman (Turkey) Stearnes	Career	At-bats: 2,217 (1923–31)
Norman (Turkey) Stearnes	Career	Hits: 783 (1923–31)*
Norman (Turkey) Stearnes	Year	Hits: 118 (1925)
Norman (Turkey) Stearnes	Year	Hitting streak: 19 (1924)
Norman (Turkey) Stearnes	Career	Batting average: .353 (1923–31)**
Norman (Turkey) Stearnes	Career	Doubles: 143 (1923–31)
Norman (Turkey) Stearnes	Career	Triples: 79 (1923–31)
Norman (Turkey) Stearnes	Year	Triples: 13 (1923)
Norman (Turkey) Stearnes	Career	Home runs: 140 (1923–31)***
Norman (Turkey) Stearnes	Year	Home runs: 24 (1928)
Norman (Turkey) Stearnes	Career	Slugging percentage: .678 (1923–31)
Norman (Turkey) Stearnes	Career	Stolen bases: 67 (1923–31)
Edgar Wesley	Year	Batting average: .424 (1925)
Edgar Wesley	Year	Slugging percentage: .810 (1925)

*Stearnes' 1,323 Negro League hits is third all-time.
**Stearnes' Negro League batting average of .3514 is behind only Josh Gibson's .3518 and Jud Wilson's .3516.
***Stearnes is third all-time in Negro League homers with 207; his HR-per-AB ratio is fourth among all Negro Leaguers with at least 40 home runs.

STARS TEAM PITCHING LEADERS

Name	Year/Career	Record
Andy (Lefty) Cooper	Career	Games pitched: 229 (1920–27, 1930)
Andy (Lefty) Cooper	Career	Games started: 139 (1920–27, 1930)
Andy (Lefty) Cooper	Career	Complete games: 87 (1920–27, 1930)
Andy (Lefty) Cooper	Career	Innings pitched: 1,152.2 (1920–27, 1930)
Andy (Lefty) Cooper	Career	Wins: 91 (1920–27, 1930)*
Andy (Lefty) Cooper	Career	Losses: 48 (1920–27, 1930)
Andy (Lefty) Cooper	Career	Hits allowed: 1,083 (1920–27, 1930)
Andy (Lefty) Cooper	Career	Walks allowed: 185 (1920–27, 1930)
Andy (Lefty) Cooper	Career	Strikeouts: 388 (1920–27, 1930)
Andy (Lefty) Cooper	Career	Saves: 24 (1920–27, 1930)
Andy (Lefty) Cooper	Year	Saves: 6 (1924 and 1925)
Albert Davis	Year	Hits allowed: 192 (1929)
Nelson Dean	Career	Runs per game**: 3.65 (1930–31)
Nelson Dean	Year	Runs per game**: 3.29 (1930)
William Force	Year	Games pitched: 38 (1923)
William Force	Year	Strikeouts: 108 (1922)
Bill Holland	Year	Games started: 23 (1922)
Bill Holland	Year	Complete games: 18 (1921)
Bill Holland	Year	Innings pitched: 204 (1922)
Bill Holland	Year	Wins: 16 (1922)
Bill Holland	Year	Losses: 13 (1922)***
Jack Marshall	Year	Walks allowed: 54 (1928)

*Cooper's 131 Negro League career victories are seventh overall, and his .708 winning percentage is fifth-best among all Negro League pitchers with at least 50 wins.
**Surviving statistics make it impossible to determine whether runs scored upon were earned or unearned.
***Holland totaled more losses—99—than any other Negro League hurler, but is also eighth overall with 127 wins compiled during a 21-year career (1920–40).

NOTABLE FEATS BY STARS PLAYERS

Six hits in a game: Stack Martin, April 28, 1928, vs. Cleveland; Hollie Harding, May 30, 1928, vs. Birmingham; Ed Rile, July 30, 1928, vs. St. Louis.

Three triples in a game: Norman (Turkey) Stearnes, June 17, 1923 (second game), vs. Milwaukee.

Three home runs in a game: Norman (Turkey) Stearnes, September 3, 1927, vs. Cuban Stars (West).

DETROIT'S ROLE IN MAJOR LEAGUE VS. NEGRO LEAGUE EXHIBITIONS

1909:The Tigers, with Ty Cobb and Sam Crawford, played Negro League all-stars in two exhibition series in Cuba as part of a barnstorming tour. The Tigers lost both series by 4-2 margins to the Habana and the Almandares teams. Cobb was overshadowed by Negro League stars Henry "Pop" Lloyd and "Home Run" Grant Johnson. Even worse, every time Cobb tried to steal a base, Negro League catcher Bruce "Buddy" Petway threw him out. Petway, as player-manager, hit .390 against the Tigers. Petway played for the Negro National League's Detroit Stars 1919–25. But the biggest highlight, at least for Cuba, was a 2-1 11-inning no-hitter pitched by Almandares' Eustaquio (Bombin) Pedroso November 18, 1909.

1922: The Tigers played a three-game exhibition series against the St. Louis Giants in the fall. The Giants, behind the talents of centerfielder Oscar Charleston, took the first two contests.

1923: The Detroit Stars played the St. Louis Browns in a three-day series at Mack Park in Detroit in October and won the first two games, including overcoming a six-run deficit to win the first game. After such continued poor showings against Negro Leaguers, Commissioner Kenesaw Mountain Landis barred individual teams from scheduling games with Negro League clubs, although barnstorming "all-star" teams were OK. The Stars' Turkey Stearnes hit .313 and smashed four home runs, according to surviving statistics, in games against major-leaguers.

1927: The Tigers and the Detroit Stars agreed to a postseason barnstorming tour. The Tigers went 2-11 on the tour. Not every Tiger was part of the barnstorming effort. Ty Cobb, by then with the Philadelphia Athletics, refused to take part. The Detroit Stars had brought back their retired catcher and manager— Bruce Petway.

BLACK BALL IN DETROIT AFTER THE NEGRO NATIONAL LEAGUE STARS

1935: The Detroit Cubs were a semipro team without a league affiliation playing a barnstorming schedule.

1937: The Detroit Stars name was revived and played in the East-West League, according to *Black Baseball in Detroit* by Larry Lester, Sammy J. Miller and Dick Clark. The name Stars appeared again in 1941 in the pro ranks, but little is known about this aggregation.

1938: Heavyweight boxing champion and Detroiter Joe Louis had wanted to buy into a Negro League team but shied away when he heard of gangster involvement in the league. Instead, he formed a softball team, the Brown Bombers (his nickname), and played first base in the club's exhibitions.

1939–40: A different edition of the Detroit Stars played semi-pro ball.

1941: The Detroit Black Sox was another all-black team about which little more is known.

1941–44: The Motor City Giants were another semipro outfit.

1942: The Detroit Giants was the name of the Motor City's entry in the Negro Major League. It played its games at two sites: the old Motor City Speedway at E. Eight Mile Rd. and Schoenherr in northeast Detroit, and Bob Sage's Sports Park at Livernois and Elmhurst on Detroit's west side.

1947: Two clubs played in Detroit: a team using the name of the Wolves, and the Detroit Senators. The Senators were a semipro team managed by Hall of Famer Cool Papa Bell and featured David Pope, who had a four-year major league career with the Cleveland Indians and the Baltimore Orioles.

1954–57: The Detroit Stars emerged anew, playing in the Negro American League. Ted Rasberry was the team's owner-manager and a part-time player. He also owned the Kansas City Monarchs, becoming the first person to own two teams in the same league. The Stars never fared as well as the Monarchs.

1958: Thanks to Harlem Globetrotters star Leon "Goose" Tatum buying a share in the ownership, a new club was formed and christened the Detroit Clowns.

1959: The team's name reverted to the Stars after the Clowns experiment was judged to be unsuccessful.

1960: The home team had two homes: Detroit and New Orleans. By this time, Negro League ball was on its last legs as every major league team had found room for at least one black player on its roster.

TIGERS' SPRING TRAINING SITES

1901	Detroit
1902	Ypsilanti, Mich.
1903–04	Shreveport, La.
1905–07	Augusta, Ga.
1908	Hot Springs, Ark.
1909–10	San Antonio
1911–12	Monroe, La.
1913–15	Gulfport, Miss.
1916–18	Waxahachie, Tex.
1919–20	Macon, Ga.
1921	San Antonio
1922–26	Augusta
1927–28	San Antonio
1929	Phoenix*
1930	Tampa, Fla.
1931	Sacramento, Calif.
1932	Palo Alto, Calif.
1933	San Antonio
1934–42	Lakeland, Fla.
1943–45	Evansville, Ind. (necessitated by wartime travel and fuel restrictions)
1946–	Lakeland**

*The Tigers were the first team to train in Arizona.
**Detroit and Lakeland have the longest continuous spring training relationship of any major league club.

TIGER GREATS HONORED AT THE TIGERTOWN COMPLEX IN LAKELAND

With baseball diamonds: Ty Cobb, Mickey Cochrane, Charlie Gehringer, Hank Greenberg, Harry Heilmann

With a plaque: Al Kaline

With artwork outside Joker Marchant Stadium: Norm Cash, Al Kaline, Alan Trammell, Lou Whitaker

THE TIGERS TAKE JAPAN

Following the Tigers' 1962 season, they played an 18-game exhibition series in Japan over 38 days October 14–November 20 before an estimated 407,500 fans. Using a 21-man squad, the Tigers racked up a 12-4-2 record, including a seven-game winning streak. Tops in hitting were Bubba Morton (.347), Al Kaline (.343), Norm Cash (.342) and Billy Bruton (.333). Meanwhile, pitchers Jim Bunning, Phil Regan and Paul Foytack each won two games. ABC's "Wide World of Sports" carried highlights from the exhibition series. During the trip, U.S. baseball commissioner Ford Frick and Japan baseball commissioner Yushi Uchimura worked out the terms of player exchanges between the two countries, giving each commissioner the final approval for a player to play in the other's country. Foreign player limits in 1962 were three per team. Among the onetime big leaguers playing in Japan in 1962 were Don Newcombe and Larry Doby. The game-by-game results (Tigers' score first):

Date	Place	Score	Attendance
October 14	Honolulu	11-2	3,608
October 15	Honolulu	9-3	2,047
October 21	Naha, Okinawa	9-0	4,000
October 24	Seoul, South Korea	8-0	20,000
October 27	Tokyo	12-1	27,000
October 30	Tokyo	3-3 tie	32,000
October 31	Tokyo	2-3	39,500
November 1	Sapporo	6-2	20,000
November 4	Osaka	7-3	30,000
November 5	Nagoya	4-6	26,000

Date	Place	Score	Attendance
November 6	Osaka	11-4	15,000
November 7	Osaka	3-0	15,000
November 8	Tokyo	13-8	13,000
November 9	Hiroshima	8-1	8,000
November 10	Fukuoka	6-4	20,000
November 11	Shimonoseki	10-0	15,000
November 13	Shizuoka	12-7	10,000
November 14	Utsonomiya	3-6	18,000
November 15	Sendai	4-3	32,000
November 17	Tokyo	0-4	39,000
November 18	Tokyo	3-3 tie	29,000
November 20	Tokyo	7-2	19,000

FIRST INTERLEAGUE GAMES VERSUS EACH OPPONENT

Team	Date	Result
Montreal	June 13, 1997	L, 3-4
Florida*	June 16, 1997	L, 3-7
NY Mets*	June 30, 1997	W, 14-0
Philadelphia*	August 29, 1997	W, 7-2
Atlanta	September 1, 1997	W, 4-2
Milwaukee^	June 5, 1998	L, 3-7
Houston*	June 8, 1998	L, 5-9
St. Louis	June 22, 1998	L, 1-4
Chi. Cubs*	June 24, 1998	W, 7-6 (11 innings)
Cincinnati*	June 26, 1998	L, 3-4
Pittsburgh	June 30, 1998	W, 3-0
Arizona	June 5, 2001	W, 5-2

*Game played in Detroit (others on the road)
^First game with Milwaukee as a member of the National League; the teams played 397 games in the American League from 1970–1997.

In an early example of cross-training, pitchers Mickey Lolich and John Hiller work out in the infield with badminton racquets during spring training in the 1960s. Joker Marchant Stadium in Lakeland, Fla., is in the background. (Photo courtesy Ernie Harwell Collection/Burton Historical Collection, Detroit Public Library)

TIGERS WHO PLAYED FOR THE DETROIT CAESARS

Norm Cash
Jim Northrup

The Detroit Caesars, owned by current Tigers owner Mike Ilitch, played their games in the late 1970s at a field in then-East Detroit (now Eastpointe). In their short life, they were the perennial champions of the American Professional Slo-Pitch Softball League. Cash and Northrup, having retired from pro baseball, were brought in to lend the team some name players and increase the gate. While their softball averages were fatter than their major league averages, they paled in comparison to teammates who hit the ball at a .700 clip.

TIGERS IN THE SENIOR LEAGUE

Hitters

Ike Blessitt
Sal Butera
Marty Castillo
Al Cowens
Steve Dillard
John Grubb
Tim Hosley
Ron Jackson
Dalton Jones
Steve Kemp
Wayne Krenchicki
Ron LeFlore
Dwight Lowry
Bill Madlock
Jerry Manuel
Dan Meyer
Bob Molinaro
Jim Morrison
Ricky Peters
Leon Roberts
Champ Summers
Mark Wagner

Pitchers

Fernando Arroyo
Jack Billingham
Joe Coleman
El Glynn
Jack Lazorko
Mike Marshall
Sid Monge
Dave Rozema
Jim Slaton
Milt Wilcox

Managers

Gates Brown
Pat Dobson
Leon Roberts

The Senior Professional Baseball Association was a league for players 35 or older (34 in the second year), but only 32 for catchers. It was based in Florida (with teams in California and Arizona in the second year) and took place over the winter months. They played 1-1/2 seasons, 1989–90 and 1990–91, folding around Christmas 1990.

TIGERS FARM TEAMS*

City	League	Lev	Years	#Yrs
Michigan				
Flint	Central	A	1948–50	3
Muskegon	Michigan State	C	1940–41	2
West Michigan	Midwest	A	1997–	5
Alabama				
Birmingham	Southern Association	AA	1957–61	5
Birmingham	Southern	AA	1981–85	5
Montgomery	Southeastern	B	1947	1
Montgomery	South Atlantic	A	1953	1
Montgomery	Alabama-Florida	D	1957–62	6
Montgomery	Southern	AA	1965–80	16
Tallassee	Alabama State	D	1941	1
Troy	Alabama State	D	1947–49	3
Arkansas				
Hot Springs	Cotton States	C	1939–40	2
Little Rock	Southern Association	AA	1948–55	8
Newport	Northeast Arkansas	D	1939	1
California				
Bakersfield	California	C	1953	1
San Francisco	Pacific Coast	AA	1941	1
Visalia	California	A	1996	1

City	League	Lev	Years	#Yrs
Colorado				
Denver	American Assn./PCL	AAA	1960–62	3
Florida				
Daytona Beach	Florida State	A	1965–66	2
GCL Tigers	Gulf Coast	R	1995–	7
Jacksonville	Southern	AA	1995–2000	6
Lakeland	Florida State	A	1963–64, 1967–	37
Orlando	Florida State	D	1957	1
Palatka	Florida State	D	1936, 1956	2
Panama City	Alabama-Florida	D	1955–56	2
Sarasota	Gulf Coast	R	1968	1
Georgia				
Augusta	South Atlantic	B	1936, 1941–42	3
Augusta	South Atlantic	A	1955–58	4
Macon	South Atlantic	A	1981–82	2
Thomasville	Georgia-Florida	D	1947–50	4
Thomasville	Georgia-Florida	D/A	1962–63	2
Valdosta	Georgia-Florida	D	1954–58	5
Idaho				
Idaho Falls	Pioneer	C	1954–58	5
Illinois				
Decatur	Three-I	B	1932	1
Decatur	Midwest	D	1958–61	4
Moline	Miss. Valley	D	1932	1
Springfield	Three-I	B	1935	1
Indiana				
Evansville	American Association	AAA	1974–84	11
Richmond	Ohio-Indiana	D	1950–51	2
Terre Haute	Three-I	B	1955–56	2
Iowa				
Clinton	Midwest	A	1972–75	4
Davenport	Three-I	B	1951–52	2
Sioux City	Western	A	1937	1
Sioux City	Western	D	1939	1

City	League	Lev	Years	#Yrs
Kentucky				
Fulton	Kitty	D	1939–42	4
Louisiana				
Alexandria	Evangeline	D	1936	1
Lake Charles	Evangeline	D	1937	1
Shreveport	Dixie/E. Dixie	C	1933–34	2
Maryland				
Hagerstown	Interstate	B	1941–44, 1947–48	6
Massachusetts				
Brockton	Northeast	B	1933	1
Lynn	New England	B	1949	1
Pittsfield	Canadian-American	C	1942	1
Quincy	Northeast	B	1933	1
Minnesota/Wisconsin				
Duluth/Superior	Northern	C/A	1960–64	5
Mississippi				
Greenville	Cotton States	C	1954–55	2
Greenwood	E. Dixie	C	1934	1
Jackson	Cotton States	C	1936, 1953	2
New Hampshire				
Nashua	Northeast	B	1933	1
New Jersey				
Trenton	Eastern	AA	1994	1
New Mexico				
Hobbs	West Texas/New Mexico	D	1938	1
New York				
Batavia	NY Penn	A	1968–71	4
Buffalo	International	AAA	1940–49, 1952–55	14
Elmira	Eastern	A	1941–42	2
Glens Falls	Eastern	AA	1986–88	3
Jamestown	NY Penn	D	1941–42, 1944–56	15
Jamestown	NY Penn	D/A	1961–65	5

City	League	Lev	Years	#Yrs
Jamestown	NY Penn	A	1994–98	5
Niagara Falls	NY Penn	A	1989–93	5
Oneonta	NY Penn	A	1999–	3
Rome	Canadian-American	C	1948–49	4
Syracuse	Eastern	A	1956	1
Syracuse	International	AAA	1963–66	4
Utica	Canadian-American	C	1941	1

North Carolina

City	League	Lev	Years	#Yrs
Clinton	Tobacco State	D	1948	1
Durham	Carolina	B	1948–61	14
Fayetteville	South Atlantic	A	1987–96	10
Gastonia	South Atlantic	A	1986	1
Kinston	Coastal Plain	D	1952	1
Rocky Mount	Carolina	A	1965–72	8
Statesville	Western Carolina	A	1965–66	2
Winston-Salem	Redmont	B	1937, 1941–42	3

Ohio

City	League	Lev	Years	#Yrs
Tiffin	Ohio State	D	1936	1
Toledo	American Association	AA/AAA	1937–39,1949–51	6
Toledo	International	AAA	1967–73, 1987–	21

Oklahoma

City	League	Lev	Years	#Yrs
Muskogee	Western Association	C	1946	1

Ontario

City	League	Lev	Years	#Yrs
London	Eastern	AA	1989–93	5
Toronto	International	AA	1932–33	2

Oregon

City	League	Lev	Years	#Yrs
Portland	Pacific Coast	AA	1935	1

Pennsylvania

City	League	Lev	Years	#Yrs
Butler	Middle Atlantic	C	1949–50	2
Charleroi	Penn. State Assn.	D	1934–36	3
Erie	NY Penn	D/A	1957–59, 1967	4
Erie	Eastern	AA	2001–	1
Lancaster	Eastern	A	1958	1
Nazareth	North Atlantic	D	1947	1

OTHER TEAMS, OTHER LEAGUES

City	League	Lev	Years	#Yrs
Wilkes-Barre	Eastern	A	1954	1
Williamsport	Eastern	A	1946–52	7

South Carolina

City	League	Lev	Years	#Yrs
Anderson	Western Carolina	A	1973	1

Tennessee

City	League	Lev	Years	#Yrs
Knoxville	South Atlantic/ Southern Association	A/AA	1959–64	6
Nashville	American Association	AAA	1985–86	2

Texas

City	League	Lev	Years	#Yrs
Beaumont	Texas	A/A1	1930–42	13
Dallas	Texas	AA	1946–47	2
Ft. Worth	Texas	B/A	1919–29	11
Henderson	West Dixie	C	1935	1
Henderson	East Texas	C	1937, 1939–40	3
Lubbock	West Texas/New Mexico	C	1946–47	2
Texarkana	Cotton States	C	1941	1
Victoria	Texas	AA	1960	1

Virginia

City	League	Lev	Years	#Yrs
Bristol	Appalachian	R	1969–94	26

Washington

City	League	Lev	Years	#Yrs
Seattle	Pacific Coast	AAA	1948	1

West Virginia

City	League	Lev	Years	#Yrs
Beckley	Mountain State	D	1937	1
Charleston	Middle Atlantic	C	1934–38	5
Charleston	American Association	AAA	1956–59	4
Huntington	Middle Atlantic	C	1932–33	2

Wisconsin

City	League	Lev	Years	#Yrs
Milwaukee	American Association	AA	1936	1
Wausau	Wisconsin State	D	1951–53	3

The Tigers have had farm teams in thity-three states and one Canadian province.
*The levels of the minor leagues went from AA-D (through 1945), AAA-D (1946–62), and
AAA-Rookie (1963–present).

NUMBER OF TIGER FARM
TEAMS BY YEAR

Year	Teams
1919–31	1
1932	5
1933	6
1934	4
1935	6
1936–37	9
1938	5
1939	8
1940	6
1941	13
1942	9
1943	2
1944	3
1945	2
1946	7
1947	11
1948–49	12
1950	9
1951–52	8
1953	7
1954	8
1955–56	10
1957	9
1958	10
1959	7
1960–61	8
1962–63	6
1964	5
1965	6
1966–67	5
1968–73	6
1974–75	5
1976–80	4
1981–82	5
1983–85	4
1986–88	5

Year	Teams
1989–95	6
1996	7
1997–	6

Note how the number of farm teams the Tigers have had has fluctuated over time. The Tigers acquired their first farm team in 1932, quickly growing to twelve affiliates before World War II broke out. After the war, the Tigers rebuilt their farm system, but as television started bringing major-league games into distant communities, minor league baseball was deeply wounded. The Tigers dropped to a low of four affiliates in the 1970s and '80s. The expenses of running a minor-league system in an era of ballooning salaries led the club to cut costs. But the Tigers eventually recognized that the minor leagues were less of an expense than an investment. The majors has also standardized the alignment of minor leagues and developmental leagues in Arizona, California, the Dominican Republic, plus winter ball opportunities in Latin America. It's also helped that minor-league baseball has developed as an inexpensive family alternative to give greater incentive for parent clubs to sign affiliation agreements.

A MICHIGAN-BASED BASEBALL LEAGUE YOU MAY HAVE OVERLOOKED

The American Amateur Baseball Congress, headquartered in Marshall, Michigan supports amateur baseball by sponsoring major national tournaments for different age divisions: Roberto Clemente (ages 8-under), Willie Mays (ages 10-under), Pee Wee Reese (ages 12-under), Sandy Koufax (ages 14-under), Mickey Mantle (ages 16-under), Connie Mack, (ages 18-under) and Stan Musial (unlimited age).

LISTS EVEN WE WOULD HAVE TO CALL MISCELLANEOUS

So help us! Even though most everything in baseball can be quantified, we just couldn't find ways to package the nuggets found in this chapter any other way, from geography to war service to brawls, forfeits, suspensions and ejections, to prison time, to cup-of-coffee Tigers, to all sorts of feats of derring-do between the white lines and then some. We recommend you take in these lists during a commercial break in any Tigers game.

TIGERS HAILING FROM MICHIGAN

Adrian: Jack Feller, Fritz Fisher, Rube Kisinger, Mike Marshall
Ann Arbor: Rick Leach, Lou Schiappacasse, Pat Sheridan
Bellaire: Roger Mason
Bloomingdale: Red Killefer
Breckenridge: Jim Northrup
Coleman: Vern Ruhle
Corunna: Earl Rapp
Dallas: Slicker Parks

MISCELLANEOUS LISTS

Detroit: Ike Blessitt, Bob Bruce, Ed Cicotte, Leo Cristante, Jerry Davie, Bill Fahey, Bill Freehan, Frank Fuller, Ted Gray, Lenny Green, Altar Greene, Ray Herbert, Fred Holdsworth, Willie Horton*, Art James, Chick Lathers, Ron LeFlore, George Lerchen, Dick Littlefield, Don Lund, Leo Marentette, John McHale Sr., Hal Newhouser, Frank Okrie, Billy Pierce, Dick Radatz, Dennis Ribant, Bill Roman, Frank Scheibeck, Frank Tanana, Gary Taylor, Tom Tresh, Bill Zepp
Evart: Wish Egan
Flat Rock: Fred Gladding
Flint: Scott Aldred, Steve Boros
Fowlerville: Charlie Gehringer
Grand Haven: Howard Bailey
Grand Rapids: Al Platte, Dave Rozema, Mickey Stanley
Hamtramck: Steve Gromek, Bill Nahorodny
Hastings: Lew Post
Holland: George Zuvernik
Hopkins: Frank Kitson
Howell: Hank Perry
Jenison: Benny McCoy
Kalamazoo: Neil Berry
Kalkaska: Emil Frisk
Lansing: Larry Foster, Jim Stump
Lawton: Charlie Maxwell
Lincoln Park: Larry Pashnick
Ludington: Danny Claire
Manistee: Dave Campbell
Melvindale: Al Cicotte
Moline: Stubby Overmire
Montague: Ira Flagstead
Montrose: Alex Main
Mt. Clemens: Gary Ignasiak
Oakville: Lou Vedder
Otsego: Phil Regan
Oxford: Elijah Jones
Pontiac: Kirk Gibson
Romulus: Charlie Lau
Saginaw: Archie Yelle
St. Joseph: Dave Machemer
South Haven: Dave Gumpert
Sterling Heights: Dave Borkowski

Terris Center: Luke Hamlin
Utica: Duke Maas
Vicksburg: Leon Roberts
Wayne: Ed Fisher
Wyandotte: John Martin, Ed Mierkowicz
Ypsilanti: Arch McCarthy, Frank Owen

*Born in Arno, Virginia, but grew up in Detroit.

Detroit's Jewish Tigers

Brad Ausmus
Jose Bautista
Lou Brower
Richard Conger
Harry Eisenstat
Al Federoff
Murray Franklin
Joe Ginsberg
Izzy Goldstein
Hank Greenberg
Harry Kane (born Harry Cohen)
Gabe Kapler
Alan Koch
Elliott Maddox
Bob Melvin
Dave Roberts
Saul Rogovin
Larry Rothschild
Dick Sharon
Larry Sherry
Steve Wapnick

THIRD BASEMEN SPARKY ANDERSON USED TO TRY TO DISPLACE TOM BROOKENS*

Chris Pittaro
Glenn Wilson (one spring training game in 1984)
Barbaro Garbey
Howard Johnson
Marty Castillo
Darrell Evans
Darnell Coles
Lou Whitaker (spring training 1985, with Pittaro at second)
Chris Brown (in spring 1989, Brookens was dealt to the Yankees; Brown, acquired from San Diego, was such a bust he was gone from the majors for good by mid–1989)

*Others who played third base during Brookens' tenure, but were never considered serious threats to his playing time, included Doug Baker, Enos Cabell, Mark DeJohn, Doug Flynn, Julio Gonzalez, Johnny Grubb, Mike Heath, Richie Hebner, Mick Kelleher, Ray Knight, Wayne Krenchicki, Torey Lovullo, Scotti Madison, Bill Madlock, Jim Morrison, Matt Nokes, Stan Papi, Luis Salazar, Harry Spilman, Mark Wagner, Jim Walewander and John Wockenfuss.

GREAT TIGERS-WHITE SOX BRAWLS

August 22, 1968: Dick McAuliffe went after pitcher Tommy John after a pitch was thrown at his head. In the fight with McAuliffe John tore a ligament in his pitching shoulder (NOT the muscle that requires "Tommy John" surgery). McAuliffe was suspended for five days and fined $250.

June 20, 1980: Grounding out to shortstop, Tigers outfielder Al Cowens, instead of running to first base, charged the mound to get at Chisox pitcher Ed Farmer, who had broken Cowens' jaw with a pitch the year before when Cowens was with Kansas City. Cowens was ejected, and Farmer threatened to seek criminal charges against Cowens. But Cowens and Farmer ended their feud Sept. 1 by shaking hands as they brought out the lineup cards prior to a game in Detroit, earning a standing ovation from the crowd.

April 22, 2000: Twice the Tigers charged the mound after retaliatory pitches by Chisox hurlers. Tigers pitcher Jeff Weaver, who had already hit two batters, was out of the game. But when Tigers third baseman Dean Palmer was plunked by Jim Parque, that set off one melee. And when Shane Halter was hit in the ninth inning by Bobby Howry, a second brawl ensued. Detroit outfielder Bobby Higginson struck White Sox closer Keith Foulke, opening up a nasty gash around his eye. Palmer, ejected for his role in the first brawl, came out of the clubhouse for the second and was suspended eight games. Eight Tigers and five White Sox were suspended, Detroit getting the worst of it; the heaviest penalty fell on Tigers first base coach Juan Samuel, suspended ten games (down from fifteen on appeal).

Tiger	Games
Juan Samuel	10
Phil Garner	8
Dean Palmer	8
Bobby Higginson	5
Robert Fick	4
Juan Encarnacion	3
Doug Brocail	3
Karim Garcia	3 (was sent to the minors, then traded to Baltimore before he could serve his suspension)
Total	44 games

GREAT TIGERS-WHITE SOX FORFEITS

May 2, 1901: The Tigers were ahead 7-5, Chicago stalled to keep the game from reaching regulation length, and the umps awarded the game to Detroit. It was the first AL forfeit.

July 12, 1979: The second game of a planned twi-night doubleheader at Comiskey Park was forfeited to the Tigers. The between-games promotion was "Disco Demolition Night," for which fans paid 98 cents to get into the stadium; there were more than 50,000 in attendance, some of them throwing LPs like they were Frisbees. The highlight was supposed to have been the between-games dynamiting of disco records on the playing field by Chicago (and onetime Detroit) rock disc jockey Steve Dahl. About 6,000 fans stormed the field to exult after the explosion, further tearing up the field. It was the last AL forfeit.

OTHER FORFEITS INVOLVING THE TIGERS

May 31, 1901: The Tigers scored on a close play at the plate in the bottom of the ninth inning to tie its game with Baltimore at 5-5. Baltimore (which would move to New York) players charged onto the field to protest. As the umpire turned to walk away, one Baltimore player threw a bat at him and another threw a ball at him. The ump merely continued to walk to a bench, sat down, and pulled a watch out of his pocket. When Baltimore didn't clear the field in time, he awarded a forfeit to Detroit.

August 21, 1901: Home-team Baltimore, not having learned its lesson three months before, protested a close call at first base in Detroit's favor by charging out of the dugout again. One player spat into the umpire's eyes. The ump forfeited the game. Incensed, fans joined players in attacking the umpire; several fans were arrested for their role in the fracas. Detroit was leading 7-4 in the bottom of the fourth when the mess started.

August 8, 1903: Hall of Famer Nap Lajoie cost his Cleveland team, which was already down 6-5 with two out in the bottom of the 11th inning, the game when he protested that the ball in play was so dirty it couldn't be seen. The umpire refused to replace it. Lajoie, at a fan's urging, tossed the ball over the fence, and the umpire awarded the game to the Tigers.

August 22, 1905: The Washington Senators had just scored the go-ahead run on a close play in a 2-1 game with two out in the top of the 11th inning in a game at Bennett Park, and the Tigers rushed the field. When they refused to clear the field in time, the umpires forfeited the game to Washington.

June 13, 1924: The umpires forfeited a Tigers-Yankees game in Detroit to New York after umpire Billy Evans was unable to clear the field after a 30-minute melee of both teams—and rambunctious fans. It started when the Yanks' Bob Meusel, after getting hit in the back by a Bert Cole pitch, threw his bat at Cole and charged the mound.

DENNY MCLAIN'S 1970 SUSPENSIONS

McLain was first suspended February 19, 1970, by Commissioner
Bowie Kuhn for his involvement with bookmakers. In the 1960s,
there was great speculation—never confirmed—that a broken
toe McLain suffered late in the 1967 season came at the hands
(or the heels) of bookmakers. He was the first major-leaguer
suspended by the commissioner since 1924.

Denny returned to the Tigers and pitched his first game July 1,
1970. He went 3-5 in his 1970 season, shortened still further by a
30-day suspension by Tigers general manager Jim Campbell
August 28 after McLain doused sportswriters Jim Hawkins of the
Detroit Free Press and Watson Spoelstra of the Detroit News
with buckets of water. The suspension also included a $500-per-
day fine. Campbell lifted the suspension after a week.

But before McLain could return to the lineup, Kuhn suspended
him a third time, this time indefinitely, for carrying a gun. Kuhn
lifted the suspension October 9 to allow the Tigers to trade
McLain to the Washington Senators; baseball rules prohibited the
movement of suspended players from one franchise to another.

BROTHER VS. BROTHER

Tigers pitcher Jim Perry started against his brother Gaylord,
pitching for Cleveland, on July 3, 1973. It was the first time in
American League history two brothers opposed each other on
the mound. Neither pitcher finished the game, and the Tigers
lost 5-4. Oddly, the Coveleski brothers, Detroit's Harry and
Cleveland's Stanley, never pitched against each other, even
though Harry had 51 starts for Detroit 1916–18 and Stan had 90
starts for Cleveland in the same time frame—and teams played
each other 22 times a season then.

Who to cheer for when sons play on opposing teams can be a
nettlesome dilemma for parents, but in a September 4, 1974,
game, Graig Nettles hit a first-inning homer for the Yankees,
while brother Jim hit a second-inning home run for Detroit.
The Tigers lost to New York 10-7.

Pat Underwood, making his first start in the major leagues for the Tigers, was sent to pitch against his brother, Tom, hurling for the Toronto Blue Jays, May 31, 1979. Tom pitched well but Pat was even better, shutting out the Jays over 8.1 innings and leading the Tigers to a 1-0 victory.

THE AMERICAN LEAGUE'S CATCHER-UMPIRE BROTHER DUO

In 1972, Tom Haller, ex of the Los Angeles Dodgers, donned the Old English "D" as well as the "tools of ignorance." His brother was American League umpire Bill Haller. There was one game that season where Tom Haller caught while Bill Haller called balls and strikes as the home plate umpire. Baltimore Orioles manager Earl Weaver objected to two Hallers behind the plate at the same time, but nothing came of it.

TIGERS WITH BASEBALL FATHERS-IN-LAW

Denny McLain: Lou Boudreau, shortstop and player-manager of the 1948 World Series champion Cleveland Indians.

Skeeter Webb: Steve O'Neill, who managed the Tigers 1943-48. Webb played under O'Neill—and won a World Series with him in 1945.

TIGERS SONS OF HALL OF FAMERS

Dave Sisler, pitcher; his dad was AL batting champ George Sisler.

TIGERS WHO WERE REGULARS AT MORE THAN ONE POSITION (COUNTING THE OF AS ONE POSITION)

Player	Position 1	Position 2
Oscar Vitt	3B 1915–18	2B 1913
Dick McAuliffe	SS 1963–66	2B 1967–73
Mickey Tettleton	C 1991–92	RF 1994
Travis Fryman*	3B 1991, 1993–97	SS 1992–93

*Fryman was the regular 3B and SS in 1993. How? He played more games at each position (SS, 81; 3B, 69) than any other Tiger.

TIGERS WHO SERVED DURING WORLD WAR I

Ernie Alten
Del Baker
Bernie Boland
Tioga George Burns
Joe Cobb
Ty Cobb*
George Cunningham
Howard Ehmke
Bert Ellison
Frank Fuller
Harry Heilmann
Bill James
Hughie Jennings**
Willie Mitchell
Fred Nicholson
John "Red" Oldham

*Never saw action, but was commissioned a captain in the Army's Gas and Flame Division.
**Too old to serve, he volunteered in 1919 as a Knights of Columbus worker, arriving in France just prior to the signing of the Treaty of Versailles.

TIGERS WHO SERVED DURING WORLD WAR II

Name	Full Seasons Missed
Al Benton	1943–44
Jimmy Bloodworth	1944–45
Tommy Bridges	1944
Hoot Evers	1943–45
Murray Franklin	1943–45
Charlie Gehringer	1943–45*
Johnny Gorsica	1945
Hank Greenberg	1942–44
Ned Harris	1944–45
Pinky Higgins	1945
Billy Hitchcock	1943–45
Fred Hutchinson	1942–45
Johnny Lipon	1943–45
Barney McCosky	1943–45
Dutch Meyer	1943–44
Les Mueller	1942–44
Pat Mullin	1942–45
Bob Patrick	1943–45
Rip Radcliff	1944–46
Harvey Riebe	1943–45
Birdie Tebbetts	1943–45
Virgil Trucks	1944
Dick Wakefield	1945
Hub Walker	1942–44
Hal White	1944–45
Joe Wood	1944–45

Hal Newhouser, classified 4F, worked nights in a defense plant.
*Gehringer never returned to the majors.

TIGERS WHO SERVED DURING THE KOREAN WAR

Name	Full Seasons Missed
Ray Herbert	1952
Frank House	1952–53
Art Houtteman	1951
J. W. Porter	1953–54

I'VE HEARD OF "LITTLE BALL," BUT THIS IS TOO MUCH!

The pinch-hitter: Eddie Gaedel, St. Louis Browns
Gaedel's uniform number: 1/8
His height: 3 feet, 6 inches
His bat length: 17 inches
Who he hit for: Leadoff hitter Frank Saucier
The Tigers pitcher: Bob Cain
The Tigers catcher: Bob Swift
The outcome: A walk on four straight pitches
Gaedel's pinch-runner: Jim Delsing
The mastermind: Browns owner and general manager Bill Veeck
Where it happened: Sportsman's Park, St. Louis
When it happened: August 19, 1951 (second game), first inning
Two days later, the commissioner's office banned Gaedel.

A TALE OF TWO CITIES

When rioting erupted in Detroit July 23, 1967, a July 25–27 series with the Orioles was canceled in Detroit and moved to Baltimore. In the first game of the series, the teams could play only an inning and a half before rain came down and forced the cancellation of the game a second time—the first time the same game has been canceled in two cities.

SOME TIGERS WHO EXCELLED AT OTHER SPORTS

Elden Auker was all-conference in three sports at Kansas State and was offered a football contract by the Chicago Bears. He intended to play both pro sports, "But (owner Frank) Navin said no. I liked football better but I chose baseball because the season was already underway and I could make four hundred fifty dollars a month."

Norm Cash was also drafted by the Chicago Bears.

Tony Clark played basketball at San Diego State University and the University of Arizona.

Hoot Evers was a basketball star at the University of Illinois.

Bill Freehan was an end prospect for the University of Michigan football team before he signed a baseball contract.

Charlie Gehringer lettered in basketball at Michigan—but not in baseball.

Kirk Gibson was an All-American wide receiver at Michigan State University and drafted by football's St. Louis Cardinals.

Richie Hebner was a Scholastic All-American in hockey at Norwood (Mass.) High School and drafted by the Boston Bruins.

Frank Howard starred in basketball at Ohio State University.

Al Kaline, like many star high school athletes, played other high school sports in addition to baseball. But Kaline's basketball squad at Baltimore Southern High School won the Maryland state championship.

Rick Leach was starting quarterback at the University of Michigan.

Don Lund won nine varsity letters at Michigan and played pro football.

John McHale Sr. played football at Notre Dame.

Ed Rakow was a quarterback for the Bloomfield Rams in a semipro Pittsburgh-area league. He lost the starting job in 1956 to future Pro Football Hall of Famer Johnny Unitas.

Joe Sparma was a quarterback at Ohio State University.

Ron LeFlore, who persevered through a troubled youth to become an
All-Star in his home town. (Photo courtesy National Baseball Hall of
Fame Library, Cooperstown, N.Y.)

Charlie Dressen, Bob Fothergill, Tom Yewcic and Russ Young played pro baseball and pro football.

DETROIT'S BASEBALL-NBA CONNECTION

Dave DeBusschere: A top two-sport player at the University of Detroit, he pitched 1962–63 with the White Sox (36 G, 10 starts, 1 CG (shutout), 102.1 IP, 34 BB, 53 K, 2.90 ERA) before turning to basketball full-time for the Detroit Pistons. In 1964, at age 24, he became player-coach, the youngest ever in NBA history. He was relived of his coaching duties in 1967, and traded in 1969 to the New York Knicks, where he won NBA crowns in 1969 and 1973.

Ron Reed: A two-sport standout at Notre Dame, Reed played 1965–67 with the Pistons—under DeBusschere. The 6'6" guard-forward played 118 games and averaged 8.1 points per game before sticking with baseball as a starter with Atlanta (1966–75) and St. Louis (1975) and a reliever with Philadelphia (1976–83) and the White Sox (1984). He finished with a 146-140 lifetime record, a 3.46 ERA, 751 games, 236 starts, 55 complete games, and eight shutouts. He led the NL with 13 relief wins in 1979.

Red Rolfe: Manager of the Tigers 1949–52, he also coached 44 games for the Toronto Huskies of the fledgling NBA in 1946–47, going 17-27 as the fourth—and last—Huskies coach that year. As the Tigers' skipper, Rolfe went 278-216 in three seasons and part of a fourth.

THE TIGERS
AS THE BEST TEAM IN BASEBALL

In major-league history, there have been only five seasons when just one team played ball either above .600 or below .400. Each time it happened was in the American League. Four of those five teams were over .600. Only two of those four teams went on to win the World Series. Both times it was the Tigers, in 1968 (103-59, .636) and 1984 (104-58, .642). The 1959 White Sox and the 1990 A's won the AL crown but lost the World Series, and the

1958 Senators finished under .400 while the other major-league teams played between .400 and .600. The eight-team Federal League achieved parity in 1914, its first season. In 2000, all 30 AL and NL teams played between .400 and .600 for the first time.

WHEN JIM CAMPBELL CLOSED THE TIGER STADIUM BLEACHERS

June 17, 1980: Bleacher creatures pelted Milwaukee outfielders Gorman Thomas and Sixto Lezcano with such debris as batteries. The bleachers were reopened June 30 with a more restrictive beer-sales policy and more stringent security.

May 4, 1985: Bleacher rowdies, despite two pleas over the public address system, failed to stop their profane variant on a Miller Lite beer commercial which showed fans chanting the beer's attributes: "Less filling!" "Tastes great!" The 11,000-seat bleachers—the largest such section in any major-league park—stayed closed for nearly a month, reopening June 2 in time for a 4-3 win over California. With the reopening came more changes: only light beer offered at nearby concession stands—and a smaller cup for the same price as a regular-size, full-strength beer.

STRUCTURAL CHANGES AT THE CORNER OF MICHIGAN AND TRUMBULL

1896: George Van Der Beck, owner of Detroit's Western League franchise, acquired the property that now holds Tiger Stadium. He named the ballpark he built there Bennett Park after Charlie Bennett, a popular player for the 1880s-era Detroit Wolverines of the National League, who lost his legs in a freak train mishap. Its home plate was in present-day Tiger Stadium's rightfield corner.

1911: Tigers owner Frank Navin razed Bennett Park to prepare for a new stadium.

1912: Navin Field, seating 23,000, opened April 20.

1923: The park's original grandstands were double-decked, bringing seating capacity to 30,000. Navin also built a press box up on the roof behind home plate.

1936: Walter Briggs, who owned the Tigers after Navin's death, tore down the first-base pavilion and replaced it with a double-decked grandstand extending into right field, bringing seating capacity to 36,000.

1937: The third-base pavilion was removed. In its place was a double-decked grandstand and a two-tiered centerfield bleacher section, making Briggs Stadium—the new name—entirely double-decked.

1946: The warning track was added in the outfield.

1948: Light standards were added to the grandstand roofs, and 1,458 incandescent bulbs affixed to them in preparation for the Tigers' first-ever home night game.

1953: The bullpens were moved from behind the centerfield fence to inside the foul lines near the outfield corners.

1955: Some box seats in the rightfield corner were removed.

1977: After Tiger Stadium caught fire February 1—firefighters confined the fire to the third-level press box—the club rebuilt it before the season began. (Tigers general manager Jim Campbell was heard to say, "What a shame it happened in the winter when the writers weren't around.")

1977: On October 31, construction started on a $15 million modernization project at Tiger Stadium that would span three years. The project would renovate clubhouses and put in a new press box, electronic scoreboard and luxury boxes. The project was able to take place because the Tigers had sold the stadium to the city (for a dollar!), making the ballpark eligible for federal funds. However, a 90-cent ticket surcharge was added to the price of all tickets to pay for the renovation.

1980: Blue and orange plastic seats replaced the green seats that had been a stadium mainstay for more than a half-century.

1993: The exterior of the stadium along Michigan Avenue, which had served as a parking lot for players, was transformed into "Tiger Plaza," with added concessions, attractions and a patio for fans.

The Tigers' Hoped-For Dome Home

On January 12, 1972, Tigers owner John Fetzer announced the Tigers had signed a 40-year lease for a $126 million domed stadium that would be built on the riverfront. The stadium would seat 52,000 for baseball and 60,000 for football. The site is now occupied largely by Joe Louis Arena, home to the Detroit Red Wings. It never got built because a bond issue failed at the polls and lawsuits were filed alleging chicanery in how the stadium would be funded. The Tigers stayed put.

Great Tigers On-Field Props

Germany Schaefer came to second base for a game in 1906 in one inning wearing a raincoat. The umpire made him go to the dugout and take it off before resuming play. In another game when he thought the umpires should call it on account of darkness, he came out to second with a lantern. In yet another game, he wore a fake black mustache onto the field, only to be ejected.

Dick McAuliffe in 1968, so sure that Ray Oyler (who hit .135 that year) would make the third out of the inning, went to the on-deck circle without a bat but stood in it wearing his glove.

Norm Cash, having been struck out twice already by California's Nolan Ryan July 15, 1973, came to the plate with a table leg instead of a bat. The umpire made him get a regulation bat. Ryan struck out 17 and blanked Detroit, 6-0. In another game, Cash offered the umpire a pair of novelty sunglasses with battery-operated wiper blades.

Great Hats in the Dugout

Manager Billy Martin used a hat from which he pulled his lineup at random in the first game of an Aug. 13, 1972, doubleheader vs. Cleveland to snap the Tigers out of a four-game losing streak. The Tigers won, 3-2, but lost the nightcap, 9-2, with a regular batting order. The lineup:

Norm Cash, 1B
Jim Northrup, RF

Willie Horton, LF
Ed Brinkman, SS
Tony Taylor, 2B
Duke Sims, C
Mickey Stanley, CF
Aurelio Rodriguez, 3B
Woodie Fryman, P

FIVE BIGGEST YEAR-TO-YEAR IMPROVEMENTS BY THE TIGERS

Year	From	To	Plus	Comment
1997	53–109	79–83	26	Rebound to respectability.
1961	71–83	101–61	26	Tigers outscored Maris/Mantle Yanks.
1934	75–79	101–53	26	Start of something big: 4 pennants, 15 of 17 winning seasons.
1907	71–78	92–58	20-1/2	Cobb comes into own; first pennant.
1915	80–73	100–54	19-1/2	First 100-win team to not win flag.

FIVE BIGGEST YEAR-TO-YEAR DROPS BY THE TIGERS

Year	From	To	Down	Comment
1989	88–74	59–103	29	Tigers' '80s dynasty falls apart.
1920	80–60	61–93	26	Hughie Jennings' last year managing.
1952	73–81	50–104	23	Caps 45-game drop over 2 years; first last-place finish.
1951	95–59	73–81	22	End of the 1930s–40s run.
1902	74–61	52–83	22	Other AL clubs raiding NL rosters.

FAMOUS TIGER FANS

Patsy O'Toole: In the 1930s, he was so loud he got the nickname "The All-American Earache." To him, all the Tigers were "great guys" and opponents "bums." His trademark rallying cry: "Boy, oh boy, oh boy, oh boy! Keep cool wit' O'Toole!" His real name

was Samuel Ozadowski. Before he got a job as Detroit mayor
Frank Murphy's errand boy, he was a newsboy, boxer, whisky
salesman and ticket seller. During the Tigers' 1934 pennant
drive, he so got under Yankees pitcher Lefty Gomez' skin that
Gomez had to be restrained by several players lest he do
O'Toole bodily harm.

Joe Diroff: Nicknamed "The Brow" because of his bushy eye-
brows, he supported all Detroit pro teams unquestioningly over
three decades, meeting the clubs at airports as they came home
from road trips. His clothing nearly obscured by buttons and
pennants, Diroff wandered throughout the stands, rousing the
fans with a wide assortment of G-rated cheers, among them
"Strawberry Shortcake, Gooseberry Pie."

TIGERS ON THE ALL-TIME
YEARS OF SERVICE LIST

Rank	Player	Years
2.*	Deacon McGuire	26 (2 with Wolverines, 3 with Tigers; 1,781 games total)
8.**	Ty Cobb	24 (22 with Detroit; 3,033 games total)
26.***	Al Kaline	22 (all with Detroit; 2,834 games total)
26.***	Joe Niekro	22 (2 with Detroit; 702 games total)
53.+	Darrell Evans	21 (5 with Detroit; 2,687 games total)
53.+	Waite Hoyt	21 (2 with Detroit; 674 games total)
53.+	Frank Tanana	21 (8 with Detroit; 638 games total)
84.++	Bobo Newsom	20 (3 with Detroit; 600 games total)
84.++	Alan Trammell	20 (all with Detroit; 2,293 games total)

*Tied with Tommy John.
**Tied with Steve Carlton, Rick Dempsey, Dennis Eckersley, Carlton Fisk, Phil Niekro and Pete Rose.
***Tied with 25 others.
+Tied with 30 others.
++Tied with 25 others.

TIGERS' LONGEST CONSECUTIVE-GAME STREAKS

Player	Games	Dates
Charlie Gehringer	511	September 3, 1927–May 7, 1931
Charlie Gehringer*	504	June 25, 1932–August 11, 1935
Rocky Colavito	458	June 21, 1960–May 21, 1963
Ed Brinkman	434	September 26, 1971–August 9, 1974**

*Pete Rose is the only other player with two 500-game streaks.
**Does not include 1972 postseason; Brinkman played just one game.

THE LONGEST-TENURED TIGERS BALLPLAYERS

Name	Years
Ty Cobb	22
Al Kaline	22*
Alan Trammell	20*
Charlie Gehringer	19*
Lou Whitaker	19*
Tommy Bridges	16*
Norm Cash	15
Sam Crawford	15
Hooks Dauss	15*
Bill Freehan	15*
Harry Heilmann	15
John Hiller	15*
Willie Horton	15
Hal Newhouser	15
Mickey Stanley	15*
Donie Bush	14
Dick McAuliffe	14
Jack Morris	14
Dizzy Trout	14

*Entire big-league career with Detroit.

TIGERS WHO PLAYED WITH DETROIT IN THREE DECADES

Player	Years
Donie Bush	1908–21
Ty Cobb	1905–26
Charlie Gehringer	1924–42
Kirk Gibson	1979–87, 1993–95
Johnny Groth	1946–52, 1957–60
John Hiller	1965–70, 1972–80
Chief Hogsett	1929–36, 1944
Fred Hutchinson	1939–41, 1946–53
Al Kaline	1953–74
Jack Morris	1977–90
Hal Newhouser	1939–53
Dan Petry	1979–87, 1990–91
Oscar Stanage	1909–20, 1925
Alan Trammell	1977–96
Dizzy Trout	1939–52
Vic Wertz	1947–52, 1961–63
Lou Whitaker	1977–95

TIGERS WITH ONLY ONE SEASON IN THE MAJORS

1901: Ed High
1902: Ed Fisher, Peter LePine, Arch McCarthy, Lou Schiappacasse
1904: Charlie Jaeger
1905: Gene Ford, Charlie Jackson, Walt Justis, Frosty Thomas
1908: Clay Perry
1909: Kid Speer
1910: Frank Browning, Art Loudell, Marv Peasley, Dave Skeels
1911: Jack Lively
1912: Ed Irvin, Bill Leinhauser, Red McDermott, Jim McGarr, Con McGarvey, Pat McGehee, Hank Perry, Jack Smith, Al Travers, Bun Troy, Hap Ward, Charlie Wheatley
1913: Al Clauss, Charlie Harding, Les Hennessy, Lefty Lorenzen, Steve Partenheimer, Pepper Peploski, Al Platte, Erwin Renfer, Carl Zamloch

1914: Ed McCreery
1915: Razor Ledbetter
1918: Joe Cobb, Ben Dyer, Herb Hall
1920: Ernie Alten, Harry Baumgartner, John Bogart, Danny Claire, Red Cox, Cy Fried, John Glaiser, Lou Vedder, Mutt Wilson
1921: Sam Barnes, Slicker Parks, Joe Sargent, Suds Sutherland, Jim Walsh
1922: John Mohardt
1924: Willie Ludolph
1925: Andy Harrington, Bill Moore
1927: Rufus Smith, Jim H. Walkup
1929: Augie Prudhomme
1930: Joe Samuels, Johnny Watson, Hughie Wise
1931: Lou Brower, Orlin Collier
1932: Izzy Goldstein, Bill Lawrence
1934: Steve Larkin, Icehouse Wilson
1935: Hugh Shelley
1936: Salty Parker
1938: Woody Davis, Joe Rogalski
1940: Scat Metha
1941: Earl Cook, Boyd Perry
1943: Joe Wood
1944: Bubba Floyd, Jack Sullivan
1945: Russ Kerns, Bob Maier, Carl McNabb, Milt Welch, Walter Wilson
1946: Anse Moore
1949: Bob Mavis
1952: Alex Garbowski
1953: John Baumgartner, Frank Carswell, Milt Jordan
1954: George Bullard
1955: Van Fletcher, Bill Froats, Harry Malmberg
1956: Jim Brady, Buddy Hicks
1957: Tom Yewcic
1958: Jack Feller
1959: Jerry Davie, Jim Proctor, Ron Shoop
1961: Manny Montejo
1962: Tom Fletcher, Doug Gallagher
1963: Bob Dustal, Larry Foster
1964: Fritz Fisher
1965: Jackie Moore, Vern Holtgrave

1966: Arlo Brunsberg, Don Pepper
1968: Jon Warden
1970: Dennis Saunders, Ken Szotkiewicz
1971: Jack Whillock, John Young
1972: Ike Blessitt, Paul Jata, Don Leshnock, Phil Meeler, Bob Strampe
1973: Gary Ignasiak
1974: Reggie Sanders
1975: Ike Brookens, Art James
1977: Bob Adams
1979: Altar Greene
1980: Roger Weaver
1982: Mark DeJohn
1984: Scott Earl
1989: Jeff Datz, Ramon Peña, Rob Richie
1991: Mike Dalton, Dan Gakeler
1994: Phil Stidham
1995: Pat Ahearne, Ben Blohmdahl, Sean Whiteside
1998: Brian Powell
1999: Luis Garcia, Beiker Graterol
2000: Mark Johnson, Rod Lindsey,
2001: Jermaine Clark, Nate Cornejo, Brandon Inge, Matt Miller, Heath Murray, Jarrod Patterson, Adam Pettyjohn, Luis Piñeda, Pedro Santana, Victor Santos, Chris Wakeland

DETROIT'S ONLY KNOWN "PHANTOM" BALLPLAYER

"K. John Drennan." He had been created as the result of a typographical error in a 1904 box score in which "Drennan" played first base in one game. His name appeared in The Official Encyclopedia of Baseball, the first authoritative baseball compendium, published in 1951, of every known ballplayer. Later research showed the player really was pitcher Wild Bill Donovan, who was filling in at first; he put in eight games there in 1904.

TIGERS WHO APPEARED ONLY AS A PINCH-RUNNER

Alex Garbowski, 1952
Bob Mavis, 1949
Ben Steiner, 1947

TIGERS WHO APPEARED ONLY AS A PINCH-HITTER

Joe Cobb, 1918 (no relation to Ty)
Doc Daugherty, 1951
George Freese, 1953
Andy Harrington, 1925
Russ Kerns, 1945
Em Lindbeck, 1960
Carl Linhart, 1952
Carl McNabb, 1945
Bill Nahorodny, 1983
Cy Perkins, 1934
Icehouse Wilson, 1934

To date, no Tiger has served only as a designated hitter.

THE 1912 REPLACEMENT GAME

The Tigers' 24-2 "Ty Cobb" loss to Philadelphia was May 18, 1912. The Tigers players had protested Cobb's indefinite suspension for climbing into the stands to pummel heckler Claude Lueker in New York three days before and voted to strike. Faced with a $5,000 fine for failing to field a team, club owner Frank Navin ordered manager Hughie Jennings to sign up local amateurs and semipros. Aloysius Travers, Bill Leinhauser, Dan McGarvey, Billy Maharg (whose real name was Graham, "Maharg" spelled backwards), Jim McGarr, Pat Meany, Hap Ward and Ed Irvin put on Tiger uniforms. Two Detroit coaches, Joe Sugden, 41, and Deacon McGuire, 48, completed the lineup. Travers, a seminary student who would later become a priest, pitched a complete game for Detroit, giving up 26 hits and 24 runs in eight innings. Irvin hit two triples in three trips to the plate and closed his major league career with a record 2.000 slugging average. Irvin would die in a 1916 bar brawl. Only one replacement Tiger ever played another major league game: Maharg would bat once for the Phillies in 1916. He would also be involved as a conspirator in the Black Sox scandal of 1919. The Tigers returned to the field two days later after Cobb counseled them not to risk being banned for life by AL president Ban Johnson for continuing the strike.

TIGERS PITCHERS WHO DOUBLED AS TIGERS POSITION PLAYERS

George Cunningham—Played 20 games in the outfield in 1918 and one more in 1921 in addition to 123 appearances as a pitcher, 1916–21.

Wild Bill Donovan—Played the outfield for 13 games, first base for 10 games, second base for six games, and shortstop for two games, 1903–06 and 1912, in addition to 261 mound appearances.

Emil Frisk—Two outfield appearances in 1901 in addition to 11 appearances pitching.

Frank Kitson—Played five games in the outfield in 1903. He was a Detroit starting pitcher, 1903–05.

George Mullin—Had 13 outfield appearances plus three at first base 1902–07 and 1909–10 in addition to being the Tigers' workhorse starter for most of his 12 seasons with the club (1902–13).

Joe Yeager—After sliding from a 12-11, 2.61-ERA season in 1901 to a 6-12 record in 1902 with a 4.81 ERA, he moved to third base in 1903, playing 107 games there and pitching only once that season. In four more big-league years with the New York Highlanders and the St. Louis Browns, Yeager never pitched again.

TIGERS POSITION PLAYERS WHO DOUBLED AS TIGERS PITCHERS

Ty Cobb—Two games in 1918, one game in 1925 (he picked up the save!), 5 innings pitched, ERA of 3.60.

Ben Dyer—Two games in 1918, 1.2 innings pitched, 0.00 ERA.

Bobby Veach—One game in 1918, 2 innings pitched, 4.50 ERA.

Joe Yeager—He pitched 46 games 1901–03: 41 starts, 37 complete games, two shutouts, 348.2 innings pitched, 18-24 record. In six years (including three with Brooklyn) he compiled a 33-49 record in 94 games and 80 starts. He played 10 big-league seasons overall, with 295 games at third base, 83 at short-stop and two in the outfield. It's easy to see why he's included in both this category and the one preceding.

Mark Koenig—He pitched five games 1930–31, including one start in 1930. He was 0-1 in his appearances with an 8.44 ERA. In his last mound appearance vs. the Philadelphia Athletics, September 22, 1931—save for the walks—was a little better. Koenig's line score: 4 IP, 3H, 0R, 0 ER, 6BB, 1K.

Shane Halter—One game on October 1, 2000, as part of his nine-positions-in-one-game stunt. He faced one batter at the top of the eighth inning, walking him on five pitches after getting the first pitch over the plate. The runner did not score, leaving Halter with an ERA of -.--. It's not 0.00 because he didn't retire the batter he faced, and it's not infinity because the batter he put on base didn't score.

SHANE HALTER'S NINE-POSITION GAME

The Tigers' Shane Halter, in the last game of the 2000 season (October 1), played all nine positions in the field against the Minnesota Twins. He handled the ball in every position but right field. Here's the order in which Halter played the nine positions: first base, third base, right field, center field, left field, shortstop, catcher, pitcher, second base.

He played one inning for the first seven positions, walked the first hitter up in the eighth, then moved to second base for the rest of the game. Halter had played all positions but pitcher for the Tigers before the season's final game. He was kept from trying the stunt until the Tigers had clinched third place in the American League Central Division. He had wanted to be the designated hitter, but manager Phil Garner thought it would cause too many lineup headaches. Halter became only the fourth major leaguer—all in the American League—to play all nine positions in a single game. The others were the Kansas City Athletics' Bert Campaneris in 1965, the Minnesota Twins' Cesar Tovar in 1968, and the Texas Rangers' Scott Sheldon in 2000.

PARKS THE TIGERS OPENED

New League Park, Cleveland: Detroit 5, Cleveland 0, April 21, 1910, as Ed Willett threw a shutout before a crowd of 19,867 fans.

Navin Field (later to become Briggs Stadium and Tiger Stadium), Detroit; Detroit 6, Cleveland 5 (11 innings), April 20, 1912.

Municipal Stadium, Kansas City: Athletics 6, Detroit 2, April 12, 1955.

District of Columbia Stadium (later to become RFK Stadium), Washington: Washington 4, Detroit 1, April 9, 1962.

Atlanta-Fulton County Stadium, Atlanta: Milwaukee Braves 6, Detroit 3, April 9, 1965. The exhibition was played before the start of the Braves' lame-duck season in Milwaukee.

New Comiskey Park, Chicago: Detroit 16, Chicago 0, April 18, 1991.

Tropicana Field, St. Petersburg, Fla.: Detroit 11, Tampa Bay 5, March 31, 1998.

Comerica Park, Detroit: Detroit 5, Seattle 2, April 11, 2000.

TIGERS PLAYING THE FIRST NIGHT GAME EVER IN DIFFERENT PARKS

Shibe Park (later Connie Mack Stadium), Philadelphia: Detroit 5, Philadelphia 0, June 20, 1939.

Municipal Stadium, Cleveland: Cleveland 5, Detroit 0, June 27, 1939.

Briggs Stadium (later Tiger Stadium), Detroit: Detroit 4, Philadelphia 1, June 15, 1948. Attendance was 54,480.

Tropicana Field, St. Petersburg, Fla.: Detroit 11, Tampa Bay 6, March 31, 1998.

Comerica Park, Detroit: Seattle 4, Detroit 0, April 12, 2000.

TIGERS WITH UNUSUAL PRE-TIGERS BASEBALL CARDS

Gus Zernial (Topps, 1952): He's wearing a pink undershirt and giving the high sign, and holding a bat that has five baseballs stuck to it.

Aurelio Rodriguez (Topps, 1969): A batboy stood in for Rodriguez.

Billy Ripken (Fleer, 1989): An obscenity was written on the knob of his bat.

OUR FAVORITE TIGER STADIUM EMPLOYEES

Herbie "Love Bug" Redmond. While the grounds crew tending to the infield went stolidly about their work during the Tigers' win-starved years of the 1970s, Redmond shook his hips and waved his cap as part of his crowd-pleasing routine.

Then there's the Coca-Cola vendor whose name is not known. He most often plied his trade in the left field corner of the lower deck. He would have a running call and response pitch:

Vendor: "Beep beep beep."

Fans: "Ice cold Coke."

Vendor: "Beep beep beep."

Fans: "Ice cold Coke."
Vendor: "Ice cold Coke."
Fans: "Beep beep beep."

WHEN TY COBB LOST A FIGHT

It was 1906 against Tigers catcher Boss Schmidt. Cobb kept goading Schmidt into a fight by dumping a glass full of tooth-picks into his suit, kicking his suitcase out of his hand and down a train platform. But after Cobb had an altercation with a laun-dry woman, Schmidt waited until he and Cobb were on the practice field. Although Cobb jumped atop Schmidt, the power-ful catcher easily bested the young outfielder who wouldn't cry uncle. Schmidt also topped Cobb in a later rematch.

THE TIGERS' MOST NOTABLE SEASON-ENDING INJURIES

Hank Greenberg, 12 games into defending the Tigers' 1935 World Series championship, broke his wrist on a collision at first base with Washington Senators hitter Jake Powell. The bone Greenberg broke was the same bone that had sidelined him dur-ing Game Two of the 1935 World Series.

Pitcher Dave Rozema, joining a bench-clearing brawl in a game against Minnesota May 14, 1982, tried to imitate the kung fu kick popular on TV and movie action dramas of the time. He failed miserably at it; the resulting knee ligament damage put him out of commission for the rest of the season.

THE TIGERS' WORST CAREER-ENDING INJURY

Catcher-manager Mickey Cochrane was beaned on a 3-1 count by a fastball that got away from Yankees pitcher Irving "Bump" Hadley in New York, May 25, 1937. Cochrane had touched up Hadley for a home run his previous time up, but

Hadley said, "The ball sailed—I don't know why—it just did."
The pitch knocked Cochrane out cold and he didn't regain
consciousness until after being carried by teammates to the
dugout. X-rays revealed a triple skull fracture. Cochrane
reportedly hovered between life and death for three days. He
returned to manage the Tigers two months later, but heeded
doctors' orders against playing on the field. Mickey lasted
another year as manager before Tigers owner Walter Briggs
fired him in August 1938.

OLD TIGERS PROMOTIONAL DAYS

The Tigers were one of the last teams to have frequent give-
away promotions. Instead, they focused on days or nights out
for community groups, among other events:
Shrine Night (always a twi-night doubleheader with a ceremony
    between games)
Father-Son/Father-Child Game (the Tigers always lost this one big,
    often with Detroit weathercaster Sonny Eliot umpiring)
Beeper Ball Game (for blind people, with a beeping softball-like ball
    that they could hear)
Polish-American Night
Irish-American Night
Lutheran Night
Knights of Columbus Night
American Legion Night
Veterans of Foreign Wars Night
Windsor Night
DeMolay Night
B'nai B'rith Night
Elks Night
Kiwanis Night
Current promotions that have a chance to be remembered by
a new era of Tigers fans includes Friday Night Fireworks and
Kids Run the Bases.

A MAJOR-LEAGUE BASEBALL ORGANIZATION FOUNDED IN DETROIT

The Baseball Writers Association was started October 14, 1908, during the Tigers-Cubs World Series, at the Ponchartrain Hotel in Detroit as a response by newspaper reporters to what they considered shabby treatment by the front offices of teams in both leagues. Chapters formed in the other cities where the AL and NL had teams, and the group's name eventually expanded to the Baseball Writers Association of America.

TIGERS IN THE PEN—AND WE DON'T MEAN THE BULLPEN!

Gates Brown was in prison in Ohio for breaking and entering before he signed with the Tigers, who beat the Indians in a bidding war, straight out of the Mansfield (Ohio) State Reformatory in 1960. Prison team coach Chuck Yarman had written letters to several clubs; they liked what they saw. Brown once returned to the high school in his home town, Crestline, Ohio, to talk to students. During as assembly, the principal asked him, "Gates, I'm sure some of our students would be interested to know: What did you take when you were in school?" Brown answered, "Overcoats, mostly."

Pinky Higgins, who collected 12 straight hits in 1938, one year before he joined the Tigers, was convicted of vehicular homicide after he struck and killed a highway worker in 1968. Paroled after serving two months, he died of a heart attack the day after his release.

Jerry Priddy, a Tigers second baseman from 1950–54, was charged in 1973 with extortion. He had threatened to put a bomb on a ship, and then called the company to arrange a payoff. He was found guilty and sentenced to nine months in prison.

Ron LeFlore was serving a 5-to-15-year term in Southern Michigan Prison in Jackson, Michigan, for the 1966 robbery of Dee's Bar on Detroit's east side. They had gotten away with nearly $35,000, but the driver of the getaway car forgot to put his lights on. A police car saw the vehicle, and LeFlore was busted. LeFlore had been in trouble early; at age 12, he stole $1,500 from a grocery store. Because he goaded the prison guards, LeFlore often found himself in solitary confinement. But while in solitary, he strengthened himself by doing pushups and situps. Invited to try out for the prison baseball team, he proved to be a natural. Another inmate at Jackson wrote to Jimmy Butsicaris, who owned the Lindell AC—a downtown bar where Detroit's pro athletes often hung out after games—with his brother, Johnny, and was best man at one of Billy Martin's weddings. Martin invited LeFlore to try out at Tiger Stadium after he was released in 1972. But LeFlore got a weekend furlough and worked out with the team. The Tigers signed LeFlore for $5,000 and, with the promise of a job, LeFlore was released from prison a month early. He broke into the majors the following year as a 26-year-old rookie and would become an All-Star.

Ferris Fain's California farm was raided in 1988 and authorities confiscated more than $1 million in marijuana. Fain, then 66, swore he never smoked and that the crop was grown solely for profit.

Denny McLain had a 1985 racketeering conviction overturned on grounds of judicial prejudice while he was in prison serving a 23-year sentence. Making his way back to Michigan, he quit his job as a morning-drive talk-radio host to acquire a meat-packing company in Chesaning, Michigan. There he was convicted of embezzlement in 1996 after the workers' pension fund had been raided, and sentenced to eight years in prison.

BIBLIOGRAPHY

ARTICLES

Anderson, William M. "Baseball at the Corner." Michigan History Magazine. September–October 1999.

Associated Press. "Gibson HR Clears Tiger Stadium Roof." San Francisco Chronicle. June 15, 1983.

Bragg, Brian. "To baseball gladiators, Detroit is the pits." Detroit Free Press. June 19, 1980.

Bullion, Harry. "Record Games Won by Tigers From Boston," Detroit Free Press. August 25, 1919.

Chass, Murray. "Without Warning, The Field Is Leveling Regardless of Payroll Disparity." New York Times. Sept. 17, 2000.

Denlinger, Kenneth. "Fans Blast Nats' Short For Trade." The Washington Post. October 10, 1970.

———. "McLain Welcomes Chance, Plans to Stick to His Pitching." The Washington Post. October 10, 1970.

The Detroit News. "He Who Laughs Last." July 9, 1918.

Donovan, Leo. "Services Monday for W. O. Briggs." Detroit Free Press. January 18, 1952.

Eichorn, George. "Gervin To Be Honored." The Monitor, Detroit. May 17, 2001.

Ewald, Dan. "Trade ends in red faces, hot water." The Detroit News. December 4, 1974.

Gage, Tom. "Tigers swing 2-for-2 deal, cut Leach." The Detroit News. March 25, 1984.

Greene, Sam. "13 Hits (12 in Row) Boost Dropo to .296." The Detroit News. July 16, 1952.

———. "Demeter Traded for Norm Cash." The Detroit News, April 14, 1960.

———. "Tigers Trade Boy for Veteran, 32." The Detroit News. November 12, 1948.

Guidi, Gene. "Big night, and Horton has `willies.'" Detroit Free Press. June 1, 1985.

"Hall of Fame Gallery." The Daily Star, Oneonta, N.Y., July 21, 2000.

Holway, John. "Negro League." Self-published. 2001.

Howe, Dean. "A night to reminisce with former Tiger greats," The Flint Journal, Flint, Mich., April 26, 2001.

Khan, Ansar. "Easley hits for cycle in Tigers' 9-4 win." Ann Arbor News. June 9, 2001.

Knobler, Danny. "Blair resigned that he'll go to bullpen when Mlicki returns." Ann Arbor News. September 4, 2000.

———. "Tigers, Red Sox used record-tying 42 players in 7-6 Sox Win." Ann Arbor News. September 16, 2000.

———. "Heams thrilled with gold medal, hopes to be with Tigers in 2001." Ann Arbor News. October 1, 2000.

———. "Wild 12-11 win sends Tigers out on a good note." Ann Arbor News. October 2, 2000.

———. "Subbing out for pinch runner didn't halt end to Tigers win streak." Ann Arbor News. May 6, 2001.

Lapointe, Joe. "Obscene chant leads Tigers to close bleachers." Detroit Free Press. May 5, 1985.

———. "Sick and tired of it, Jim Campbell says." Detroit Free Press, June 19, 1980.

———. "The brews of summer are under fire: Beer, baseball marriage going flat?" Detroit Free Press. May 5, 1985.

———. "Tiger fans object to Campbell decision." Detroit Free Press, May 6, 1985.

Lardner, R. W. "The Longest Way 'Round the Bases Isn't the Best Way Home in Baseball." Chicago Tribune. August 1, 1910.

McClure, Sandy. "Rowdyism nothing new in Tiger Stadium stands." Detroit Free Press. May 6, 1985.

McGraw, Bill. "Foul chants absent as bleachers reopen." Detroit Free Press. June 3, 1985.

Middlesworth, Hal. "Hoeft Hurls Tigers Past Senators." Detroit Free Press. June 7, 1958.

Salsinger, H. G. "The Umpire." The Detroit News, December 11, 1933.

——— "The Umpire." The Detroit News, July 10, 1951.

Saylor, Jack, "Tigers' Offense Sputters Anew, 6-2, Late Rush Falls Short for Lynn." Detroit Free Press. September 2, 1988.

Smith, Lyall. "No-Hitter Escapes Houtteman." Detroit Free Press, April 27, 1952.

———. "'Demeter Better Than Rocky.'" Detroit Free Press. December 6, 1963.

Spoelstra, Watson. "Sherry's Bubbly Bull-Pen Work Leaves Tigers Smacking Lips," The Sporting News, May 9, 1964.

———. "It doesn't thrill Ted." The Detroit News. October 10, 1970.

———. "Senators' owner succeeds at last." The Detroit News. October 10, 1970.

———. "Trade rebuilds Tigers' infield." The Detroit News. October 10, 1970.

———. "Why Kuhn lifted ban." The Detroit News. October 10, 1970.

Sylvester, Curt. "Bleachers to reopen soon." Detroit Free Press May 31, 1985.

"Today in Baseball," The Washington Post, July 13, 2000.

"Today in Baseball," The Washington Post, July 16, 2000.

"Today in Baseball," Los Angeles Times, July 20, 2000.

"Today in Baseball," The Washington Post, August 1, 2000.

341

BIBLIOGRAPHY

"Today in Baseball," The Washington Post, August 8, 2000.
"Today in Baseball," The Washington Post, August 14, 2000.
"Today in Baseball," The New York Times, August 30, 2000.
Untitled, Chicago Tribune, September 26, 1940.
Untitled, Philadelphia Daily News, September 26, 1908.
Untitled, The Washington Post, September 23, 1906.
Zurawik, Dave. "Tigers to reopen bleachers—carefully: Beer sales curbed, beach balls banned." Detroit Free Press. June 29, 1980.

AUDIO

Harwell, Ernie, and Ray Lane. "Year of the Tiger '68." Revere, Mass.: Fleetwood Recording Co. Inc. 1968.
Smith, Fred. *Tiger Trivia*. Okemos, Mich.: Force Publishing. 1998.

BOOKS

Alexander, Charles. *Ty Cobb*. New York: Oxford University Press. 1984.
Alvarez, Mark, ed. *The National Pastime: A Review of Baseball History*. Cleveland: Society for American Baseball Research. 2001.
Anderson, William M. *The Detroit Tigers: A Pictorial Celebration of the Greatest Players and Moments in Tigers History*, updated edition. Detroit: Wayne State University Press. 1999.
Arrow Street Guide to Metropolitan Detroit. Worcester, Mass.: Arrow, 1975.
Bak, Richard. *Cobb Would Have Caught It: The Golden Age of Baseball in Detroit*. Detroit: Wayne State University Press. 1991.
———. *Turkey Stearnes and the Detroit Stars: The Negro Leagues in Detroit, 1919–1933*. Detroit: Wayne State University Press. 1994.
———. *Ty Cobb: His Tumultuous Life and Times*. Dallas: Taylor. 1994.
———. *A Place for Summer: A Narrative History of Tiger Stadium*. Detroit: Wayne State University Press. 1998.
Barfknecht, Gary W. *Michillaneous*. Davison, Mich.: Friede Publications. 1982.
———. *Michillaneous II*. Davison, Mich.: Friede Publications. 1987.
Bartell, Dick, with Norman Macht. *Rowdy Richard*. Berkeley, Calif.: North Atlantic Books. 1987.
Betzold, Michael. *Tiger Stadium: Where Baseball Belongs*. Detroit: Tiger Stadium Fan Club. 1988.
Betzold, Michael and Ethan Casey. *Queen of Diamonds*. West Bloomfield, Mich.: Altwerger and Mandel. 1992; updated edition, West Bloomfield, Mich.: Northmont Publishing. 1997.

BIBLIOGRAPHY

Blake, Mike. *Baseball's Bad Hops and Lucky Bounces*. Cincinnati: Betterway Books. 1995.

Butler, Hal. *Stormin' Norman Cash*. New York, Julian Messner. 1968.

————. *The Willie Horton Story*. New York: Julian Messner. 1970.

————. *Al Kaline and the Detroit Tigers*. Chicago: Henry Regnery Company. 1973.

Carter, Craig, ed. *The Sporting News Complete Baseball Record Book*, 2000 edition. St. Louis: The Sporting News. 2000.

————, ed. *World Series Records 1903–1980*. St. Louis: The Sporting News Publishing Co. 1980.

Conner, Floyd. *Baseball's Most Wanted: The Top 10 Book of the National Pastime's Outrageous Offenders, Lucky Bounces, And Other Oddities*. Washington: Brassey's. 2000.

Connors, Martin, and Jim Craddock, eds. *VideoHound's Golden Movie Retriever 1998*. Detroit, New York, Toronto, London: Visible Ink Press. 1998.

Davis, Al, and Elliot Horne. *The All-Lover All-Star Team and 50 Other Improbable Baseball All-Star Lineups*. New York: William Morrow and Company. 1990.

Detroit Tigers roster books and press-TV-radio/media/information guides, 1949–56, 1962, 1966–67, 1969–2001.

Detroit Tigers 1970 Yearbook.

Dickson, Paul. *The Dickson Baseball Dictionary*. New York: Avon Books. 1989.

Driscoll, David, and the Mayo Smith Society. *Tiger Tracks: 1988*. London, Ontario: self-published. 1988.

Ewald, Dan. *John Fetzer: On a Handshake—The Times and Triumphs of a Tigers Owner*. Champaign, Ill.: Sagamore Press. 1997.

Falls, Joe. *Baseball's Great Teams: Detroit Tigers*. New York: MacMillan. 1975.

————. *So You Think You're a Die-Hard Tiger Fan*. Chicago: Contemporary Press. 1986.

Falls, Joe, and Irwin Cohen. *So You Love Tiger Stadium Too . . . Give It a Hug*. Grand Ledge, Mich.: Connection Graphics. 1999.

Fidrych, Mark, and Tom Clark. *No Big Deal*. Philadelphia and New York: J. B. Lippincott Co. 1977.

Fleming, G. H. *The Dizziest Season: The Gas House Gang Chases the Pennant*. New York: William Morrow and Co. 1984.

Freehan, Bill, edited by Steve Gelman and Dick Schaap. *Behind the Mask: An Inside Diary*. New York: The World Publishing Co. 1970.

Gibson, Kirk, with Lynn Henning. *Bottom of the Ninth*. Chelsea, Mich.: Sleeping Bear Press. 1997.

Green, Jerry. *The Year of the Tiger: The Diary of Detroit's World Champions*. New York: Coward-McCann. 1969.

Greenberg, Hank, with Ira Berkow. *The Story of My Life*. New York: Times Books. 1989.

Harrigan, Patrick. *The Detroit Tigers: Club and Community, 1945–1995*. Toronto: University of Toronto Press. 1997.

BIBLIOGRAPHY

Harwell, Ernie. *Tuned to Baseball*. South Bend, Ind.: Diamond Communications. 1985.

———. *Diamond Gems*. Ann Arbor, Mich.: Momentum Books Ltd. 1991

———. *The Babe Signed My Shoe*. South Bend, Ind.: Diamond Communications. 1994.

Hawkins, John C. *This Date in Detroit Tigers History: A Day-by-Day Listing of the Events in the History of the Detroit Tigers Baseball Team*. New York: Scarborough/Stein and Day. 1981.

Hill, Art: *"I Don't Care If I Never Get Back": A Baseball Fan and His Game*. New York: Simon and Schuster. 1980.

Hirshberg, Al. *The Al Kaline Story*. New York: Julian Messner. 1964.

James, Bill. *The Politics of Glory: How Baseball's Hall of Fame Really Works*. New York: MacMillan. 1994.

James, Bill, John Dewan, Neil Munro, Don Zminda, eds. *Stats Inc. All-Time Baseball Sourcebook*. Skokie, Ill.: Stats Inc. 1998.

James, Bill, John Dewan, Neil Munro, Don Zminda, eds. *Stats Inc. All-Time Major League Handbook*. Skokie, Ill.: Stats Inc. 1998.

Jordan, David. *A Tiger in His Time: Hal Newhouser and the Burden of Wartime Ball*. South Bend, Ind.: Diamond Communications. 1990.

Kahn, Roger. *Memories of Summer*. New York: Hyperion. 1997.

LeFlore, Ron, with Jim Hawkins: *Breakout: From Prison to the Big Leagues*. New York: Harper & Row. 1978.

Lester, Larry, Sammy J. Miller, Dick Clark. *Black Baseball in Detroit*. North Lincoln, Ill.: Arcadia Publishing. 2000.

Lieb, Frederick G. *The Detroit Tigers*. New York: G. P. Putnam's Sons. 1946.

Lynn, Ed. *Hitter: The Life and Turmoils of Ted Williams*. San Diego: Harcourt Brace and Company. 1993.

Lyons, Jeffrey, and Douglas B. Lyons. *Curveballs and Screwballs*. New York: Random House Puzzles & Games. 2001.

Macht, Norman L. *Ty Cobb*. New York Chelsea House Publishers. 1993.

The Mayo Smith Society. *Tiger Tracks: 1989*. London, Ontario: self-published. 1989.

Mazer, Bill, with Stan and Shirley Fischler. *Bill Mazer's Amazin' Baseball Book*. New York: Zebra Books. 1990.

McCallum, John. *Ty Cobb*. New York: Praeger. 1975.

McCollister, John. *The Tigers and Their Den: The Official Story of the Detroit Tigers*. Lenexa, Kan. Addax Publishing Group, 1999.

McLain, Denny, and Dave Diles. *Nobody's Perfect*. New York: Dial Press. 1975.

McLain, Denny with Mike Nahrstedt. *Strikeout: The Story of Denny McLain*. St. Louis: The Sporting News Publishing Co. 1988.

Moffi, Larry. *This Side of Cooperstown: An Oral History of Major League Baseball in the 1950s*. Iowa City: University of Iowa Press. 1996.

BIBLIOGRAPHY

Nemec, David. *Great Baseball Feats, Facts & Firsts (1995 edition)*. New York: Signet Books. 1995.

Nemec, David and Saul Wisnia. *100 Years of Major League Baseball: American and National Leagues, 1901–2000*. Lincolnwood, Ill.: Publications International Ltd. 2000.

Newhouser, Hal. *Pitching to Win*. Chicago: Ziff-Davis. 1948.

Okrent, Dan, and Steve Wulf. *Baseball Anecdotes*. New York: Putnam. 1994.

Poremba, David Lee. *Baseball in Detroit 1886–1968*. Charleston, S. C.: Arcadia Press. 1998.

Pugh, David. *The Book of Baltimore Orioles Lists*, new edition. Baltimore: American Literary Press. 1999.

Reichler, Joseph A., ed. *The Baseball Encyclopedia, 7th edition, revised, updated and expanded*. New York: Macmillan, 1988.

Rubin, Louis D. Jr., ed. *The Quotable Baseball Fanatic*. New York, N.Y: The Lyons Press. 2000.

Rubin, Robert. *Ty Cobb: The Greatest*. New York: Putnam. 1978.

Rucker, Mark, and Peter C. Bjarkman. *Smoke: The Romance and Lore of Cuban Baseball*. Champaign, Ill.: Total Sports. 1999.

Slocum, Frank. *Topps Baseball Cards: The Complete Picture Collection 1951–1985—A 35-Year History*. 1986.

Smalling, R. J. "Jack." *Baseball America's Baseball Address List Number 9*. Durham, N. C.: Baseball America Inc. 1996.

Smith, Fred. *Fifty Years With the Tigers*. Lathrup Village, Mich.: self-published. 1983.

———. *Tiger S.T.A.T.S.* Lathrup Village, Mich.: self-published. 1991.

Soloman, Burt. *The Baseball Timeline*. New York: Dorling Kindersley Publishing Inc. 2001.

The Sporting News. *Official Baseball Guide*, published annually 1947–2000. St. Louis: The Sporting News Publishing Co.

Stang, Mark, and Linda Harkness. *Baseball By The Numbers*. Lanham, Md.: The Scarecrow Press. 1997.

Stanton, Tom. *The Final Season: Fathers, Sons, And One Last Season in a Classic American Ballpark*. New York: Thomas Donne Books/St. Martin's Press. 2001.

Stats Inc. *Stats Inc. Major League Handbook 2000*. Morton Grove, Ill.: Stats Inc. 1999.

Sullivan, George, and David Cataneo. *Detroit Tigers: The Complete Record of Detroit Tigers Baseball*. New York: Macmillan. 1985.

Thorn, John, Pete Palmer, Michael Gershman and David Pietrusza: *Total Baseball: The Official Encyclopedia of Major League Baseball, 5th edition*. New York: Viking. 1997.

BIBLIOGRAPHY

Thorn, John, Pete Palmer, Michael Gershman, eds. *Total Baseball: The Official Encyclopedia of Major League Baseball*, 7th edition. Kingston, N.Y.: Total Sports Publishing. 2001.

Walker, G. Jay. *The Encyclopedia of the Senior Baseball League*. Self-published. No date.

Wickett, Bill and J. J, Carter, editors. *Detroit Pistons Media Guide, 1999–2000*. Auburn Hills, Mich.: The Detroit Pistons Basketball Co. 1999.

Wills, Maury, as told to Steve Gardner. *It Pays to Steal*. Beverly Hills, Calif.: Book Company of America. 1963.

Zminda, Don. *From Abba Dabba to Zorro: The World of Baseball Nicknames*. Morton Grove, Ill.: Stats Publsihing. 1999.

MAGAZINES AND NEWSPAPERS

Bayoff, Mike, Melanie Waters, Tyler Barnes, executive eds. *Tigers Magazine*, 2000 season, no. 2.

Bayoff, Mike, Melanie Waters, Tyler Barnes. *Tigers Magazine*, 2000 season, no. 4.

The Sporting News, weekly editions, 1968.

NEWSLETTERS

Amateur Baseball News, Vol. 51, No. 5, May 2000.

OTHER PUBLICATIONS

"Bill James 2000 Baseball Calendar." New York: Workman Publishing. 1999.

Franklin Total Baseball personal computer, 1994 edition.

WEB SITES

http://usimdb.com.

http://www.baseball1.com.

http://www.baseballhalloffame.org.

http://www.hankgreenbergfilm.org.

http://www.netcolony.com/sports/bunko/minor.

html.http://www.people.fas.harvard.edu/~kay/soundgarden/.

http://www.silentera.com/PSFL/data/C/College1927.html.

http://wso.williams.edu/~jkossuth/cobb/soundgarden.htm.

Society for American Baseball Research. McConnell/Tatersoll Home Run Log. Maintained by Dave Vincent.

INDEX OF NAMES

348

INDEX

355

INDEX

INDEX

362

365

INDEX

INDEX

INDEX OF DATES

INDEX

371

INDEX

TITLES IN THE GREAT LAKES
BOOKS SERIES

Seasons of Grace: A History of the Catholic Archdiocese of Detroit, by Leslie Woodcock Tentler, 1990

The Pottery of John Foster: Form and Meaning, by Gordon and Elizabeth Orear, 1990

The Diary of Bishop Frederic Baraga: First Bishop of Marquette, Michigan, edited by Regis M. Walling and Rev. N. Daniel Rupp, 1990

Walnut Pickles and Watermelon Cake: A Century of Michigan Cooking, by Larry B. Massie and Priscilla Massie, 1990

The Making of Michigan, 1820–1860: A Pioneer Anthology, edited by Justin L. Kestenbaum, 1990

America's Favorite Homes: A Guide to Popular Early Twentieth-Century Homes, by Robert Schweitzer and Michael W. R. Davis, 1990

Beyond the Model T: The Other Ventures of Henry Ford, by Ford R. Bryan, 1990

Life after the Line, by Josie Kearns, 1990

Michigan Lumbertowns: Lumbermen and Laborers in Saginaw, Bay City, and Muskegon, 1870–1905, by Jeremy W. Kilar, 1990

Detroit Kids Catalog: The Hometown Tourist, by Ellyce Field, 1990

Waiting for the News, by Leo Litwak, 1990 (reprint)

Detroit Perspectives, edited by Wilma Wood Henrickson, 1991

Life on the Great Lakes: A Wheelsman's Story, by Fred W. Dutton, edited by William Donohue Ellis, 1991

Copper Country Journal: The Diary of Schoolmaster Henry Hobart, 1863–1864, by Henry Hobart, edited by Philip P. Mason, 1991

John Jacob Astor: Business and Finance in the Early Republic, by John Denis Haeger, 1991

Survival and Regeneration: Detroit's American Indian Community, by Edmund J. Danziger, Jr., 1991

Steamboats and Sailors of the Great Lakes, by Mark L. Thompson, 1991

Cobb Would Have Caught It: The Golden Age of Baseball in Detroit, by Richard Bak, 1991

Michigan in Literature, by Clarence Andrews, 1992

Under the Influence of Water: Poems, Essays, and Stories, by Michael Delp, 1992

The Country Kitchen, by Della T. Lutes, 1992 (reprint)

The Making of a Mining District: Keweenaw Native Copper 1500–1870, by David J. Krause, 1992

Kids Catalog of Michigan Adventures, by Ellyce Field, 1993

Henry's Lieutenants, by Ford R. Bryan, 1993

Historic Highway Bridges of Michigan, by Charles K. Hyde, 1993

Lake Erie and Lake St. Clair Handbook, by Stanley J. Bolsenga and Charles E. Herndendorf, 1993

Queen of the Lakes, by Mark Thompson, 1994

Iron Fleet: The Great Lakes in World War II, by George J. Joachim, 1994

Turkey Stearnes and the Detroit Stars: The Negro Leagues in Detroit, 1919–1933, by Richard Bak, 1994

Pontiac and the Indian Uprising, by Howard H. Peckham, 1994 (reprint)

Charting the Inland Seas: A History of the U.S. Lake Survey, by Arthur M. Woodford, 1994 (reprint)

Ojibwa Narratives of Charles and Charlotte Kawbawgam and Jacques LePique, 1893–1895. Recorded with Notes by Homer H. Kidder, edited by Arthur P. Bourgeois, 1994, co-published with the Marquette County Historical Society

Strangers and Sojourners: A History of Michigan's Keweenaw Peninsula, by Arthur W. Thurner, 1994

Win Some, Lose Some: G. Mennen Williams and the New Democrats, by Helen Washburn Berthelot, 1995

Sarkis, by Gordon and Elizabeth Orear, 1995

The Northern Lights: Lighthouses of the Upper Great Lakes, by Charles K. Hyde, 1995 (reprint)

Kids Catalog of Michigan Adventures, second edition, by Ellyce Field, 1995

Rumrunning and the Roaring Twenties: Prohibition on the Michigan-Ontario Waterway, by Philip P. Mason, 1995

In the Wilderness with the Red Indians, by E. R. Baierlein, translated by Anita Z. Boldt, edited by Harold W. Moll, 1996

Elmwood Endures: History of a Detroit Cemetery, by Michael Franck, 1996

Master of Precision: Henry M. Leland, by Mrs. Wilfred C. Leland with Minnie Dubbs Millbrook, 1996 (reprint)

Haul-Out: New and Selected Poems, by Stephen Tudor, 1996

Kids Catalog of Michigan Adventures, third edition, by Ellyce Field, 1997

Beyond the Model T: The Other Ventures of Henry Ford, revised edition, by Ford R. Bryan, 1997

Young Henry Ford: A Picture History of the First Forty Years, by Sidney Olson, 1997 (reprint)

The Coast of Nowhere: Meditations on Rivers, Lakes and Streams, by Michael Delp, 1997

From Saginaw Valley to Tin Pan Alley: Saginaw's Contribution to American Popular Music, 1890–1955, by R. Grant Smith, 1998

The Long Winter Ends, by Newton G. Thomas, 1998 (reprint)

Bridging the River of Hatred: The Pioneering Efforts of Detroit Police Commissioner George Edwards, by Mary M. Stolberg, 1998

Toast of the Town: The Life and Times of Sunnie Wilson, by Sunnie Wilson with John Cohassey, 1998

These Men Have Seen Hard Service: The First Michigan Sharpshooters in the Civil War, by Raymond J. Herek, 1998

A Place for Summer: One Hundred Years at Michigan and Trumbull, by Richard Bak, 1998

Early Midwestern Travel Narratives: An Annotated Bibliography, 1634–1850, by Robert R. Hubach, 1998 (reprint)

All-American Anarchist: Joseph A. Labadie and the Labor Movement, by Carlotta R. Anderson, 1998

Michigan in the Novel, 1816–1996: An Annotated Bibliography, by Robert Beasecker, 1998

"Time by Moments Steals Away": The 1848 Journal of Ruth Douglass, by Robert L. Root, Jr., 1998

The Detroit Tigers: A Pictorial Celebration of the Greatest Players and Moments in Tigers' History, updated edition, by William M. Anderson, 1999

Father Abraham's Children: Michigan Episodes in the Civil War, by Frank B. Woodford, 1999 (reprint)

Letter from Washington, 1863–1865, by Lois Bryan Adams, edited and with an introduction by Evelyn Leasher, 1999

Wonderful Power: The Story of Ancient Copper Working in the Lake Superior Basin, by Susan R. Martin, 1999

A Sailor's Logbook: A Season aboard Great Lakes Freighters, by Mark L. Thompson, 1999

Huron: The Seasons of a Great Lake, by Napier Shelton, 1999

Tin Stackers: The History of the Pittsburgh Steamship Company, by Al Miller, 1999

Art in Detroit Public Places, revised edition, text by Dennis Nawrocki, photographs by David Clements, 1999

Brewed in Detroit: Breweries and Beers Since 1830, by Peter H. Blum, 1999

Detroit Kids Catalog: A Family Guide for the 21st Century, by Ellyce Field, 2000

"Expanding the Frontiers of Civil Rights": Michigan, 1948–1968, by Sidney Fine, 2000

Graveyard of the Lakes, by Mark L. Thompson, 2000

Enterprising Images: The Goodridge Brothers, African American Photographers, 1847–1922, by John Vincent Jezierski, 2000

New Poems from the Third Coast: Contemporary Michigan Poetry, edited by Michael Delp, Conrad Hilberry, and Josie Kearns, 2000

Arab Detroit: From Margin to Mainstream, edited by Nabeel Abraham and Andrew Shryock, 2000

The Sandstone Architecture of the Lake Superior Region, by Kathryn Bishop Eckert, 2000

Looking Beyond Race: The Life of Otis Milton Smith, by Otis Milton Smith and Mary M. Stolberg, 2000

Mail by the Pail, by Colin Bergel, illustrated by Mark Koenig, 2000

Great Lakes Journey: A New Look at America's Freshwater Coast, by William Ashworth, 2000

A Life in the Balance: The Memoirs of Stanley J. Winkelman, by Stanley J. Winkelman, 2000

Schooner Passage: Sailing Ships and the Lake Michigan Frontier, by Theodore J. Karamanski, 2000

The Outdoor Museum: The Magic of Michigan's Marshall M. Fredericks, by Marcy Heller Fisher, illustrated by Christine Collins Woomer, 2001

Detroit in Its World Setting: A Three Hundred Year Chronology, 1701–2001, edited by David Lee Poremba, 2001

Frontier Metropolis: Picturing Early Detroit, 1701–1838, by Brian Leigh Dunnigan, 2001

Michigan Remembered: Photographs from the Farm Security Administration and the Office of War Information, 1936–1943, edited by Constance B. Schulz, with Introductory Essays by Constance B. Schulz and William H. Mulligan, Jr., 2001

This Is Detroit, 1701–2001, by Arthur M. Woodford, 2001

History of the Finns in Michigan, by Armas K. E. Holmio, translated by Ellen M. Ryynanen, 2001

Angels in the Architecture: A Photographic Elegy to an American Asylum, by Heidi Johnson, 2001

Uppermost Canada: The Western District and the Detroit Frontier, 1800–1850, by R. Alan Douglas, 2001

The Iron Hunter, by Chase S. Osborn, 2002

Windjammers: Songs of the Great Lakes Sailors, by Ivan H. Walton with Joe Grimm, 2002

Detroit Tigers Lists and More: Runs, Hits, and Eras, by Mark Pattison and David Raglin, 2002